THE SINGAPORE PUZZLE

2nd Edition

Edited by Michael Haas

Library of Congress Cataloging-in-Publication Data

The Singapore puzzle / edited by Michael Haas
    p. cm.
    Includes bibliographical references and index

    I 1. Singapore—Politics and government. II. Haas, Michael, 1938-

Library of Congress Catalog Card Number: 2014904396
ISBN: 978-0-9839626-4-9

First published in 2014

Publishinghouse for Scholars, P. O. Box 461267, Los Angeles, CA 90046

Table of Contents

Tables

Preface to the First Edition

In 1971, during my second of two visits to Singapore, I was on sabbatical researching the subject of regional cooperation in Asia. At the conclusion of an interview with a prominent head of a regional organization headquartered in the island republic, I was gratuitously briefed on the virtues of Singapore, which I was told was "clean as a hound's tooth from top to bottom." Considerable economic progress was evident by 1978, the time of my next sabbatical, and the same official justifiably beamed with pride over the advances of the country.

When I returned in 1985, however, that official had been sacked for the temerity of allowing an opposition candidate to use the auditorium of the organization to make a speech. In 1987, when I returned on a Fulbright grant for the summer, I took a bus home from the Institute of Southeast Asian Studies after a busy day, turned on the television, and observed as an announcer began to explain how authorities had uncovered a "Marxist conspiracy to overthrow the government." As the summer progressed, news reports were dominated by various revelations about the so-called conspiracy, including obviously scripted televised confessions.

I grew up in Hollywood during the 1950s, when various luminaries of the film industry were accused of being Communist or otherwise were blacklisted for their courage in defying those who placed the label "un-American" on anyone with left-wing views. Thus, the Singapore "conspiracy" of 1987 was an obvious déjà vu that stimulated my interest. In subsequent publications, I have analyzed Singapore, a country that had so much promise while focusing on matters of economics in the 1970s, yet which seems of late to have become a rather nasty place due to overpoliticization.

By 1995, a critical mass had clearly emerged among independent Singapore watchers. After checking into the feasibility of an edited book with many authors, I decided to work on this book.

I am editing this book and penning a couple of chapters for several reasons. First of all, I admire many Singaporeans at a personal level; they are the sort who make friends for life. Second, the economic success of Singapore is an important achievement that I would hope could be emulated elsewhere to bring up the world's standard of living. Third, I spent most of my life in perhaps the only part of the world that resembles Singapore, and I can understand many problems of the country from my life in Hawai'i for more than three decades.

In 1959, both Hawai'i and Singapore achieved self-rule, that is, autonomy in most matters but defense and foreign affairs. As is true of Singapore, Hawai'i is a multiracial society dominated by one political party, a place where Asian-Pacific values are in daily conflict with Western Values. This similarity assisted me in interpreting developments in Asia, for example my *The Asian Way to Peace: A Story of Regional Cooperation* (1989), which I completed while on a Fulbright Research appointment at the Institute of Southeast Asian Studies in Singapore.

But Hawai'i is unlike Singapore. Although multiracial, Hawai'i is known for the "aloha spirit," a feeling of humility and acceptance of other cultures, Chinese ways of thinking dominate Singapore politics. Also in contrast, the dominant political party in Hawai'i wins elections by consistently running intelligent candidates and platforms; attempts to discredit or sue members of the opposition, as in Singapore, would be counterproductive in Hawai'i in light of the aloha spirit. Finally, representatives of gentler Asian-Pacific cultures in Hawai'i are often offended by brash Western ways of doing things, but the aloha spirit is basically syncretic, so efforts of Singapore's Westernized leaders to trumpet the superiority of "Asian Values" over "Western Values" seems a strange project indeed.

In short, I believe that Hawai'i presents a challenge and perhaps a model for Singapore. In 1971, when I first visited Singapore, there was a real chance for a society that could celebrate diversity of racial groups, a dominant party that could achieve legitimation by simply doing an excellent job of governance, and the forging of a syncretic Eurasian culture that could impress the world. Today, I am sorry to report that the Singapore government has painted itself into a corner wherein Chinese ethnocentrism, electoral dictatorship, and anti-communitarianism (that is, opposition to a balance between collectivist and individualist cultures) now prevail. Moreover, the second generation of leaders in Singapore seems intent on governing as in the checkered past, thus inviting opprobrium in a world that is increasingly democratic.

Although I issued many invitations to contribute chapters to this volume, not everyone was willing to write on the subject. I regret that Singaporeans were reluctant, but I could well understand the fear that swept across the face of one Singapore scholar whom I asked across the table during lunch in 1996. That Lau Teik Soon and Augustine Tan also turned down my invitation is doubtless also due the fear that someone in the government would be angered by their collaboration with some of the authors in this book and that they would ultimately suffer reprisals.

What has emerged in this volume, nevertheless, constitutes a coherent picture of a Singapore that is baffling to many. I wish at this time to thank the contributors for their eloquence, and I am especially indebted to Clark Neher for answering my call for an essay to present a balanced case for Singapore.

The purpose of the book is to engage in critical scholarly discussion by identifying peculiarities and explaining why Singapore has taken a singular path. The task of the reader will be to judge how well this objective has been accomplished in the pages to follow.

Michael Haas

Preface to the Second Edition

After *The Singapore Puzzle* was published, I had occasion to promote the sale of the book in Hongkong during early March 1999 alongside Christopher Lingle, who was then employed at the City University of Hongkong. After making a few remarks, we fielded questions, and afterward sold all copies of the book that we possessed. Three Singaporeans came forward to ask further questions, two from the *Straits Times* and one gentleman who presumably was sent from the Consulate of Singapore. The journalists were most interested in my comments about members of the opposition in Singapore, with whom I had no contact whatsoever, though I did comment that Chiam See Tong appeared to be playing a constructive role, well respected by PAP parliamentarians. The third gentleman just shook my hand.

I heard nothing from Singapore regarding the book until I received a missive later in 1999 from Ambassador-at-Large Tommy Koh. He evidently took exception to my statement in the book that he expressed the view one day at Stanford University that Richard Deck, author of Chapter 7, should be purged from the Stanford graduate program. Prior to writing me, Koh contacted the president of Stanford to determine whether there was a report of such a statement in Deck's academic file. Koh then enclosed in a letter to me the missive from the Stanford president stating that there was no such record on file. Copies of the letter that he sent me were also mailed to the president of Stanford, the president of the University of Hawai'i, and to my publisher. Rather than acknowledging receipt to Mr. Koh, who reportedly had ambitions to become United Nations Secretary-General some day, I informed Deck that his academic file was not filed in the manner of a dossier prepared by Singapore's notorious Internal Security Department (ISD). I can now report, thanks to the intervention of Mr. Koh, that Deck's file at Stanford has now been modified to document the statement in question.

Subsequently, I was informed that *The Singapore Puzzle* was banned from sale in the bookstores of the island republic. Although the only objection to the book from anyone in the Singapore government came from Mr. Koh, I doubt that efforts to add to Richard Deck's academic file will release the book from its embargoed status in the freeport of Singapore. Instead, I suspect that the points raised in the book were too embarrassing for the ruling elites, who as usual have decided to show their intellectual cowardice by restricting the free flow of information—and trade.

Since *The Singapore Puzzle* came out, two volumes of Lee Kuan Yew's autobiography have been published. As is customary in the autobiographies of controversial leaders, the aim is to provide a sanitized and self-congratulatory account of events that will be contradicted in due course by more unbiased scholars. A few points in his *From Third World to First: The Singapore Story: 1965-2000; Memoirs of Lee Kuan Yew* (Singapore Press Holdings, Times Editions, 2000) conflict with statements in *The Singapore Puzzle*, so I have decided to call attention to some of the divergences below as they relate to contributors to the book.

For a respected leader who has gone to court so often to win defamation lawsuits, common courtesy presumably might guide Lee Kuan Yew in avoiding defamation of others. But, of course, nobody will be surprised that he has libeled some of the authors of chapters in *The Singapore Puzzle*.

Whereas Lee has claimed that Christopher Lingle left Singapore to "avoid being cross-examined" in a libel suit (p. 155), Lingle instead left the country in fear of his life, as he had every reason to believe. Based on the experience of academic Chia Thye Poh, he could have been incarcerated, tortured, and held in detention for many years for merely holding an opinion. Further, Lee imagined that Lingle's unwelcome article attacked him personally, solely citing the following quote (p. 154): "Intolerant regimes in the region reveal considerable ingenuity in their methods of suppressing dissent . . . Others are more subtle: relying upon a compliant judiciary to bankrupt opposition politicians." Since the article was written in 1994, when Lee was no longer prime minister, only a paranoiac, neurotic, or megalomaniac could have possibly construed these words to be a personal attack. Indeed, in the court action to which Lee referred, the Singapore government itself provided the evidence of the truth of Lingle's statement, which Lee claimeds to be false. Thus, Lee's autobiography shows contempt not only for Lingle but distrust of the very government that was so compliant in defending him in court.

Lee also asserted (p. 152) that an article in the *Far Eastern Economic Review*, then edited by Derek Davies, libeled him when an article quoted a priest, Edgar d'Souza (whom Lee maligns, calling him a "renegade priest"), for claiming that the government, by detaining Catholic layworkers, was attacking the Catholic Church itself. A later account written by D'Souza was also published in the *Review*. Lee did not like what d'Souza said, demanded that Davies apologize for quoting d'Souza, and then sued Davies (not d'Souza) for libel when Davies refused to apologize. Furthermore, Lee stated (p. 152) that Davies "did not give evidence [in court during the libel lawsuit] because he would have been cross-examined." Clearly, Lee pretended that he does not understand that it is common practice for journalists to quote a wide range of opinions on controversial matters. There was no point in having Davies provide hearsay testimony, since he was not the reporter who interviewed D'Souza. Moreover, Lee's suit was based on the view that D'Souza's opinion was not factual (p. 222), thus demonstrating that Lee saw no distinction between a fact and an opinion. Indeed, the judge in the Singapore court that awarded in Lee's favor also conflated fact with opinion, thus again demonstrating the truth of Lingle's thesis.

The most fantastic fabrications of Lee Kuan Yew relate to Francis Seow (pp. 149-150, 253). Lee first imagined that sixteen Catholics and six professionals, only one of whom was a lawyer, secured such influence in the Law Society as to elect Seow as president. In 1990, he referred to the twenty-two in a Singapore court as inconsequential "do-gooders" who might someday become Marxists, but now in his book they contradictorily had become a "Marxist group" that canvassed the Law Society for Seow. If we believe Lee's new assessment, he should turn himself in to Singapore authorities for the crime of perjury, but of course a compliant judiciary would fail to convict him.

Moreover, Lee asserted that the Law Society had never commented on government action before, whereas in 1969 the Law Society objected to abolition by trial by jury. Lee objected to Seow's influence in the Law Society for "attacking government legislation," when in fact the Law Society was empowered by the Legal Profession Act to comment on pending and existing legislation. What upset Lee was the Law Society's comments on proposed amendments to the Newspaper and Printing Presses Act, which for Lee was criticism "on political grounds."

Next, Lee claimed that an American diplomat encouraged Seow to run as an opposition candidate for office, that Seow was assured of diplomatic asylum in case he ran into trouble in Singapore, and that therefore the Internal Security Department recommended detaining Seow. First, how would Lee know the subject of conversation between two persons in a private meeting? The answer is that Seow, after seventy-one days of detention and torture, signed a statement to secure his release that he has later denied, so Lee's claim is that truth emerges from the finely honed skills of Singaporean terroristic interrogation but not from a statement made freely out of confinement. Second, Seow had already decided to run for parliament before he met the American diplomat. Third, in a televised press conference Goh Chok Tong, then deputy prime minister, stated that ISD recommended against arresting Seow, who has amply demonstrated that his release from detention depended upon a decision by Lee Kuan Yew, not ISD.

Further, Lee questioned how Seow could have paid back a loan to a private Singapore bank in 1986. Seow, in the income tax investigation that the Singapore government then launched against him, responded in a sworn statement that his source of funds was his girlfriend, who had substantial assets. Lee, relying on malicious gossip from her former boyfriend, disputed Seow. Since the confidentiality of Singaporean banking transactions has been breached before by Lee, he could have checked out the facts but instead preferred defamatory hearsay.

A number of years ago, Richard Deck tried to help Dr. Chee Soon Juan, leader of the Singapore Democratic Party and head of the pan-Asian NGO Alliance for Reform and Democracy in Asia (ARDA), while he was in prison. He was ill and not receiving proper medical care. According to Deck,

> I contacted the staff of the late U.S. Representative Tom Lantos, who then served as Chairman of the House's International Affairs Committee (as it was then named—it is now the House's Foreign Affairs Committee), and requested their intervention. The Committee's Asian affairs staffer was tasked with contacting the Singaporean embassy in D.C. and making the intercession. When my name was mentioned, the Singaporean official launched into a diatribe against me. According to the Lantos staffer

whom I originally contacted, they "threatened to do all kinds of terrible things to you" if I should ever should return to Singapore. In the event, the intervention was successful because Dr. Chee was released from prison and hospitalized, where he staged a full recovery. The Singaporean government's opinion of me was not enhanced because I twice gave speeches and offered testimony on Capitol Hill before the joint House-Senate Human Rights Caucus; I advocated the expansion of human rights and democracy in Asia (once in the context of ARDA's *Asia Democracy Index* [2005], when I served as that publication's Editorial Board Director). I also visited Congressional offices on behalf of ARDA, once with Dr. Chee in tow.

Nevertheless, neither Richard Deck nor Clark Neher nor I have been libeled in Lee's autobiography. Nor have we been arrested or sued, though Deck was watched by ISD while in Singapore and his mail was conspicuously opened, and his physical condition deteriorated after he left Singapore. Evidently, we are less "naughty" than Davies, Lingle, and Seow.

Nevertheless, *The Singapore Puzzle*, which contains eight carefully written essays, is banned from bookstores in Singapore because, though nonlibelous, the truth evidently hurts much too much, while Lee's autobiography comes across as a rather clumsy effort to answer critics by rewriting history.

Why a second edition? Hoping to find that the earlier problems have been corrected so that I can write a more positive book on Singapore, I have written Epilog sections for all the original chapters to update the narratives. When asked, none of the contributors to the first edition expressed a desire to revisit their essays. I am indebted to ABC-Clio Press for permission to issue a second edition, which perhaps will not be subjected to censorship and, by becoming an e-book, will be more available at a reduced cost.

Michael Haas

THE SINGAPORE PUZZLE

2nd Edition

1

The Singapore Puzzle
Michael Haas

Singapore is an island republic with economic, political, and social characteristics that are puzzling to many observers. For example, the third most prosperous country, with highly paid top governmental officials, wants trade benefits that are accorded only to the poorest countries in the world. A cane strikes the posterior of an American teenager after he is tortured into confessing that he sprayed removal paint on a car, and the government admits that such uses of torture are customary. The father of the country, who has immensely favorable press coverage internationally, nevertheless has the distinction of being the most successful libel litigant in history. In addition, as the country becomes more economically prosperous, human rights violations appear to have increased. These and other paradoxes are obvious to many commentators, but explanations are elusive. Contributors to this volume, nevertheless, are prepared to offer some facts and observations that will help to answer the puzzle—and many subpuzzles.

Singapore's rulers are aware that their country puzzles outsiders. From time to time, they offer explanations, though critics of Singapore scoff at these as mere rationalizations. In my judgment, the official explanations, many of which tend to focus on past historical circumstances, should be taken seriously. For this reason, I have asked critics and defenders of Singapore to contribute essays to this book. My aim is to stimulate a debate that will focus on objective facts about various aspects of Singapore, yet permit various authors an opportunity to provide alternative explanations for puzzles of the island republic.

One might ask, "Why Singapore?" "What is so important about a small piece of real estate in the world today?" Singapore, as the various chapters in this book will attest, has decided to challenge the notion of universal human rights, arguing that rapid economic development requires the suppression of such rights as elections with viable alternative choices and information sources, due process before the law, and the freedom to associate with citizens and noncitizens without fear of reprisals—for a time, all in the name of the triumph of "Asian Values" over the "effete West." A tiny country with the lofty ambition of challenging all the industrial democracies may seem absurdly megalomaniacal. But Singapore has undertaken to proselytize for its viewpoint among Third World nations, and it is gaining converts at a rapid rate. In short, Singapore's assault on democracies appears to be one of the primary battlegrounds in the post-Cold War era.

The Puzzle(s)

The history of Singapore is littered with enigmas of Churchillian proportions, sometimes wrapped within mysteries. As this book is not a general review of Singapore nor of all public policies of the country, what appears in the pages to follow is an effort to identify and explain the main paradoxes of Singapore. After this introductory chapter, I provide a historical account of some of the headline events of the country, when in many cases the Singapore government acted in a peculiar manner (Chapter 2). Then the case for Singapore is stated (Clark Neher in Chapter 3). The subsequent four chapters focus on specific aspects of Singapore's economic and political systems—the economy (Christopher Lingle and Kurt Wickman in Chapter 4), the press (Derek Davies in Chapter 5), the judiciary (Francis Seow in Chapter 6), and foreign policy (Richard Deck in Chapter 7). In the final chapter I attempt an explanation of the various puzzles based on mass society theory (Chapter 8).

The puzzles may be classified under a few general headings—the economy, the culture, the media, the judiciary, foreign affairs, the political system, the society, the leadership, and the future of Singapore.

Economic puzzles. In Chapter 3 Clark Neher states the case for Singapore. Perhaps the most commonly posed question is how Singapore, a Third World country at the time of independence, could rise to First World status, a feat that even Lee Kuan Yew once thought to be impossible.[1] Since Singapore's state directed so much of the economic transformation of the country, what were the successful policies, if any, that should be emulated elsewhere? The puzzle is particularly baffling because, in most parts of the world, "revolutions from the top" have failed.[2] What has Singapore's polity done correctly, while other elite-led economic transformation programs have failed? Chris Lingle and Kurt Wickman address this puzzle in Chapter 4.

Lingle and Wickman also seek to provide a label for Singapore's economic system, which leaders insisted for a time was "socialist." Today, however, the government appears to favor a "free market" form of economy while retaining government control of certain corporations. The authors seek to answer the question by analyzing how the economy works in practice. Similarly, we may ask whether Singapore is "developing" or has become "developed"?

In Chapter 5, Derek Davies describes an incident in which Lee Kuan Yew bullied bankers, including a representative of the Chase Manhattan Bank, into revealing transactions in public, an action repeated on a few other occasions.[3] What is puzzling is that Singapore, which seeks to be an international banking center, is a country where the principle of confidentiality of transactions has been so brazenly violated.

Cultural puzzles. Singaporeans clearly practice Western competitive individualism in their economic pursuits, through frequent job hopping[4] for example. So the campaign to replace so-called decadent "Western Values" with traditional "Asian Values" arrived too late and, if successful, might have lowered productivity by encouraging workers to adopt conformist rather than innovative orientations. Indeed, Lee Kuan Yew and Goh Keng Swee originally encouraged Singaporeans to be individualistic achievers.[5] Lingle and Wickman attempt to characterize what the Singapore government meant by "Asian Values," but the entire campaign of what Lingle elsewhere calls "cultural protectionism" was denounced by Foreign Minister Sinnathamby Rajaratnam 1977, and then embraced two decades later.[6] What, then, are "Asian Values," and why were they promoted by the elites of Singapore?

Puzzles about the media. Singapore's economy seeks to be competitive in nearly all products but one—newspapers. Competition among newspapers has been characterized by former journalist Rajaratnam as "wasteful."[7] Thus, another puzzle relates to the contradiction between Lee Kuan Yew's rise to power as an advocate of a truly free press while Singapore endured a pro-British colonial press and his later efforts to control the press of independent Singapore, as recounted in detail by Derek Davies in Chapter 5. The line between fair and unfair criticism in the press puzzles Singaporeans, some of whom find to their later chagrin that the line has been redrawn after they have tried to act responsibly.

Although Lee Kuan Yew wanted to end foreign ownership of his country's press, he did not apply the same reasoning when the government-controlled *Straits Times* undertook to invest in *Business Day* of Bangkok and the *South China Morning Post* of Hongkong.[8] For that matter, the *Straits Times* has published acerbic columns of William Safire about Singapore, whereas routine reporting by foreign news publications has been subject to various forms of restriction. Thus, another puzzle is why the foreign press has been hounded so much over the years.

Yet another puzzle identified by Davies is the novel claim that the Singapore government has the "right of reply. That is, in the event that a foreign news source prints something deemed inaccurate or offensive, the government claims that a press release in rebuttal is a condition of allowing that periodical to continue to circulate freely within Singapore. Nonetheless, if the controlled press in Singapore government presents something inaccurate or offensive to ordinary citizens, no "right of reply" is granted.[9] Indeed, when some of the twenty-two detainees of 1987 claimed that they were tortured, they were rearrested and released only when they recanted.

Puzzles about the judiciary. Why does the criminal justice system, which appears to operate quite admirably in ordinary cases, so often wreak political vengeance upon individuals who appear to pose very little threat to the state? In Chapter 6, Francis Seow demonstrates how Lee Kuan Yew, an anticolonial champion of the rights of the individual, brought about a postcolonial destruction of the independence of the judiciary. What is particularly baffling is not only that the criminal justice system has been compromised but also that Singapore appears to be the only country in the world that proudly admits using torture as a routine aspect of police interrogation.

Another mystery identified by Seow is that the Singapore government continues to employ preventive detention, a tool once designed to fight the Malayan Communist Party, long after serious threats to the survival of the island republic have disappeared. Efforts of the government to use preventive detention in 1987 to arrest so-called "Marxists" lacked credibility inside and outside Singapore. Yet the government still appears to believe that it can fool everyone with the claim that preventive detention is vital to the survival of the country.

Implicitly, Seow asks why the Singapore government clobbers so many persons. A long train of scapegoats defines the political history of Singapore unlike anywhere else in the world. Why such melodrama out of all proportion to the perceived threat?

Foreign policy puzzles. In regard to Singapore's security, another puzzle is that leaders of the Lilliputian state presume that a small island can defend itself in the missile age. In Chapter 7, Richard Deck poses this Alice in Wonderland question.

Students of international relations will recognize that the best way for a city-state to achieve security is to deter attack, and the logic of deterrence clearly suggests the need to court the friendship of adjacent countries. Yet the history of the foreign policy of Singapore, as chronicled by Deck, repeatedly demonstrates an abrasiveness that has alienated neighboring countries, contrary to the security needs of the country.

A second way to deter adversaries from attack would presumably be to have powerful allies. Accordingly, a recent foreign policy puzzle is why Singapore chose to annoy the United States during the 1990s. For example, though Singapore's per capita income is higher than that of Britain, the island republic sought to qualify for Washington's generalized system of preferences (GSP), a privilege not accorded to Britain, and then complained bitterly when its GSP privileges were rescinded. Singapore's leaders also have complained stridently, without evidence, that the United States government has interfered in its internal affairs, yet the same leaders vigorously lobby in Washington on behalf of its own interests. The rebuff of President Bill Clinton, who asked that American student Michael Fay be spared of caning in 1994, yet another a case in point, soured friendly relations between Singapore and the United States. But why?

Puzzles about the polity. Many other puzzles lie more subliminally. One puzzle that pervades all the chapters in this book is how to classify the political system of the country. In 1968, Lee insisted that the best method for preventing a Communist victory in Singapore and elsewhere was to uphold "free choice of a people, by secret ballot, at periodic intervals."[10] Today, critics use such terms as "authoritarian," "corporatist," "fascist," "phobocracy," and "totalitarian," while friends use such terms as "Asian democracy," "communitarian democracy," and "consociational democracy."[11] Which term applies?

Despite Lee's democratic rhetoric in the colonial era, later statements show contempt for ordinary Singaporeans. For instance, he once said, "We decide what is right. Never mind what the people think." A few months later then Deputy Prime Minister Goh Chok Tong indicated that Singapore's "intellectual elite" will continue to make the key decisions, while the proper role for the "rest of the nation [is to] conform."[12] Accordingly, yet another puzzle is why a majority of the voters has supported the People's Action Party (PAP) despite these insults, whereas for PAP the mystery is why so many voters cast ballots in opposition to the party in power.

One of the most basic puzzles is why Singapore has become even less democratic while advancing economically. That political freedom is a precondition to economic prosperity is one of the most basic findings of the social sciences.[13] Similarly, the government's insistence that human rights are a luxury for rich countries is belied by the fact that Singapore is one of the most affluent countries in the world. According to Lee Kuan Yew a decade ago, "We have now achieved enough of the material basics of life to be able to give more attention to socio-psychological and spiritual needs."[14] Why, then, does the Singapore government continue to espouse the view that it must assign higher priority to achieving economic growth than to providing more political freedom?

Social puzzles. Social problems in Singapore, from discourtesy to juvenile delinquency, concern the leadership of the country very deeply. One such puzzle is the campaign to encourage female college graduates to marry male counterparts, ostensibly to enhance the gene pool with geniuses. The campaign persists though biologists have long known that two intelligent parents will produce less intelligent offspring, a phenomenon known as "regression of the mean."[15] Besides, Lee Kuan Yew has referred to the National University of Singapore as less than "reputable,"[16] so the marriage policy evidently applies to those who study abroad, where Lee expects that they will encounter corrupting Western influences if not overseas employment.

Although Lee Kuan Yew once argued strongly for a "Malaysian Malaysia," still another puzzle is why the Singapore government has never advocated a "Singaporean Singapore."[17] Whereas half the population of Hawai`i marries across ethnic lines and enjoys high social status, Eurasians in Singapore, accounting for only 2.4 percent of the population, tend to be ignored.[18] Differing educational streams, divided by language and religion, were an early innovation in Singapore, but they institutionalized social divisions. The effort in the 1980s to encourage schoolchildren to take courses in religion further divided ethnic and religious groups. When religion courses were later discontinued in favor of an "Asian Values" approach to morals education at schools divided by ethnicity and religion, Chinese Confucianists played a dominant role in defining the content.[19] Meanwhile, government leaders from time to time make statements that praise Chinese yet denigrate Indians and Malays,[20] and also claim that they seek ethnic harmony. In short, the Singapore government puzzles many observers, who wonder why the leaders shoot themselves in the foot on matters of ethnoreligious diversity and harmony.

Governmental campaigns and harsh penalties evidently do not solve all the social problems of the country. The bewilderment of the government over matters of social alienation is yet another puzzle to add to the list.

Puzzles about the leadership. Perhaps the most intriguing mystery of all is Lee Kuan Yew himself. Statements early in his career demonstrated a commitment to democracy, a free press, and the rule of law. Yet later statements and actions, reported in this book and elsewhere, show that he repudiated his earlier ideals. One of the most difficult if important puzzles to unravel is what has made the man tick—and backtrack in his later career.

Puzzles about the future. The final puzzle to be explored herein concerns the future of Singapore. What will happen after Lee Kuan Yew fades from the scene? Will Singapore's economy be left behind in the world economy? Can Singapore become more democratic—and, if so, how?

Other puzzles. Other puzzles could be added to the list. In a society with so many restrictions on news acquisition, rumors inevitably substitute for facts.[21] For example, Lee Kuan Yew is rumored to have been born in Indonesia. Alleged sex escapades of Lee Hsien Loong are also the subject of incredible fantasy reports. Rather than rumors, the aim in this volume is to present and analyze facts.

The Contributors

To attempt to solve puzzles about Singapore, some twenty in all, I have relied on the eloquence and experience of several contributors to this book. Each author has a story to tell about Singapore based on unique personal and sometimes unhappy contacts with the government. Although the essays are factual in general, painful experiences in Singapore may occasionally motivate acerbic comments.

Political scientist Clark D. Neher, author of Chapter 3, is former Director of the Center for Southeast Asian Studies at Northern Illinois University. He has done field work for Singapore's well-respected Institute of Southeast Asian Studies (ISEAS), and he has included a chapter on Singapore in *Southeast Asia in the New International Era* (2013), which is now in its fifth edition.[22]

Christopher Lingle and Kurt Wickman, coauthors of Chapter 4, are former visiting economics professors at the National University of Singapore (NUS), where they learned that their lectures were attended by informers, who were assigned the responsibility of monitoring lectures as well as students. In early 1994, after they coauthored an op-ed for the *International Herald Tribune*[23] which questioned the validity of economic data produced by the People's Republic of China, they were summoned to the office of Dean Edward Chew, chastised for the indiscretion, and informed of a directive that all their publications should be cleared by the dean before being sent off to publishers with a byline indicating that they were employed at NUS.

Later in 1994, Lingle as sole author decided to ignore the directive and wrote in the *Tribune* again, criticizing unnamed dictatorships in Asia with compliant judiciaries.[24] This time he was interrogated at work and had his papers at home searched. He then fled the country, resigned his university position, though he had another eleven months remaining on his contract, and he lost as a codefendant in a lawsuit with the *Tribune*, thereby forfeiting approximately US$100,000 in fines and wages. His *Singapore's Authoritarian Capitalism* (1996) provides some details on his experience as well as an analysis of how Singapore's economy works.[25]

Wickman served out his full assignment from 1992 to 1994 and returned to teach at City University, Stockholm, and now is an economics professor at Gavle University and Chulalongkorn University. He later published a book and several essays on Singapore.[26]

Derek Davies, author of Chapter 5, was distinguished by serving from 1964 to 1990 as the editor of *Far Eastern Economic Review*, a newsweekly that he built from relative obscurity into the premier Asian news periodical. As his chapter recounts in part, Davies has been in Singapore on several occasions to advance the cause of freedom of the press. In 1976, after several of his correspondents encountered difficulties with the government, he sought an appointment with Lee Kuan Yew to resolve the difficulties. Lee, however, was interested in no such resolution, and a repeat visit in 1985 was to no avail. The *Review's* problems multiplied over the years, including the arrest and detention of several reporters, restrictions on the sale of the periodical, and denials to *Review* journalists of entry into Singapore, even once for a family reunion. In 1988, the case of *Lee Kuan Yew v Derek Davies* was filed before a Singapore court. Lee believed that he was defamed by an article on how Lee allegedly bullied the Catholic hierarchy after so many of its layworkers had been arrested in Operation Spectrum. Predictably, Lee won the case, and the Singapore court assessed Davies S$230,000 (then US$165,000), with interest at 6 percent per annum from the approximate date when the news article appeared. The *Review*'s publisher, Dow Jones & Company, then secured Davies's resignation. After a stint at the East-West Center in Honolulu, he volunteered for a retirement in Europe. He died in 2002.

Francis T. Seow, author of Chapter 6, has a long and distinguished career in Singapore, recounted in *To Catch a Tartar* (1994), a book so eloquent as to invite a filmscript. After joining the Singapore Legal Service in 1956, his performance attracted the attention of Lee Kuan Yew, who played a godfather role in arranging for his appointment as Solicitor-General in 1967, a post that he resigned in 1969 to go into private practice. His legal skills and political courage so gained the admiration of many Singaporeans that in 1986 he was elected president of the Law Society, which he hoped would advise parliamentarians regarding proposed legislation. When Seow defended political detainees and chose to run for office as an opposition candidate in 1988, he was arrested as an alleged agent of the American government. After seventy-two days of detention, including physical and psychological torture, he was released. While in the United States for medical treatment, the Singapore government accused Seow of financial improprieties. He then accepted an invitation to be a Fellow at Yale Law School in 1989. The following year, he became a Fellow at the East Asian Legal Studies Program, Harvard School of Law. In addition to *To Catch a Tartar* (1994), Seow has written *The Media Enthralled* (1997), and *Beyond Suspicion: The Singapore Courts on Trial* (2006).

Richard A. Deck, author of Chapter 7, first visited Singapore for three weeks in early 1975 as an undergraduate honors student studying Japan's role in Southeast Asia. He returned as a Stanford University graduate student from November 1986 to December 1988 as a Fellow in International Peace and Security on a grant to study at the National University of Singapore and to write his dissertation at the nearby Institute of Southeast Asian Studies. During his stay, especially after the expulsion of American diplomat E. Mason Hendrickson, he was wiretapped, his mail was opened, and he was placed under surveillance, evidently because Lee Kuan Yew did not agree with statements that he made on television regarding the Iran-Contra scandal. Further, for the sin of having the television set on while studying at home, Lee characterized Deck as an example of a "decadent American." Upon his return to Stanford, he was diagnosed and treated for post-traumatic stress syndrome due to the harassment. Tommy Koh, Singapore's ambassador to the United States, even journeyed to Stanford in a vain attempt to have Deck kicked out of the graduate program. Deck attributes his heart attack in 1994 and current cardiopulmonary disability directly to the stress of being hounded while in Singapore. He has written prodigiously about Singapore and other matters.[27]

My own interest in Singapore, as noted in the Preface to the first edition, began with two one-week trips to the island republic in 1971, followed by week-long revisits in 1978 and 1985, all while on sabbatical from my position as a political science professor at the University of Hawai`i. In 1987, I returned for a summer on a Fulbright Research Fellowship at ISEAS to write a book about Asian regional cooperation, which emerged as *The Asian Way to Peace* (1989). While in Singapore during the height of Operation Spectrum, I attended an

ISEAS seminar and sat next to an exuberant American, whom I much later learned at a Stanford alumni party in San Francisco was Richard Deck. The evident absurdity of the Operation Spectrum docudrama staged for Singapore television in 1987 and the preposterousness of letters to the editor of the *Far Eastern Economic Review* penned by Singaporean government officials thereafter prompted me to write a critical column for the *Far Eastern Economic Review* in 1988.[28] My essay in turn occasioned yet another governmental riposte,[29] and not long afterward the Singapore government asked the Fulbright Commission to stop recommending political scientists for fellowships in Singapore. Thereafter, I wrote a few obscure academic essays on Singapore.[30] I returned to the country for short stopovers in 1989 and 1994, the latter visit happening to coincide with the day when Michael Fay was released from custody. I have assumed the task of presenting the Singapore puzzle out of respect for the successes of the country and chagrin over the excesses.

Epilog

Writing in 2014, some of the puzzles identified earlier are still puzzles, but others have been mitigated. The concept of "Asian Values," for example, is no longer trumpeted. Other changes are presented within Epilogs in later chapters.

Statistical indicators also have changed. In 1998, Singapore was the ninth most prosperous country; today, the International Monetary Fund reports that the island republic has risen to third place.[31] Data on the average salaries of top government officials are not available today, though they have recently been cut in response to public pressure.[32] Singaporeans of mixed race accounted for 0.5 percent in 1998, but that figure rose to 2.4 percent in 2012.[33]

Although I have kept most of the text reflecting the occupational status of the contributors at the time of the first edition, the section About the Contributors at the end of the book provides updates.

Notes

1.   Quoted in C. M. Turnbull, *A History of Singapore, 1819-1988*, 2nd edn. (Singapore: Oxford University Press, 1989), 267.
2.   Ellen Kay Trimberger, *Revolution from Above, Military Bureaucrats and Development in Japan, Turkey,*

Egypt, and Peru (New Brunswick, NJ: Transaction Books, 1978).

3. Other instances are described in Francis T. Seow, *To Catch a Tartar: A Dissident in Lee Kuan Yew's Prison* (New Haven, CT: Yale University Southeast Asia Studies, 1994), 180.

4. Christopher Lingle, *Singapore's Authoritarian Capitalism: Asian Values, Free Market Illusions, and Political Dependency* (Fairfax, VA: Locke Institute, 1996), 100.

5. *Straits Times*, 1 May 1981; Goh Keng Swee, "Social, Political and Institutional Aspects of Development Planning," in *The Economics of Modernization*, ed. Goh Keng Swee (Singapore: Asia Pacific Press, 1972).

6. Christopher Lingle, *Singapore's Authoritarian Capitalism*, 7; Sinnathamby Rajaratnam, "Asian Values and Modernization" in *Asian Values and Modernization*, ed. Seah Chee Meow (Singapore: Singapore University Press, 1977). See also Fareed Zakaria, "A Conversation with Lee Kuan Yew," *Foreign Affairs*, LXXIII (March/April, 1994): 109-116.

7. *Straits Times*, 18 July 1984.

8. Francis T. Seow, *The Media Enthralled* (Boulder, CO: Rienner, 1997), 119.

9. For example, "Seow Reveals the Human Rights Connection, Amnesty and Asiawatch Knew Detainees Had Not Been Assaulted," *Sunday Times* (Singapore), 22 May 1988.

10. Alex Josey, *Democracy in Singapore: The 1970 By-Elections* (Singapore: Asia Pacific Press, 1970), 12.

11. See Lingle, *Singapore's Authoritarian Capitalism*; Beng-Huan Chua, *Communitarian Ideology and Democracy in Singapore* (London: Routledge, 1995); Narayan Ganesan, "Democracy in Singapore," paper presented at the annual convention of the Association of Asian Studies, Honolulu, April, 1996; Chua Beng Huat, *Communitarian Ideology and Democracy in Singapore* (London: Routledge, 1999).

12. *Straits Times*, 20 April 1987; Steve Vines, "The Deepening Tendency to Control," *Honolulu Star-Bulletin & Advertiser*, 1 September 1987, E1.

13. Seymour Martin Lipset, "Some Social Requisites of Democracy," *American Political Science Review*, LIII (1959): 69-105; Adam Przeworski and Fernande Limongi, "Political Regimes and Economic Growth," *Journal of Economic Perspectives*, VII (1993): 3-21; Michael Haas, *Improving Human Rights* (Westport, CT: Praeger, 1994); John B. Londregan and Keith T. Poole, "Does High Income Promote Democracy?," *World Politics*, XLIX (1996): 1-30.

14. "Out of the Recession—Thanks to Younger Leaders, Workers," *Straits Times*, 9 August 1987, 13.

15. L. C. Dunn and Th. Dobzhanski, *Heredity, Race, and Society* (New York: Mentor, 1955, 99; Theodosius Dobzhanski, *Genetic Diversity and Human Equality* (New York: Basic Books, 1973).

16. Quoted in Seow, *The Media Enthralled*, 65.

17. The question is raised in James Cotton, "Political Innovation in Singapore: The Presidency, the Leadership and the Party," in *Singapore Changes Guard: Social, Political and Economic Directions in the 1990s*, ed. Garry Rodan (New York: St. Martin's Press, 1993), 12.

18. Michael Haas, ed. *Multicultural Hawai`i: The Fabric of a Multiethnic Society* (New York: Garland, 1998); Michael Hill and Lian Kwen Fee, *The Politics of Nation Building and Citizenship in Singapore* (London: Routledge, 1995), 235, 239.

19. Ibid., 8-9; Chua, *Communitarian Ideology and Democracy in Singapore*, 35; John Clammer, "Deconstructing Values: The Establishment of a National Ideology," in *Singapore Changes Guard*, ed. Rodan, 42.

20. *Straits Times*, 11 August 1987; *Straits Times Weekly*, 20 June 1992; Seow, *To Catch a Tartar*, 139; David Brown, "The Corporatist Management of Ethnicity in Contemporary Singapore," in *Singapore Changes Guard: Social, Political and Economic Directions in the 1990s*, ed. Barry Rodan (New York: St. Martin's Press), 24.

21. Chua, *Communitarian Ideology and Democracy in Singapore*, 50-54.

22. Robert A. Dayley and Clark D. Neher, *Southeast Asia in the New International Era*, 5th edn. (Boulder, CO: Westview, 2013).

23. Christopher Lingle and Kurt Wickman, "Don't Trust the Reports of Supercharged Growth," *International Herald Tribune*, 19 January 1994.

24. Christopher Lingle, "The Smoke over Parts of Asia Obscures Some Profound Concerns," *International Herald Tribune*, 7 October 1994.

25. See also Christopher Lingle, *The Rise and Decline of the Asian Century: False Starts on the Path to the Global Millennium* (Barcelona: Editions Siroco, 1997).

26. Kurt Wickman, *Singapore: Föredöme eller skräckexempel?* (Stockholm: Timbro, 1995); "*Uländers väg från fattigdom till västånd*" (Stockholm: Timbro, Rapport 11, 1994); "Demokratisk omvandling asiatisk våg," *Gefle Dagblad*, XVI (#12, 1994); "Some General Relations in the Development of Trade Between Asia and the European Community 1985-1991," *Journal of European Studies*, III (January-June, 1995): 69-95; "Singapores mörka sidor," *Smedjan* (October, 1995): 45-46; "Nedgång i Ostasien: Besvär i Sverige," *Gefle Dagblad*, XXIII (#2, 1997). See also Wickman's earlier essay, "The Asian Challenge," *Asian Journal of Political Science*, I (December, 1993): 190-195. Lingle and Wickman jointly authored "Index Undermined by Singapore System," *Australian Financial Review*, III (#1, 1997); and "Mixing Wealth with Tyranny," *Journal of Commerce*, III (#1, 1997).

27. See Richard A. Deck, "Singapore's Strategic Culture," in *Conflict, and Strategic Culture in the Asia-Pacific Region*, eds. Russell Trood and Kenneth Booth (London: Macmillan, 1997).

28. Michael Haas, "Dissent and the Demand for Democracy in Singapore," *Far Eastern Economic Review*, 10 March 1987, 24-26.

29. Martin Marini, "The Enemy Within," *Far Eastern Economic Review*, 24 March 24, 7 (letter). See also Lau Teik Soon, "Conclusive Evidence," *Far Eastern Economic Review*, 31 March 1988, 9 (letter); Lau Teik Soon, "Witty and Wise," *Far Eastern Economic Review*, 21 April 1998, 6 (letter); Michael Haas, "Different Department," *Far Eastern Economic Review*, 5 May 1988, 4-5 (letter).

30. Michael Haas, "The Politics of Singapore in the 1980s"; "Third World Sub-Fascism and Corporate Dominance: The Case of Singapore," *Asian Perspective*, XIV (1990): 31-42; "U.S.-Singapore Relations: Democracy Versus Sadistocracy." See also Michael Haas, "Singapore: Taunting West with Boast of 'Prosperous Totalitarianism'," *Honolulu Advertiser*, 16 October 1994, B3.

31. International Monetary Fund, *World Economic Outlook Database*, www.imf.com, accessed 14 January 2014.

32. Agence France Press, "Singapore to Cut Salaries of Top Officials," *Jordan Times*, January 4, accessed 14 January 2014. Adverse publicity was provided in an article by Chua Beng Huat, "Singapore in 2007: High Wage Ministers and the Management of Gays and the Elderly," *Asian Survey*, XLVIII (2008): 55-56.
33. "Singapore," *wikipedia.com*, accessed 14 January 2014.

2

A Political History
Michael Haas

The purpose of the present chapter is to identify some of the historical events that have colored contemporary Singapore. Government leaders frequently justify present actions by referring to past traumas. The chapter develops neither the case for nor against Singapore but attempts to show that the country has faced many challenges, some more serious than others.

Early History

Singapore is a republic consisting of the island of Singapura, which consists of some 240 square miles (about the same size as Corfu, Guam, and the Isle of Man, and nearly half the size of Long Island, New York), and about sixty islets located between Indonesia and Malaysia at the southern end of the Straits of Malacca. Singapura is linked by a Causeway to the southernmost part of the Malay peninsula, the Malaysian state of Johore Bahru. Indonesia's Riau Islands are a short distance away by boat. Water is piped in from Malaysia.

For the indigenous Malays, Singapore was a fishing village. In due course, Chinese settlers found the island to be a useful location for trade, and they have been migrating to Singapore ever since. Today, the population of about 5.5 million is multiethnic; the principal ethnic groups are Chinese (77 percent), Malays (14 percent), and Indians (8 percent). Those with ancestry from India were recruited by the British as contract laborers in the nineteenth century. Singapore's principal religions are Buddhism/Taoism (44 percent), Christian (18 percent), Islam (15 percent), and Hinduism (5 percent).

The ambitious Sir Stamford Raffles landed in 1819 and persuaded the Sultan of Riau and Johore to cede the island to the East India Company. In 1824, Britain assumed sovereignty over Singapore. In 1826, Malacca, Penang, and Singapore were absorbed into the Straits Settlements, administratively governed by British India. Finally, in 1867, the Straits Settlements became a British Crown Colony, governed directly from London.

In 1942, Japan's imperial army invaded Singapore, which surrendered after its water supply was cut off. Whereas the new Japanese rulers stressed the superiority of Asian over Western Values, the abusiveness of the occupation authorities negated the campaign to obtain willing cooperation from Singaporeans.[1] Instead, there were mass arrests, massacres, suspension of habeas corpus, torture during interrogation, and a fear among Singaporeans that anyone could be arrested at any time. Although the Malayan Communist Party (MCP) heroically sought to undermine Japanese rule, most Chinese in Singapore superficially accommodated to Japanese rule while despising their new Asian overlords.

After Japan's defeat in 1945, British colonialism returned, but the Straits Settlements was abolished, and Singapore was separated from Malaya as a Crown Colony in 1946. The MCP organized workers into trade-unions and agitated for independence. But in 1947 the British required all unions to register and prohibited the use of union funds for political purposes, and MCP's planned May Day rally was banned. Within Malaya, the MCP called for a mass struggle against British colonialism. Resulting acts of violence in Malaya during May and June 1948 prompted British authorities to declare the situation to be an Emergency in both and Malaya and Singapore. Under the Preservation of Public Security Ordinance, the British banned the MCP, restricted associations, meetings, and strikes, and allowed for preventive detention of suspected Communists, some of whom were defended eloquently by a young attorney named Lee Kuan Yew, who returned to Singapore in 1950 with a law degree from Cambridge University. The Emergency lasted until 1960.

The Movement for Independence

British plans to provide self-government to Singapore first emerged in 1953, when a commission was appointed to draw up a constitution. With the political landscape uncertain, vigorous labor and student unrest arose. In 1954, students massively protested compulsory national service, and several small strikes were also called. In 1955, workers at a bus company went on strike for higher wages and better working conditions (known as the Hock Lee Bus Company riots), and students went on strike to demand recognition for a student organization. Some of these uprisings were orchestrated by founders of the People's Action Party (PAP), which was launched in 1954 as a socialist party that sought an end to the Emergency, free compulsory education, workers' rights, and immediate independence.

The first measure of self-government came in 1955, when a constitution was proclaimed and parliamentary elections were held. David Saul Marshall, leader of the leftist Labour Front, was elected Chief Minister of Singapore in a coalition that included some centrist political parties. PAP secured only three seats (Table 2.1), one occupied by its secretary-general, Lee Kuan Yew, who began to perfect his oratorical skills, making stirring speeches for democracy, independence, and social justice. One of the earliest innovations that year was the launching of the Central Provident Fund (CPF), to which employees now contribute as much as 20 percent of their salaries, which is matched by employers (about 15 percent today), in order to provide capital for home ownership and later retirement.

In 1956, Marshall resigned because he could not accept the terms for independence proposed by London, which insisted on retaining control over British military bases on the island. As the bases then employed some 40,000 Singaporeans,[2] vital to the island's economy, his Labour Front successor, Lim Yew Hock, eventually negotiated a compromise arrangement with the British regarding security that allocated three of the seven seats on Singapore's transitional Internal Security Council to Britain, three to Singapore, and one to Malaya. While negotiations were in progress, the MCP stirred up unrest among students and even tried to oust the Lee Kuan Yew faction from PAP. In 1957, Lim Yew Hock responded to the student agitation by arresting extremists in the labor and student movements, thereby strengthening Lee's position in PAP, which in turn won City Council elections that year. Ong Eng Guan, a founding member of PAP and rival of Lee Kuan Yew, was then elected Mayor of Singapore.

Singapore achieved internal autonomy in 1959, when the British governor of Singapore was replaced by a Singaporean head of state. London then retained responsibility only for defense and foreign affairs. In elections for the Legislative Assembly, the victor was PAP, which won forty-three of the fifty-one seats (Table 2.1). During the election, PAP weakened the Labour Front by accusing its minister of education of pocketing political funds from the U.S. government that were designed to aid the party. Marshall, who resigned from the Labour Front, formed the Workers' Party but lost at the polls.

Table 2.1 People's Action Party Support, 1955-2011

Year of Election	Percent of Votes	Percent of Seats
1955	9	11
1959	53	84
1963	46	73
1968	84	100
1972	69	100
1976	72	100
1980	76	100
1984	63	97
1988	62	99
1991	61	95
1997	65	98
2001	75	98
2006	67	98
2011	60	93

Source: Alex Josey, *Democracy in Singapore: The 1970 By-Election* (Singapore: Asia Pacific Press, 1970), 34; Bilveer Singh, *Whither PAP's Dominance: An Analysis of Singapore's 1991 General Elections* (Petaling Jaya, Malaysia: Pelanduk, 1992), 5, 86; Murray Hiebert, "Ring in the Old," *Far Eastern Economic Review*, 16 January 1997, 16; "People's Action Party," *wikipedia.com*, accessed 14 January 2014.

Upon taking office as prime minister in 1959, Lee launched a brief attack on Western culture. He also he began calling newspaper editors privately whenever displeased by a news article, while in public he threatened to arrest members of the press for allegedly misreporting the news. Members of Chinese secret societies were arrested or placed under surveillance, resulting in fewer incidents of communal unrest. The government provided reorientation sessions and cut allowances to the white-collar civil service, who were drafted into performing "voluntary" manual work on Sundays. In addition, special terms for British subjects to become Singaporean citizens were withdrawn.

In the transition to self-governing status, Ong Eng Guan was transformed from Mayor of Singapore into Minister of National Development. In 1960, Lee reduced the powers of the ministry to limit Ong's power, whereupon he accused Lee of corruption and charged PAP with being undemocratic. Ong was then dismissed from the ministry, expelled from PAP, and forced to resign from the Legislative Assembly. In 1961, Ong won back his former parliamentary seat after a campaign that appeared to some to exploit Chinese chauvinistic sentiments, and he formed a rival United People's Party.

Although Lee's initial campaign rhetoric about socialism frightened the business community, PAP gained new support when his minister of finance, Goh Keng Swee, embarked on a pragmatic program of industrial development to be financed by foreign capital, as recommended in a United Nations study by Dutch economist Albert Winsemius. One economic imperative perceived by the PAP government was merger with Malaya. So in 1960 Lee's government held talks in Kuala Lumpur regarding the formation of a common market, albeit without success. In 1960, the Housing and Development Board was launched with extensive powers of land condemnation and housing construction, ultimately resulting in widespread apartment ownership. In 1961, an Economic Development Board was established, and work began on Jurong Industrial Estate, a tax haven that sought foreign investment for new industries. The government then de-registered the Communist-dominated Singapore Trades Union Congress, which was replaced by the National Trades Union Congress, a body that accepted the government's policy of limiting labor disputes so as to encourage business. In other areas of government activity, from education to health to housing, PAP enacted progressive reforms.

Britain conferred independence upon the Federation of Malaya in 1957. As Britain wanted to divest itself of colonies in Southeast Asia, Lee Kuan Yew was enlisted in a plan to add Singapore and the Borneo states of Sabah and Sarawak to the Federation of Malaya, which thereby would form the Federation of Malaysia. Leftist members of PAP opposed the plan, and in 1961 they consulted the British Commissioner-General for Southeast Asia in order to receive assurances that the constitution would remain in force if they ousted Lee from office.

Upon learning of the meeting, the prime minister charged that Britain had hatched a plot to encourage the Communists to gain control of the government so that London would have an excuse to suspend the constitution. Lee also scheduled a debate in parliament on the pending entry into Malaysia, and he received majority support. When PAP dissidents formed the Barisan Socialist Party, defections reduced PAP to 20 percent of its former members.[3] In 1962, Lee offered a referendum on the proposed terms of the merger, and 71 percent of the electorate supported Lee's position.[4] In early 1963, the Internal Security Council launched Operation Cold Store, detaining more than one hundred Barisan Socialist members, which led to protest riots; the unrest, in turn, served as a pretext to arrest more dissidents, thus crushing the party. Since then, no opposition party has ever developed a mass base. During 1963, Lee was particularly nervous about the outcome of a jury trial involving alleged financial mismanagement of union funds by a charismatic leader of a dockworkers' union (which supported bus drivers in the earlier Hock Lee riots), and by the end of the year the government abolished trial by jury in all cases except capital offenses. The union itself was de-registered in 1964.

President Sukarno of Indonesia was extremely unhappy about the formation of Malaysia, as Sabah and Sarawak were enclaves on the island of Borneo, the rest of which was Indonesian territory. The Philippines also declared that Sabah was rightfully a part of the Philippines. To support negotiations on the matter among foreign ministers of the affected countries, Malayan Prime Minister Tunku Abdul Rahman delayed the formation of Malaysia for two weeks. On August 31, 1963, when the Federation of Malaysia was originally scheduled to come into being, Lee Kuan Yew issued a unilateral declaration of Singapore's independence (the first British colony to do so since 1776) and scheduled a snap election. Controlling radio and television throughout the island, PAP won 47 percent of the vote but 73 percent of the seats in single-member districts (Table 2.1). Among Lee's rivals, David Marshall was defeated, and Lim Yew Hock did not even run for office.

Singapore in Malaysia

The Federation of Malaysia was finally launched in September 6, 1963, with Singapore a state in the federation. Indonesia's "Crush Malaysia" campaign included guerrilla and military action. Communist opponents of merger were responsible for several bomb blasts in Singapore from 1963 to 1965, and Indonesian gunboats seized some Singapore fishing boats. Malaysia then passed the Internal Security Act to supersede the Preservation of Public Security Ordinance, which was in force under British rule, thus enabling Singaporean authorities to arrest and detain suspected Communists indefinitely, without needing to charge specific persons with an offense before a judge.

Meanwhile, Lee Kuan Yew became disenchanted with the way in which the Malaysian government treated Singapore. Kuala Lumpur, which had accepted Singapore reluctantly in the first place, moved slowly on matters of economic development, which was the top priority of PAP in Singapore. Instead, the dominant party, the United Malays National Organization (UMNO), requested special treatment of Malays in Singapore. Although Lee had already allowed Malay-language schools, he refused other demands. During 1963, week-long riots broke out twice between Chinese and Malay youths, resulting in curfews; twenty-two died in the resulting communal violence.[5] Chinese students also protested changes in secondary exams that year.

In the federal elections of 1964, only one PAP delegate was elected to the Malaysian parliament—C. V. Devan Nair, an ardent anticolonialist who had been jailed by the British in the early 1950s and joined PAP before the end of the decade. Lee tried to confer with Malay civic leaders in Singapore over the heads of UMNO, which had been trounced in the 1963 elections in Singapore, but Syed Ja`afar Albar, heartened by PAP's defeat in the 1964 elections, lashed out against PAP. In mid-1964, on the birthday of Mohammed, riots broke out between Chinese and Malays, reportedly because of pro-Chinese speeches by Lee Kuan Yew; twenty-two died and at least one hundred were reportedly injured.[6]

Since PAP was being cornered into the role of a Chinese communal political party within the federation, Lee appealed to an end to communal politics, tried to form a coalition with opposition parties in Malaya, Sabah, and Sarawak, and advocated a "Malaysian Malaysia," in which the underprivileged of all races could advance economically. Although his rhetoric was reasonable to some, the way he articulated his case was far too abrasive for UMNO. He then began the practice of filing a lawsuit against a political opponent—this time, Syed Ja`afar Albar. Under UMNO pressure to arrest Lee,[7] Prime Minister Rahman then decided to expel Singapore from the federation, and the island nation achieved full independence on

August 9, 1965.

Newly Independent Singapore

Recriminations on both sides of the Causeway, which separates Malaysia from Singapore, continued for a few years. Leftists agitated students to protest the new arrangement in 1965, resulting in arrests, deportations of foreign students, and expulsions. Lee told Singaporeans to buckle down to work, and the situation eventually calmed down to the task of building a viable city-state. Barisan Socialist representatives resigned in protest over what they claimed was a sham democracy, and PAP thereafter had no opposition in parliament for the next twenty-six years. In 1966, PAP outflanked the Barisan Socialists by joining the Socialist International, a nongovernmental body that includes the British Labour Party, French Socialist Party, and similar non-Communist left-wing political parties. However, its membership was ended within a decade because of human rights concerns among the European socialists about Singapore.

In 1966, Chia Thye Poh, an academician and former Barisan Socialist parliamentarian, was arrested under the authority of the Internal Security Act for organizing a protest against the American entry into Vietnam's civil war. He was never charged with a crime, and he refused to confess of Communist leanings, so by 1989 he held the dubious distinction of being the only political detainee to have been incarcerated longer than South Africa's Nelson Mandela. Also in 1966 the government issued the Essential Information (Control of Publications and Safeguarding of Information) Regulations, which were later interpreted to mean that news leaks from government sources constituted sedition.

Also in 1967, Singapore lobbied to join the Association of South-East Asian Nations (ASEAN) along with Indonesia, Malaysia, the Philippines, and Thailand, which had originally planned to exclude the island republic.[8] ASEAN initially was established as a forum for foreign ministers to build a sense of community within the region, and in due course Singapore mended fences with Indonesia and Malaysia.

In 1967, Britain announced that it would soon phase out troops from Malaysia and Singapore, whereupon Singapore consulted Israel on how to defend such a small country. The government then instituted national service, which requires Singapore males (excluding Malays until 1985) at age eighteen to train for two and one-half years of military service, followed by a reserve status up to the age of forty. The Total Defense Doctrine, which then emerged, provided that Singapore's defense required economic, military, psychological, and social measures of various sorts. When Britain fixed the military withdrawal timetable at 1971, Lee Kuan Yew went to London to obtain a commitment to hand over various assets on the island to the government, to retrain those put out of work, and to give the government the sum of £50 million.[9] In addition, negotiations ensued for the Five Power Defence Arrangements, a set of bilateral agreements to provide security through joint consultation and military exercises with Australia, New Zealand, Malaysia, and the United Kingdom.

In 1968, PAP won all the seats in the parliamentary election (Table 2.1); only seven seats were contested. With this mandate, economic development plans were implemented, including the formation of new government corporations and government-financed joint ventures with the private sector. Urban renewal plans, adopted the previous year, went forward, gradually transforming a downtown of decaying shops into one of modern skyscrapers. In addition, new towns, with government-financed housing and recreational facilities, were built around the island, and most residents were able to buy their own apartments at reasonable prices. Drainage projects and sanitation improvements gave the island the look of immaculate gardens. Affordable health care was available to all, and life expectancy increased, though the handicapped and infirm were largely left to family and private care. Family planning programs were instituted, and the birthrate fell.

New laws permitted longer working hours, regulated wages and restricted bonuses and overtime, but required employers to place larger CPF matching contributions. There was no provision for unemployment insurance, but the government's policy of full employment was largely successful, and Singaporeans frequently changed employers in order to increase their salaries. Union membership plummeted, and strikes vanished from the landscape by 1969. Jury trials were completely abolished, also in 1969. Welfare eligibility criteria became more stringent, such that Singapore's early welfare state ceased to exist.

When it became clear that Singapore leaders had totally abandoned socialism, direct foreign investment poured into the country, and the country decreasingly depended on its role in entrepôt trade. What followed was spectacular economic growth, which enhanced the international reputation of its prime minister, Lee Kuan Yew. Locally, he was held in awe; whenever he enters a room, all persons stand at attention until he seats himself.

A multilingual educational system, with English as a second language, was revamped to steer students into technical and vocational studies. Parallel educational streams in Chinese, English, Malay, and Tamil languages assured the population that cultural diversity would be respected, although most students pragmatically enrolled in English-language schools. However, the government discouraged education along separatist communal lines in the 1970s. Lee Kuan Yew and other prominent English-educated leaders sent their children to Chinese schools, which they then claimed to be superior in instilling the values of hard work, resilience in adversity, and sacrifice for the good of the community.

The positive achievements of Singapore, however, soon became clouded with some unusual campaigns. For example, editorials decrying the declining status of Chinese education by the local newspaper *Nanyang Siang Pau* resulted in charges of sedition lodged against the top management in 1971. This was a part of a general crackdown on the press that year so that the government would not be embarrassed by adverse news stories. Several local newspaper executives and reporters were arrested and forced to confess that they were trying to stir up either communalism or sympathy for Communism. Lee Kuan Yew was particularly unhappy that mainstream newspapers in Singapore had foreign financial backing, and in 1971 a reporter for the *Far Eastern Economic Review* was the first of many to be accused of interfering in the internal affairs of the country (in this case, by reporting news about Singapore obtained from an employee of Amnesty International)[10] and then ordered to leave the country. In 1974, when a foreign journalist for the first time was found guilty of contempt of court for negative reporting, parliament amended the Newspaper and Printing Presses Act to require public offering of shares and government approval of all foreign investment in newspapers. The result was increased self-censorship among the press.

Although the ruling party won all seats in the 1972 election, opposition party candidates emerged (Table 2.1). About one-third of the electorate voted against PAP, shocking the party into contemplating measures that might head off possible defeat in the future. One apparent ploy was to accuse opposition parties of receiving foreign financing. A second reaction was the successful prosecution of an opposition candidate for defamation of Lee Kuan Yew because of a campaign statement; this tactic was repeated after nearly every election thereafter. Yet another precursor of things to come was the fine of a *Newsweek* journalist for contempt of court; the offense was to write an article in 1974 that impugned the integrity of the Singapore judiciary. The anti-PAP vote continued to annoy Lee and company in future elections.

In 1974 Tan Wah Piow, president of the University of Singapore Students Union, tried to organize a protest over the deportation of students who came to Singapore from Hongkong and Malaysia. In 1975, he was convicted of the trumped-up charge[11] of incitement to riot (though no riot took place) and jailed for a year, after which he fled to England. The university administration then abolished direct election of student government officers. Although student activism ceased, Tan was not forgotten. In 1985, with Tan out of the country for a decade, parliament passed a law stripping Singaporean citizenship from all persons out of the country for ten years, leaving him stateless. In 1987, Tan was identified as the alleged "mastermind" behind a "Marxist conspiracy" to overthrow the government. Today, he is a lawyer in Britain.

In 1976, one year after Communist movements triumphed in Indochina, Singapore joined in upgrading ASEAN: For the first time there was a summit conference of heads of government of the member countries, and Singapore assisted in wording an ASEAN treaty that was aimed at providing nonmilitary security guarantees. When Vietnamese troops entered Cambodia to drive out the Khmer Rouge in 1978, Singapore was at the forefront of ASEAN efforts to prevent the new Cambodian regime from obtaining international recognition while providing clandestine military equipment to the Khmer Rouge.[12]

In the run-up to elections in 1976, PAP candidates again accused opposition politicians of securing foreign funding for their campaigns, and Malaysia was accused of conducting a "black operation"—that is, a covert operation, to discredit the government. Many were also arrested as suspected Communists, including three Malay journalists, though Lee admitted that the latter posed no serious threat.[13] After the customary PAP victory (Table 2.1), there was a round-up of three opposition candidates. One, accused of inciting Chinese chauvinism, fled to exile in England. A second was detained for eighteen months under the Internal Security Act for the same reason. A third was jailed and fined for criminally defaming Lee Kuan Yew during a speech at an election rally.

In 1977, a further amendment of the Newspaper and Printing Presses Act enabled the government eventually to take over management of all domestic publications, including the *Nanyang Siang Pau*, whose former manager was released after five years of detention. Also that year, two foreign correspondents were arrested for alleged Communist news slanting and released after being coerced into confessions of purported Communist leanings.

In 1978, Singapore's economy changed markedly. Several laws were adopted to attract foreign businesses. Abolished were capital flows restrictions, capital gains taxes, inheritance taxes, and wealth taxes—but these applied only to foreign corporations. The economy improved, as multinational corporations set up shop in the island republic.

A Viable Opposition Emerges

In 1980, when PAP was again victorious (Table 2.1), the government promoted a "high wage" policy. In 1981, however, the voters in one district favored populist Joshua Benjamin Jeyaretnam, secretary-general of the Workers' Party, who won a seat in a parliamentary by-election. Although he secured a bare majority of the votes in the working-class district, Jeyarfetnam's victory spurred PAP to assess why the electorate was dissatisfied.

One PAP innovation was for members of parliament to engage in well-publicized "walk-abouts" in their constituencies. Residents' committees, formerly relegated to the role informal housing management bodies, were given new power, and PAP sponsored new ethnically-based organizations.

In 1982, after Lee Kuan Yew criticized the media for "inaccuracies,"[14] PAP loyalist S. R. Nathan, former director of the security and intelligence division of the Ministry of Defense, was appointed to head the *Straits Times*, the principal English language daily newspaper. In 1983, three independent Chinese-language newspapers were shut down, and all major newspapers were merged into a single holding company. Also in 1983, anti-Communist hysteria resurfaced when Tan Cay Boon was arrested for possessing a subversive document, namely, the epitaph of his brother, a former member of the MCP.[15]

In 1984, Jeyaretnam was reelected along with Chiam See Tong of the Singapore Democratic Party, and PAP's share of the vote slipped again (Table 2.1). Surprised that public discontent had increased despite favorable economic performance since the 1980 election, PAP leaders appeared on television to defend their policies to the glee of citizens, whose right to petition for the redress of grievances seemed rejuvenated.

The 1984 election also brought Lee Kuan Yew's son, Lee Hsien Loong, into parliament.

He became a Brigadier-General (thenceforward known in the press as "B. G. Lee") and second in command of the armed forces that year, a junior minister in 1985, Minister of Trade and Industry in 1986, and head of Singapore's central bank in 1997. Goh Keng Swee retired from politics in 1984, and newly elected technocrat Goh Chok Tong became First Deputy Prime Minister. Only three PAP veterans remained in the Cabinet, two of which resigned in 1988, so a new generation of technocrats had all but replaced the cadre of politics that founded independent Singapore.

Regarding the next generation, Lee launched a campaign in 1983 to enrich the genetic pool in Singapore by encouraging more college-educated women to marry male counterparts and have children. Various incentives were provided in the campaign, including a government matchmaking agency, the Social Development Unit, and preferences were granted for children of college graduates to attend Singapore's best schools.

In 1984, a course on Confucian philosophy or a religion was required of all secondary school students, with options to select the religion or philosophy of one's choice. Lee Kuan Yew publicly hoped that Confucianism would be the favorite choice, but instead Confucianism trailed Buddhism and Christianity in popularity.[16]

A sudden economic downturn in the mid-1980s prompted a series of actions, including a three-day shutdown of the stock exchange, a freeze on salary increases throughout the country for two years, an end to the "high wage" policy, a requirement that all students must learn English, a temporary reduction in the amounts employers employers were required to contribute to the CPF (from 25 to 10 percent), and a decision to privatize some government-linked corporations. The economy rebounded in 1986.

PAP once again seemed intent on identifying the sources of its decline in support. In 1985, its leaders announced that the upgrading of services at government housing would be provided last to constituencies that elected non-PAP candidates. Devan Nair, drugged with valium and charged with alcoholism and sexual harassment by Lee Kuan Yew,[17] resigned as president, and in due course went into exile as a bitter critic of the regime. Also in 1985, Jeyaretnam was charged of making false declarations of his party's accounts; the following year he was subsequently convicted, fined, imprisoned, disqualified from sitting in parliament for five years, and disbarred. After he won an appeal on his disbarment to the Privy Council in 1989, the Singapore government abolished that avenue of appeal.

An editorial about the Jeyaretnam saga in the *Asian Wall Street Journal* during 1985, questioning the independence of the judiciary, resulted in fines for "criminal contempt" for several journalists responsible. In 1986, the Newspaper and Printing Presses Act was amended to authorize government ministers to blacklist any international publication in the *Government Gazette* that supposedly interfered in Singaporean domestic politics. This meant that a ceiling on circulation could be imposed if a news story or editorial comment was thought to discredit the government and the publication refused to honor the "right of reply"—that is, to afford space in the publication for sometimes lengthy, argumentative statements in rebuttal by a Singapore government official. The aim of "gazetting" was to cut into revenues of the publications for "interfering" in domestic politics. When the Law Society (Singapore's equivalent of a national bar association) objected to the vagueness of the law, parliament amended the Legal Profession Act to prohibit the society from commenting on matters of politics unless the government asked it to so. In due course, circulation restrictions were slapped on *Asiaweek*, *The Economist*, *Far Eastern Economic Review*, and *Time*. Instead of arresting reporters and extorting confessions of "pro-Communist" leanings as in the 1970s, libel suits were filed against the foreign press, and damage awards for growing amounts were assessed.

In the early 1980s, Singapore's foreign policy showed some insensitivity toward fellow ASEAN countries. For example, in 1983, Singapore intelligence alerted Manila about the movements of Benigno Aquino, who was then assassinated upon his arrival at Manila airport.[18] In 1985, Lee publicly accused President Ferdinand Marcos of fixing judges. In 1986, the visit of Israeli President Chaim Herzog, which occasioned anti-Singaporean demonstrations in Malaysia for five weeks, prompted the Singapore defense department to conduct military exercises. Curiously, Malay citizens in Singapore were passive regarding the Herzog visit, but they took note of their second-class status in 1987, when Lee Hsien Loong noted that they would never be sent into the front line of battle in the event of war with Indonesia or Malaysia.

The United States was Singapore's next target. In early 1987, after the State Department expressed regret over the restriction imposed on the *Asian Wall Street Journal*, Singapore threatened to boot all American journalists and newspapers out of the country.[19] The threat was carried out when correspondents of Dow Jones & Company (from the *Asian Wall Street*

Journal, Far Eastern Economic Review, and the *Wall Street Journal*) were not allowed visas to enter the country from 1987 to 1993. When the *Far Eastern Economic Review* refused to distribute its weekly within Singapore rather than allow a cut in circulation, the Newspaper and Printing Presses Act was amended in 1988 to allow for the reproduction of gazetted publications for sale at cost. While this was going on, the *U.S. News and World Report* closed its office in Singapore in apparent protest.

The *Far Eastern Economic Review* ran afoul of Singapore authorities because of its coverage of Operation Spectrum. In this case, several Catholic organizations had been assisting Filipina maids who complained of mistreatment by their employers. In 1987, some twenty-two professionals, mostly Catholic layworkers, were detained for allegedly being part of a "Marxist network" linked to Tan Wah Piow with plans to overthrow the government. Some were also associated with Jeyaretnam's Workers' Party, though this was not mentioned in public by the government. After odd-sounding televised confessions, most of the twenty-two detainees, whom Lee later told a court (*Lee Kuan Yew v Derek Davies*, 1990) were inconsequential "do-gooders," were freed. However, in 1988, after some of those released were goaded by Lee Hsien Loong to claim that their confessions were obtained by physical and psychological torture (according to him, a common police method),[20] they were rearrested.

Francis Seow, attorney for two of the rearrestees and a likely opposition party candidate for election in 1988, in turn, was detained under similar circumstances, but accused falsely of serving as an agent of Washington in a supposed American plot to build a strong opposition to PAP.[21] The government's effort to stop alleged U.S. interference in Singapore domestic politics also involved expelling American diplomat E. Mason Hendrickson in 1988, ostensibly because of his luncheon meetings at public eating establishments with Seow, who says that he merely briefed the Americans on developments in Singapore politics.

Due to the fear of a greater role for religion in politics, Catholic organizations associated with the twenty-two so-called "Marxists" were closed in 1987. At the end of the year, the Christian Conference of Asia, an umbrella organization for Protestants throughout the region, was also shut down for alleged support of liberation movements; five expatriate employees were told to leave the country.

Anti-American posturing provided rally-round-the-flag rhetoric for PAP during the election of 1988. Before the election, the law was changed to introduce multimember districts, known as group representation constituencies (GRCs). Political parties were required to run slates of three candidates (raised to a ceiling of four in 1991 and six in 1996), one of which must be a minority, such as Indian or Malay. The winning GRC slates, which now account for seventy-two of the eighty-seven elected members of parliament, also sit on district town councils, which began to be set up in 1986 as a way of decentralizing the administration of public services. The S$1,500 deposit (refundable if a candidate got one-eighth of the votes) was raised to S$4,000 in 1988 and is now S$16,000.

In addition, the amended election law also provided for nonvoting Nominated Members of Parliament and Non-Constituency Members of Parliament. In the former case, parliament may invite nine of the top unelected opposition candidates to sit in parliament as nonvoting members if fewer than three members of the opposition win their races. In the latter case, up to nine nonpoliticians are invited to sit in parliament; in practice, these are leaders of interest groups, such as an environmental group, but they are not expected to represent the interests of their own group. When the votes were counted in 1988, PAP again slipped in overall support (Table 2.1).

In 1990, political detainee Chia Thye Poh was released from jail on the condition that he would return each night to a home on Sentosa Island, the location of a daytime public park. In 1992, he was allowed to live on the main island with his parents, and in 1997 he was permitted to travel abroad. In 1998, all restrictions were lifted, so he began to make political statements. He completed a doctorate in development studies in the Netherland during 2006, and died in 2012.

In 1989, parliament adopted a quota on the number of minorities allowed to live in public housing, where some 80 percent of the residents live,[22] in order to prevent the development of ethnic residential enclaves. Later that year, after a seven-year experiment, required courses in religion were abolished in favor of civics courses, and the government began to promote a curriculum and national ideology stressing shared core values, often known as "Asian Values." In 1990, after some deliberation, parliament passed the Maintenance of Religious Harmony Act, which proscribes religious organizations from engaging in politics.

Meanwhile, the photocopying of foreign newsweeklies occasioned American interest in copyright infringements taking place in Singapore, where software piracy was particularly rampant. In early 1987, Washington threatened to withdraw tariff concessions granted under the generalized system of preferences (GSP) over the issue. Singapore capitulated by agreeing to stop copyright infringement, though implementation of the agreement was rather slow. Nevertheless, in response to Congressional pressure to revoke GSP status to Third World countries that had graduated to First World status in per capita income levels, Singapore lost GSP status anyway in 1988. Despite lobbying by Singapore diplomats to reverse the GSP decision, thus interfering in the internal affairs of the United States, there was little sympathy for the country, whose per capita income then exceeded that of Britain. On the contrary, a joint congressional resolution expressed concern over the decline of human rights in the island republic. The following year, when Vice President Dan Quayle inquired why journalists from the *Asian Wall Street Journal* and the *Far Eastern Economic Review* were prevented from entering Singapore to cover his visit, First Deputy Prime Minister Goh snapped that he had no right to question the exclusion.[23] Nevertheless, after the United States military was ejected from the Philippines, Washington signed agreements in 1990 and 1992 allowing military personnel to use Singapore bivouacking, docking, and landing facilities.

With ASEAN, Singapore had usually been odd man out, less interested in the region than in the larger international economy. That changed in 1989, when the island republic reached out to Indonesia and Malaysia to form a "growth triangle" arrangement, which allows Singapore capital to invest without restrictive regulations and taxes in its two neighboring countries, thereby taking advantage of their less expensive labor and more abundant land. In 1992, Singapore was flattered by its selection as the host country for the secretariat of the Asia Pacific Economic Cooperation (APEC) organization, whose members then included ASEAN countries, Canada, China, Hongkong, Japan, Korea, México, Taiwan, and the United States and subsequently expanded to more countries in Latin America.

New Leadership

The year 1990 was a milestone in the history of Singapore. Lee Kuan Yew stepped down. Although Lee wanted Dr. Tony Tan to succeed him, the latter declined, so Goh Chok Tong, Lee's second choice, became prime minister. However, Lee remained in the Cabinet as Senior Minister. In 1991, when Goh asked voters for a vote of confidence in his promise for a "kinder, gentler Singapore," the PAP vote slipped again, and four opposition candidates were elected (Table 2.1). According to PAP's analysis, the voters rejected a "kinder, gentler Singapore," and English-speaking candidates were losing touch with non-English-speaking voters. In 1993, there was an election for the nonpartisan office of president, formerly an appointive figurehead position, but the winning candidate, who had resigned from PAP to run, garnered only 58 percent of the votes against a candidate who urged voters to vote for the former PAP member! Among the new powers of the president is the right to veto key governmental appointments and budgets, but parliament can override a veto; if the president vetoes a constitutional amendment, the voters can decided the issue by a referendum.

By 1990, when all foreign publications circulating in Singapore were required to have a permit for sale and to post a bond of US$294,000 in case of future problems, the *Asian Wall Street Journal* pulled out of the Singapore market. The bonding requirement was only imposed on the Hongkong-based *Asian Wall Street Journal*, *Asiaweek* and its Chinese-language *Yazhou Zhoukan*, and the trade publication *Media*. In 1993, *The Economist* permanently closed its Singapore office.

The "Asian Values" movement was launched worldwide during 1993, when Singapore managed to persuade the World Conference on Human Rights to adopt a final statement that rejected universalism, instead espousing the notion that each country should set its own human rights priorities. Soon, however, the government began to tout the idea that "Asian Values" are superior to "Western Values."

It was in this context that the Michael Fay incident emerged. In this case, an American teenager was arrested in 1993 for various minor crimes after being fingered by a Chinese school rival. Although the police found street signs in Fay's room at home and thus charged him with possession of stolen property, they had no hard evidence that he engaged in vandalism, in particular the use of removable spraypainting on various automobiles, including one belonging to a high government official. After interrogation in which torture was applied, he confessed that he vandalized the cars. In an apparent plea bargain, in light of the fact that he had no previous trouble with the law, the authorities dropped all charges but vandalism, and Fay expected merely to pay a fine. However, the judge sentenced Fay to eighty-three days in jail, six strokes of a rattan cane, and a fine of S$3,500 (about US$2,500), applying a law adopted decades earlier to deter Communists from painting graffiti on government buildings. A plea for leniency from President Bill Clinton, however, only served to reduce the strokes to four. Although the caning was aimed at deterring juvenile crime, statistics show that crime among teenagers actually increased after Fay's caning. Although the overall crime rate is among the lowest in the world, more than 2,000 persons are caned annually.[24]

Thereafter, Washington initiated a policy of snubbing Singapore. For example, Singapore's request in 1994 to purchase F-18 fighter aircraft was turned down; F-16s were ordered instead. Singapore's defenses then included thirty-one F-16s, seventy A-4 Super Skyhawks, fifty-three F-5s, six missile corvettes, seven missile gunboats, six anti-submarine patrol boats, 50,000 full-time soldiers, and 250,000 reservists.[25]

In 1994, two controversial essays appeared in the *International Herald Tribune*.[26] First, an op-ed essay by journalist Philip Bowring accused China and Singapore of practicing "dynastic politics." Despite a later apology for implying that Lee Hsien Loong was not appointed because of his qualifications, the newspaper was fined the equivalent of US$665,000—but not before Prime Minister Goh Chok Tong let the cat out of the bag by admitting that the essay "simply destroys what we have set out to do, and that is to have a smooth transfer of power to the next generation."[27]

Later in the year, economist Christopher Lingle was charged with contempt of court for authoring an essay in the *International Herald Tribune* that accused unnamed Asian regimes of "suppressing dissent" and relying on a "compliant judiciary to bankrupt politicians."[28] Fearing a large fine or imprisonment, two likely outcomes of the criminal case, Lingle flew to the United States, thereby resigning his position at the National University of Singapore. Curiously, the government publicly admitted to eleven cases of bankrupting opposition party members from 1971 to 1993 in support of its claim that Lingle had Singapore and Lee Kuan Yew in mind when he wrote the essay.[29] Both were fined—Lingle was fined for the equivalent of US$71,000, while the fine was US$213,000 for Lingle and the *Tribune* jointly. Then, at the end of the year, two Singaporean writers penned essays critical of the government—a general comment about the widening gap between rich and poor in Singapore in the *Jakarta Post* and an attack on the leadership style of the prime minister in the *Straits Times*. Although the two were publicly reprimanded by the government and forced to recant, no legal action was taken against them. Goh later conceded the widening gap thesis.[30]

In 1995, President Fidel Ramos threatened to sever diplomatic relations with Singapore after Flor Contemplacion, a Filipina maid, was hanged for allegedly murdering a fellow Filipina maid and a three-year-old Singaporean. Ramos was responding to public demonstrations in Manila as forensic scientists expressed the belief at an official hearing that the maid, convicted in 1991 on the basis of a confession, was too frail to have fractured four ribs and strangled the maid; indeed, Ramos had the Philippine air force fly several hundred frightened Filipina maids out of Singapore after the hanging. The inquiry concluded by accusing police of obtaining Contemplacion's confession through torture. At one point, both ambassadors were recalled. When the autopsy was referred to an American forensic expert, the judgment went in Singapore's favor, as the ribs could have been injured before the death, and the issue died down.

Later in 1995, Williams College invited Prime Minister Goh, an alumnus, to receive academic honors; protests mounted, and Goh was subjected to vigorous questioning by a hostile audience. At the end of the year, Singapore prosecuted sixty-five members of Jehovah's Witnesses, a religious sect that was banned in 1972, for conducting a meeting of an unlawful society. In the course of the police arrest, fifty copies of the Bible were seized because they were deemed "undesirable publications." Most of the Jehovah's Witnesses decided to take their message to the prisons rather than to pay fines.

In 1996, controversy raged after public disclosure that Lee Kuan Yew and his son Lee Hsien Loong were each offered S$700,000 apartments at from 5 to 12 percent below the standard prices by a housing developer. One problem was that Lee Kuan Yew's brother was a director in the corporation selling the properties, and a second problem was that notification of the sale was delayed beyond the time limit required by regulations of the Stock Exchange of Singapore regulations, which therefore criticized the sale. The two later offered to contribute the discounted amounts, of which they professed to be unaware at the time of the presale, to charity.

Outspoken Lee Kuan Yew once again annoyed neighboring Malaysia in mid-1996, when he intimated that an economically faltering Singapore might one day rejoin an economically resurgent Malaysia, provided that it abolished special treatment for indigenous peoples and accept meritocracy. After Kuala Lumpur filed a diplomatic protest for this apparent condescension as interference in internal affairs, Singapore leaders returned the volley. Then Malaysian Prime Minister Mahathir Mohamad, recalling the remark of Lee Hsien Loong that Malays in Singapore cannot serve in the frontline of battle, deconstructed the rhetoric to imply that Singaporean Chinese were being bullied again to support the ruling party, an implication in turn denied by Prime Minister Goh, who supported Lee's original remarks in a speech two months later.

Singapore, nevertheless, scored some diplomatic success outside Asia. In 1996, it hosted the first ministerial meeting of the World Trade Organization, though its offer to host the organization was turned down. Goh's proposal for an ASEAN-Europe Meeting (ASEM) bore fruit in 1996, when ministers from ASEAN and the European Union met at Bangkok. Tommy Koh, Singapore's Ambassador-at-Large, was chosen by ASEM to head the Asia-Europe Foundation.

During the campaign leading up to the election of 1997, Goh went beyond the usual PAP claim that constituencies voting for the opposition would be the last to receive needed government-financed improvements by issuing a threat that such constituencies might become "slums." When a State Department press officer criticized Goh for this statement, PAP was able to play the "David and Goliath" card to rally Singaporeans around the image of a beleaguered island state, and PAP's margin of victory increased for the first time in seventeen years (Table 2.1). Only two opposition candidates were elected; before the election, opposition parties were prohibited from disseminating their messages through videotapes, the newest form of censorship. Goh declared that his victory proved that Singaporeans "rejected a Western-style liberal democracy and freedoms, putting individual rights over that of society."[31]

Once again, there were major defamation lawsuits after the election. PAP parliamentarians referred with impunity to opposition party candidate Chee Soon Juan as "guilty of deceit" and "a proven liar" for inadvertently mixing up numbers during a parliamentary speech in 1996, for which he had to pay about S$400,000 in damages and court costs. Perhaps the most celebrated defendant was millionaire Tang Lian Hong, who had earlier criticized the Lees for purchasing discounted condos. Tang, a neophyte opposition party candidate who championed the cause of the "Chinese silent majority," was accused of being an "anti-English education, anti-Christian Chinese chauvinist"; when he attacked PAP leaders as "liars," he was sued.[32]

Thereafter, Tang reported death threats, went across the Causeway to Malaysia, flew to London to consult with lawyers, and then returned to one of his homes in Johore Bahru (though his spouse was denied permission to leave Singapore to visit him). The Singapore court next blocked Tang and his spouse from selling assets of nearly US$8 million as a bond to pay possible damages, and he ultimately lost the libel lawsuit. However, noting that the judge who decided the case was a close friend of Lee Kuan Yew and a former attorney for Lee, Tang appealed but lost, and a warrant was issued for his arrest on tax evasion charges. Even before the court assessed the amount of damages, Lee Kuan Yew had entered the history books as the most successful individual defamation litigant in history, having already been awarded more than US$2 million by Singapore courts in eight major cases, not counting several hundred thousand dollars in out-of-court settlements.[33] In this case, his award was about US$1.6 million out of a total fine of US $5.7 million.

In the second libel case, Joshua Jeyaretnam was ordered to pay US$13,000 to Prime Minister Goh for telling an election rally that Tang had filed a police report against Goh for defamation, a report that Goh later had published in full. Shocked that the award was so little, Goh appealed, and the fine was later increased.

When Tang decided to reside in Johone Bahru, Lee Kuan Yew attacked him in an affidavit filed in court for retreating to a place "notorious for shootings, muggings and carjackings."[34] Tang then released the affidavit to the press, whereupon Malaysian officials were incensed. Although Lee quickly apologized, the apology was deemed insufficient, whereupon Lee had the remark stricken from the record, though with no penalty, in contrast with the judgment against Chee Soon Juan for stating an error in parliament. Tang, who has never returned to Singapore, later took up residence in Australia with his wife.

Editorial comment in the region at this point was harsh toward the island republic, recalling Thailand's sensitivity over Singapore leaders' remarks about corruption in Bangkok, the Flor Contemplacion incident, and how twenty-eight Indonesian maids sought refuge in their embassy in Singapore with complaints about rape.[35] Malaysian authorities were not completely satisfied either, and the Cabinet in Kuala Lumpur voted to suspend all cultural, sporting, and tourism links with Singapore, temporarily as it turned out, while maintaining commercial interactions; rumors spread that Malaysia would not approve any more contracts with Singaporean firms. Tang then called upon Lee Kuan Yew to resign so that he could no longer "embarrass the Singapore people" and accused Goh's government of acting like a "limping duck" for failing to take responsibility on behalf of the government for the actions of a member of the Cabinet.

Just when the Singapore-Malaysia tiff had almost died down, the *Straits Times* reported on a count of press clippings about crime incidents in order to argue that crime in Johore Bahru was worse than in Singapore. Believing that the publication was acting on orders from the Singapore government, the Malaysian Cabinet then reacted with anger once again. International Trade and Industry Minister Rafidah Aziz invited reporters to respond with a "media war." The *New Straits Times* of Kuala Lumpur referred to a report of the United Nations Commission on Crime Prevention and Criminal Justice, based on systematic evidence, which said that crime in Singapore was higher than in Malaysia, and soon the *Straits Times* cited contrary information from the *World Competitiveness Yearbook*. Meanwhile, PAP community groups launched a tourism boycott of Malaysia, and Malaysian customs officials were holding up Singaporean vehicles for as much as ten hours at the border. Soon, the Johore Bahru chief minister proposed taking over two of the three water purification plants operated by Singaporean firms in Malaysia, and the Singapore parliament raised water rates for consumers to encourage conservation and began a study on alternative sources of water.

Later in 1997, Singapore's close ties with the military regime in Myanmar (Burma) gained notoriety. A U.S. State Department report revealed that the government-run Singapore Investment Corporation played a role in financing drug smuggling, and later information identified Ho Ching, the wife of Lee Hsien Loong, as the head of Singapore Technologies Group, which sold electronic eavesdropping equipment to the government in Yangon.[36]

Policy Changes

Nevertheless, Singapore is today the third richest country in per capita income. In 1996, the Organization for Economic Development and Cooperation (OECD) classified Singapore as a "developed" country. Quality of life indicators, such as low infant mortality, make the island republic a desirable place to live for those who have no interest in politics, and a recent survey shows that 80 percent of Singaporeans are prepared to die for their country in battle.[37] For short-term visitors, Singapore offers excellent shopping, luxurious hotels, and world-class gourmet food. The positive side of Singapore, as stated by Clark Neher (Chapter 3), is visible to all.

Signs of a possible change in iron-fisted rule appeared in mid-1997. The *Far Eastern Economic Review* was unexpectedly allowed to post a resident journalist, and its circulation was allowed to rise from 6,000 to 8,000 copies per issue, albeit still below the 10,000 level of 1987, when restrictions were first applied. In addition, the government allowed longtime political detainee Chia Thye Poh to leave Singapore in order accept a research post at the Hamburg Foundation in Germany. Nevertheless, he was still not allowed to issue public statements, attend public meetings, join or assist organizations of any kind, engage in political activities, or communicate with other former detainees. As always, these latest actions of the Singapore government remain a puzzle. In the absence of a policy statement explaining these favorable decisions, we do not know whether they presage important democratizing trends or are shrewd public relations moves that will later be revoked.

Epilog

Now we know that there was no serious democratization trend at the end of the 1990s. There were, however, other developments. The most important was the selection of Lee Hsieng Loong as the new prime minister in 2004, who had served as deputy prime ministers for fourteen years. His elevation brought to the office a member of the generation born after 1951. Differences between Goh Chok Tong and Lee Kuan Yew during those years, which may have suggested some factionalism that might propel Singapore into a more democratic direction,[38] will no longer be a problem, as father and son are of one mind.

Demographic statistics from the Singapore census has revealed some change. Percentages of ethnic groups remain about the same, but the total population has increased from 3 million to 5.5 million. There has also been a sharp increase in the Christian population from 12 percent in 1990 to 18 percent in 2010 and a considerable drop in Buddhists/Taoists from 59 to 44 percent over the same years. Lee Kuan Yew believed that Singapore's management of cultural differences was threatened by Westernization, so he thought that he could revive Confucian values by the religious knowledge program, but the program was dropped as a failure.[39]

The number of unelected members of parliament has increased. In 1999, six nominated members and three nonconstituency members were allowed. From May 2009, nine in each category have been possible, though the nonconstituency members today number three.[40] Candidates for election must post a deposit of $16,000 today, a sharp increase from $4,000 in 1996.[41]

However, an astute observer of policy making in Singapore finds that legislators are peripheral to policy making, which is elite-driven. The "priesthood" of senior civil servants have the most input, and citizen participation the least.[42]

Joshua Jeyaretnam was declared bankrupt in 2001 and therefore lost his seat in parliament. Because the Worker's Party would not assist him in his finances, he resigned from the party. In 2008, he formed the Reform Party but died later in the year.[43]

The main opposition figure today is Chee Soon Juan.[44] During the 2001 election campaign, Chee ran into Prime Minister Goh Chok Tong at a hawker centre. Using a megaphone, he asked, "Where is the S$18 billion that you have lent to [Indonesian President) Suharto]?" PAP then demanded an apology, threatening a defamation lawsuit. Chee apologized the following day, but later retracted his apology. After the election, he lost a defamation lawsuit for the remark and was ordered to pay S$300,000 to Goh and S$200,000 to Lee Kuan Yew. In 2002, he spoke out again on two occasions without first obtaining a police permit; as a result, he was fined and jailed for five days. In 2006, unable to pay Goh and Lee, he was declared bankrupt; he was disallowed from leaving the country until 2012, when the two agreed to accept a lesser amount (S$30,000) in full settlement. He raised the funds from royalties for his book *Democratically Speaking* (2012).

The 2001 election was held after terrorist attacks on the United States. Although Singapore's economy nosedived, the percentage of votes supporting PAP was the highest since 1980—75 percent of the vote (Table 2.1).

In the 2006 election, PAP slumped to 67 percent (Table 2.1) despite the new face of the ruling party. Lee Kuan Yew's eldest son, Lee Hsien Loong, ran for the first time as the incumbent prime minister. The main election issues included the usual ones—employment, cost of living, housing, public transportation, education, and the desire for an effective opposition voice in parliament. One of the sharpest criticisms was of the practice of upgrading housing only in districts that vote for PAP.[45] Chee's bankruptcy made him ineligible for office, but he tried to distribute a podcast, protested before the Singapore meeting of the World Bank, and he was again fined and jailed. While in detention, his health deteriorated, provoking international pressure to release him for medical treatment. He claimed that his food was poisoned, and a continuously illuminated light in his cell produced sleep deprivation, though the government rejected his complaint.

In 2008, he was again arrested for demonstrating without a police permit. By that time, his mistreatment by the government had gained much support abroad. Liberal International, a federation of moderate left parties, has granted his Singapore Democratic Party observer status. He has written seven books and is the subject of a documentary, *Singapore Rebel* (2004).

The election of 2011 was the most extraordinary in recent years. With only 60 percent of the votes, parliamentary support dropped from 98 percent of the seats to 93 percent, the lowest since 1963 (Table 2.1). Clearly, voting districts continue to be drawn so that PAP will have a disproportionate share of seats in parliament despite lagging public support.

The explanation for the decline might be attributed in part to the fact that opposition candidates for the first time contested nearly all seats. As further explained in the Epilog to Chapter 4, another issue was the large number of foreign workers in the country, which some citizens believed were being given preference. Social media also played an important role in getting out the opposition vote by contradicting the PAP party line that opposition candidates were inexperienced. According to Kenneth Paul Tan, opposition candidates were well-trained and personable technocrats in contrast with the stilted performances by PAP candidates.[46]

A gaffe by Lee Kuan Yew may also have been a factor. During the campaign he once again questioned the loyalty of Malay Muslims, asserting that they should avoid strict practice of their religion, reiterating a passage from his recent book *Hard Truths to Keep Singapore Going* (2011) during an interview in March conducted by American journalist Charlie Rose.[47] He later apologized, but not before Prime Minister Lee Hsien Loong declared that he was fully in charge of the government, repudiating his father's insensitive remark. One week after the election, Lee Kuan Yew resigned as Minister Mentor in the Cabinet and took an academic position at National University of Singapore. Goh Chok Tong also tendered his resignation as Senior Minister.

Rather than ending his political career with a hallowed place in history, questions have arisen about Lee Kuan Yew's narrative that Singapore's history was made by a "great man" who made tough decisions that panned out. According to Lisa Hong and Huang Jianli, the narrative which ascribes Singapore's success to Confucian (or Asian) values is an attempt to rewrite history.[48] The early political history of Singapore, they observe, involved a clash between Chinese-educated and British-educated leaders, won by the latter.[49] British-educated Lee Kuan Yew prevailed in part by painting the leftist Chinese-educated leaders as on the wrong side of the Cold War ideological contest. Accordingly, the statue of Sir Stanford Raffles has been prominently displayed to demonstrate the success of a more modern viewpoint. But many Chinese-educated leaders (Ong Pang Boon, Lee Khoon Choy, Jek Yeun Thong) originally sought a multiethnic nationalism and played down Chinese chauvinism. Later, PAP pretended that the three were Confucianists in solidarity with the Asian Values propaganda. Most leaders rewrite history in their memoirs. Lee Kuan Yew is no exception.

Notes

1. C. M. Turnbull, *A History of Singapore, 1819-1988*, 2nd edn. (Singapore: Oxford University Press, 1989), chap. 6. Much of this chapter is based on this account.
2. D. G. E. Hall, *A History of South-East Asia*, 3rd ed. (New York: St. Martin's Press, 1968), 891.
3. Pang Cheng Lian, *The People's Action Party*. (Singapore: Oxford University Press, 1971), 14.
4. *Ibid.*, 16.
5. Turnbull, A *History of Singapore*, 283.
6. T. J. S. George, *Lee Kuan Yew's Singapore*. (London: André Deutsch, 1973), 75.
7. Sources for this claim are Devin Nair, quoted in Francis T. Seow, *To Catch a Tartar: A Dissident in Lee Kuan Yew's Prison* (New Haven, CT: Yale University Southeast Asia Studies, 1994), 209, and James Minchin, *No Man Is an Island: A Study of Lee Kuan Yew's Singapore* (Sydney: Allen & Unwin, 1986), 147, 153.
8. Turnbull, *A History of Singapore*, 315.
9. *Ibid.*, 294.
10. Seow, *The Media Enthralled: Singapore Revisited* (Boulder, CO: Rienner, 1997), 180-184.
11. Minchin, *No Man Is an Island*, 264n.
12. Michael Haas, *Genocide by Proxy: Cambodian Pawn on a Superpower Chessboard* (New York: Praeger, 1991).
13. Minchin, *No Man Is an Island*, 187.
14. John A. Lent, "Testimony," House of Representatives, Committee on Foreign Affairs, Subcommittee on Human Rights and International organizations, 7 July 1988.

15. "'Scheming' Cheng," *Straits Times*, 29 June 1987, 12.
16. E. C. Y. Kuo, *Confucianism as Political Discourse in Singapore: The Case of an Incomplete Revitalization Movement* (Singapore: Department of Sociology, National University of Singapore), 61-78.
17. C. V. Nevan Nair, "An Open Letter to Lee Kuan Yew," in Seow, *To Catch a Tartar*, 274.
18. Minchin, *No Man Is an Island*, 184.
19. *Hansard*, Parliamentary Debates, 20 March 20, col. 672.
20. *Straits Times*, 22April 1988.
21. Here I wish to recant statements in my "The Politics of Singapore in the 1980s," *Journal of Contemporary Asia*, XIX (1, 1989): 66, and "Relations Between Singapore and the United States: Sadistocracy Versus Democracy," *Proceedings of the Fifteenth International Symposium on Asian Studies, 1994* (Hongkong: International Center for Asian Studies, 1995), 71, where I repeated press reports that Hendrickson suggested that Seow could run for office. Seow categorically denies any such claim in his *To Catch a Tartar*, chap. 8.
22. Murray Hiebert, "On the Offensive: Singapore's Rules May Be Strict—But They *Do* Curb Urban Blight," *Far Eastern Economic Review*, 6 February 1997, 39; "Public Housing in Singapore," *wikipedia.com*, accessed 14 January 2014.
23. Seow, *The Media Enthralled*, 182.
24. Jacqueline Wong, "Violent Youth Rebel in Singapore," *Reuters*, 7 May 1997. But see also "What Explains Singapore's Consistently Low Crime Rate?," *furrybrowndog.wordpress.com*; accessed 17 February 2014; *Country Practices on Human Rights Practices for 2011* (Washington, DC: U.S. Department of State, 2012).
25. Rene Pastor, "Singapore Seeks to Hold onto Its Troops," *Reuters*, 8 December 1996.
26. Philip Bowring, "The Claims About 'Asian Values' Don't Usually Bear Scrutiny," *International Herald Tribune*, 2 August 1994; Christopher Lingle, "The Smoke over Parts of Asia Obscures Some Profound Concerns," *International Herald Tribune*, 7 October 1994.
27. Quoted in Kieran Cooke, "Goh Battles to Bolster His Standing: For Most in Singapore, Ex-Premier Lee Is Still a Force," *Financial Times* (London), 10 January 1995, 4.
28. Lingle, "The Smoke over Parts of Asia Obscures Some Profound Concerns," *International Herald Tribune*.
29. Matthew Lewis, "Unusual Twist When Singapore Contempt Case Reopens," *Reuters*, 15 January 1995.
30. Catherine Lim, "One Government, Two Styles," *Straits Times*, 20 November 1994; Bilveer Singh, "Singapore Faces Challenges of Success," *Jakarta Post*, 6 December 1994; "Singapore PM Says Widening Income Gap a Challenge," *Reuters*, 30 April 1996. The recantations are as reported in Chua Mui Hoong, "PM: No Erosion of My Authority Is Allowed; Respect for Office Must Be Upheld," *Straits Times* (weekly edition), 10 December 1994, 1; "S'poreans Living Hand-to-Mouth? Government Asks NUS Academic to Substantiate Claims," *Straits Times* (weekly edition), 24 December 1994, 3.
31. Jason Szep, "Singapore Libel Case Sends Chill Throughout Asia," *Reuters*, 29 May 1997.
32. Tang LIan Hong, "Why I Am Speaking up for the Chinese Silent Majority," *Straits Times*, 31 December 1996, 18.
33. Mary Baker, "Lee Courts a Legal Goldmine," *Sydney Morning Herald*, 10 May 1997.

34. Quoted in Ranjan Roy, "Malaysia, Singapore Ties Strained," *Associated Press*, 14 July 1998. This news report lists several other instances of Singaporean mudslinging at Malaysia.

35. Rene Pastor, "Singapore 'Arrogance' Haunts Ties with Neighbors," *Reuters*, 22 March 1997.

36. Dennis Bernstein and Leslie Kean, "Singapore's Blood Money," *The Nation*, 20 October 1997.

37. *The Singaporean: Ethnicity, National Identity and Citizenship* (Singapore: Institute of Policy Studies, 1990).

38. William Case, "Singapore in 2003: Another Tough Year," *Asian Survey*, XLIV (2004): 115-117, notes that Goh criticized Lee Kuan Yew for being "uncompromising." and allowed opposition leader Chee Soon Juan to host an international conference in 2002.

39. Joseph B. Tammey, *The Struggle over Singapore: Western Modernization and Asial Culture* (Berlin: de Gruyter, 1986); Chua Beng Huat, *Communitarian Ideology and Democracy in Singapore* (London: Routledge, 1999), 30.

40. "Parliament of Singapore, *wikipedia.com*, accessed 14 January 2014; Narayanan Ganesan, "Singapore in 2009: Structuring Politics, Priming the Economy, and Working the Neighborhood," *Asian Survey*, L (2010) 253-289.

41. "Parliamentary Elections in Singapore," *wikipedia.com*, accessed 14 January 2014.

42. Ho Khai Leong, *The Politics of Policy-Making in Singapore* (Singapore: Singapore University Press, 2000), 220-221; Simon S. C. Tay, "Introduction." In *A Mandarin and the Making of Public Policy*, ed. Simon S. C. Tay (Singapore: Singapore National University Press, 2000), 3.

43. "Joshua Jeyaretnam," *wikipedia.com*, accessed 14 January 2014.

44. "Chee Soon Juan," *wikipedia.com*, accessed 14 January 2014.

45. Chua Beng Huat, "Singapore in 2006: An Irritating and Irritated ASEAN Neighbor," *Asian Survey*, XLVII (2007): 208-212.

46. Kenneth Paul Tan, "Singapore in 2011: A 'New Normal' in Politics?," *Asian Survey*, LII (2012): 224.

47. "MM Lee Speaks Again on Malay-Muslim Integration," *theonlinecitizen.com*, April 10, 2011, accessed 15 February 2014; Catherine Lim, "The GE 2011 Political Demise of Lee Kuan Yew: A Supreme Irony," *catherlim.sg*, 17 May 2011, accessed 15 February 2014. For an earlier remark, see Tim Huxley, "Singapore in 2001: Political Continuity Despite Deepening Recession," *Asian Survey*, XLII (2002): 158. Lee Kuan Yew's book was released by the Straits Times Publishing Company in January.

48. Lisa Hong and Huang Jianli, *The Scripting of a National History: Singapore and Its Pasts* (Hongkong: Hongkong University Press, 2008), esp. chap 5; Michael D. Barr, *Lee Kuan Yew: The Beliefs Behind the Man* (Washington, DC:: Georgetown University Press, 2000), 157.

49. Carl A. Trocki, *Singapore: Wealth, Power, and the Culture of Control* (New York: Routledge, 2006).

3

The Case for Singapore
Clark D. Neher

The case for Singapore stems from the nation's success in four areas: economic growth, political stability, compatibility of politics with culture, and international relations. From its first days of semi-independence in the 1950s to the present, Singapore has emerged as a prominent, vibrant nation-state, viewed by the peoples of both developing and industrialized countries as "the nation that works." There are few other nations in the world where economic growth has been more rapid or sustained, or where transformation from a somnolent, swampy fishing village to the world's most technologically modern city has been more dramatic.

It is difficult to generalize about Singapore because it is an urban city-state of 5.5 million persons in a land area smaller than many contemporary urban metropolises. Contrast the compactness of Singapore with the diversity of its neighbor Indonesia, with almost 200 million people speaking hundreds of languages, and scattered among thousands of islands. Clearly, the challenges in Singapore are far less complex than are those in Indonesia. Nevertheless, compared with such urban enclaves in Southeast Asia as Bangkok, Jakarta, and Kuala Lumpur, Singapore's higher per capita income and overall quality of life are strikingly clear.[1]

When viewed through American eyes, Singapore is bound to come up short. The political system, controlled as it is by the People's Action Party (PAP), is more authoritarian than Americans would find acceptable, and its emphasis on law and order, rules, and conformity have given the island state an antiseptic quality very much at odds with the more open American culture. For Singaporeans, however, the nation and its leaders have established a society that is tolerable, even agreeable, because the citizens' needs are being met. Most groups in Singapore are content to leave politics alone, as long as they do not face repression and are allowed to live their lives in more opulence than in surrounding countries.

Notwithstanding its unique qualities, by almost any balanced judgment Singapore has succeeded in meeting the needs and demands of its population. Its successes are nowhere near perfect, but no nation can claim that ideal. Nevertheless, among the world's nations today, Singapore can make as strong a case as any for having achieved a society with a superior standard of living, and the nation's population seems impressed.

Economic Growth

Every conventional measure of quality of life places Singapore among the top rank of developed societies. Singapore scores above all Southeast Asian nations (and their capital cities) in such categories as per capita gross domestic product (GDP), life expectancy, infant mortality, persons per physician, persons per television sets, and average daily caloric intake (Table 3.1). Indeed, Singapore surpasses all but several of the world's industrialized nations on these measures. Singapore's standard of living is now higher than that of its former colonizer, Great Britain.

Per capita GDP, a measure of average purchasing power, is a problematic measure because it says little about the distribution of a nation's wealth or about such basic matters as education, health, and nutrition. To present this broader view, the United Nations Development Program has devised a Human Development Index (HDI), which combines indicators of educational attainment, income indicators, and life expectancy, to yield a composite measure of quality of life. Using data for 173 nations, the HDI rank places Singapore ahead of all Southeast Asian countries. Moreover, in terms of the distribution of wealth, high levels of employment, housing, safety, and absence of such urban ills as pollution, Singapore's rank is actually underestimated. By all measures of quality of life, Singapore ranks very high.[2]

Table 3.1 Quality of Life Indicators, 1992 and 2012

Country	GDP/ Capita		Life Expectancy		Infant Mortality		Literacy Rate		Persons/ Physician		Caloric Intake/ Capita		HDI Index	
Singapore	$21,493	$60,900	76	84	4	3	92	96	667	546	3,190	2,875	85	90
Malaysia	$8,763	$16,900	72	74	12	14	89	93	2,063	1,064	2,880	2,910	79	77
Thailand	$6,870	$10,000	69	74	26	15	94	94	4,361	3,333	2,440	2,530	69	69
Indonesia	$3,690	$5,000	63	72	60	26	84	93	6,786	3,448	2,750	2,540	49	63
Philippines	$2,900	$4,300	67	72	40	18	94	95	1,016	870	2,450	2,520	60	65
Cambodia	$1,266	$2,400	52	63	110	53	38	74	9,523	4,348	2,020	2,250	18	54
Vietnam	$1,263	$3,500	67	73	34	20	92	93	2,298	820	2,250	2,770	46	61

Note: GDP = gross domestic product   HDI = UNDP's Human Development Index   na = not available

Source: Asiaweek (June 24, 1996); United Nations Development Program, Human Development Report (New York: UNDP, 1992); "List of Countries by Human Development Index," wikipedia.com, accessed 18 February 2014; United States, Central Intelligence Agency, World Factbook, 2013; Kaiser Family Foundation (kff.org), accessed 20 January 2014.

In 1965, when Singapore became independent, one would not have expected the country to develop effectively because of a lack of requisites for a strong economy. Geographically, the nation is minuscule, and there are no significant natural resources. For example, minerals, oil, and water, all viewed necessary for economic growth, are lacking and imported. What, then, is responsible for making the country work so effectively?

Singapore's rapid economic development has multiple causes. Its location, situated half way between China and India, explains why the city-state has become an important port. The harbor is naturally calm and perfectly situated for traders around the world who have brought their treasures and their ideas. As a commercial hub for Southeast Asia, shipbuilding has flourished, including early support for British naval facilities. Then, as the world economy became increasingly interdependent after World War II, Singapore took advantage of its location to become integrated, in trade and investment, with the world capitalist system.

People are Singapore's primary resource. Although ethnically diverse (77 percent Chinese, 14 percent Malay, 8 percent Indian), Singaporeans are geographically homogeneous, all living close together in just 240 square miles. The public is overwhelmingly committed to the continued stability of the society and is imbued with a work ethic famous throughout the world.

Singaporean society has been overseen by authoritarian and incorruptible leaders of an interventionist state based on a large state enterprise sector and a commitment to indigenous entrepreneurial pursuits and outside investment.[3] Government has been in the hands of Lee Kuan Yew's People's Action Party, a political structure made up of a technocratic meritocracy that controls every aspect of the cultural, economic, political, and social lives of Singaporeans. This efficient party structure has micromanaged the economy and the daily behavior of citizenry through its control over the educational system, public policy, trade unions, and virtually all political institutions. The effectiveness of these leaders is a major cause of the nation's remarkable economic growth—as well as the people's view that their lives are over-managed.

An example of effective leadership occurred in 1965, when Singapore was ousted from the Federation of Malaysia. Singapore had based its economy on an Import Substitution Industrialization (ISI) model, relying on Malaya's large domestic workforce. Following the expulsion of Singapore, the nation faced high unemployment (9.2 percent in 1966) and an economic crisis.[4]

Seeing the crisis coming, Singapore's leadership swiftly and efficiently moved from ISI to a new Export-Oriented Industrialization (EOI) strategy that worked brilliantly to transform Singapore into a flourishing commercial center for the world. The EOI formula for success was to wed Singapore's human capital with foreign investment, all under the umbrella of governmental supervisory bodies. The marriage worked, producing the offspring of high economic growth rates, low unemployment, a rise in the standard of living of virtually all classes on the island, and a new infrastructure (housing, services, transportation) second to none in Asia. A mandatory national pension program was inaugurated, and Singapore has the second highest savings rate in the world.[5] With the exception of years when the economy has suffered negative growth, Singapore has consistently posted high growth rates.

Because the trading-to-GDP ratio has been high, Singapore's economy is vulnerable to an international recession. Following the 1985 downturn, for example, when protectionist tendencies in the industrialized world hurt Singaporean exports, state intervention forced diversification; financial and business services displaced manufacturing as the leading sector of the economy, and trade partners were diversified. In 1994, the United States was the principal trading partner, followed by Japan, Malaysia, Hongkong, Thailand, Australia, and West Germany, but in 2014 China/Hongkong topped the list.[6] Singapore's leaders also diversified exports, emphasizing automotive components, computers, electronic instrumentation, machine tools, medical instruments, and precision engineering. All these adjustments were carried out to reduce Singapore's reliance on particular industries and markets.

One of the most innovative adjustments was to establish labor enterprise zones in the "Sijori growth triangle" in which Indonesia and Malaysia opened adjacent territories for Singaporean manufacturers. Corporations with headquarters in Singapore built factories in these new zones, using less expensive labor. In tandem with more liberalization of the economy, Singapore resumed an average 8 percent growth rate in 1989 but was half that figure by 2013.

Singapore's economic policy is not laissez-faire. Government statutory boards and public enterprises have promoted economic growth. These official boards have developed infrastructure (bridges, piers, roads, telephone lines, the modern airport at Changi, etc.) and have promoted investment. Other boards supervise broadcasting, finance, housing, industrial training, shipping, and urban redevelopment. These boards, staffed by experts of exceptional technical knowledge, channel foreign capital, which makes up four-fifths of all capital in manufacturing. Thus, government intrudes into areas of the economy that most Westerners consider private. However, government intervention is carried out to support rather than to impede entrepreneurial activity.

The public sector was the initial driving force of Singapore's economic development. When the nation underwent an economic turndown in the mid-1980s, some privatization began. Thirty years of extensive public sector intervention in the market has had no deleterious effects on the economy. Indeed, unlike agricultural economies, basic socioeconomic indicators have continued to rise as the public sector has put its extracted revenue into the urban state. Singaporean government planning has enhanced the nation's competitiveness and has produced more revenue. The "strong visible hand" of the public sector has not crowded out, but rather exists alongside the expansion of the private sector.[7]

While the public sector is usually defined in terms of the government sector, Singapore's government-linked companies (GLCs) provide the government with the opportunity to intervene in the market. GLCs are doing very well in terms of profitability and efficiency. The PAP government has set forth adequate reforms to ensure that the public sector plays a positive role rather than a parasitic role. When efficiency declines, the government restructures or privatizes GLCs.[8]

Singapore's state enterprises, then, do not inhibit the private sector. Moreover, many state enterprises are undergoing privatization, and can no longer be called state enterprises in the traditional sense. The statutory boards, conspicuously free from corruption, are engaged primarily in infrastructural services (housing, transportation, utilities) to support and encourage rather than to compete against the private sector.

Notwithstanding the importance of governmental involvement, foreign capital still dominates the overall economy. Despite higher workers' wages, the developed world has found that the advantages of low levels of corruption, a high standard of living, and a superior infrastructure make Singapore a popular choice for investors.[9] Such liberal investment rules as allowing 100 percent foreign ownership, maintaining political stability, and granting tax advantages further attract investors. About 75 percent of all manufacturing output in Singapore comes from foreign firms.

Singapore's economy is interdependent with the world economic system. With a diversified economy, a highly educated and technologically proficient population, the highest standard of living in Southeast Asia, superb medical care, some of the best transportation infrastructure in the world, and good relations with its neighbors, Singapore's prospects for continued high levels of economic development are excellent.

Political Stability

It is impossible to overstate the importance of political stability in explaining Singapore's remarkable economic development. "Political stability" is defined as the continuing capacity of the government to meet the changing needs of the citizenry as well as the concomitant view of the citizenry that government policy is consistent and predictable. In both respects, Singapore ranks high.

Following Singapore's expulsion from the Federation of Malaysia, the ruling political party, PAP, has always won more than 90 percent of the seats in parliamentary elections. PAP is so preeminent that elections in Singapore simply lend an aura of prestige and legitimacy to single-party rule. PAP leaders accept in principle the notion that political opposition must be tolerated and regarded as loyal.[10] Indeed, some twenty-one political parties registered in 1991, although only three parties really mattered in the general elections—PAP, the Workers' Party (WP), and the Singapore Democratic Party (SDP).

Lee Kuan Yew has argued that strong opposition parties are not essential to democracy and in fact promote disharmony. This is a profoundly traditional view, which emphasizes order and loyalty. Since independence, PAP has won every election by a landslide, notwithstanding some erosion of public support. From 1968 to 2011, PAP's percentage of the total popular vote declined from 84 percent to 60 percent. In the 1991 election, when opposition parties won four seats, the campaign included and reflected a degree of democratization not always discussed by Singapore's critics. The opposition charged PAP with unjustly raising housing prices and overtaxing private cars. They decried the widening gap between rich and poor and accused PAP of favoring children of rich parents by "streaming" them toward college. The opposition called for greater freedom of speech, press, and assembly, and rejected Lee's thesis that liberty equals instability. However, they did not call for fundamental changes in the bases of PAP rule.

The 1997 campaign featured discussions and debates about rising prices of private property, and the emigration rate of about 5 percent of the total population. Candidates noted that monthly household expenditures increased 76 percent from 1988 to 1993. Singapore's yuppies questioned whether they could reach their dream of the five Cs—a car, careers for cash, credit cards, a condominium, and a country club membership.[11] Lee Kuan Yew, in contrast, has stressed "more important" five Cs—character, commitment, courtesy, culture, and community spirit. When votes were counted, electoral support increased for PAP, which thereby felt vindicated. Nevertheless, the decline in support for PAP in later elections, especially the 2011 election, indicates that the political system is more open than before to new approaches.

Still, the corporatist nature of the political system supports the critics' view that democratic ways are weak. Interest groups are rarely autonomous; they are controlled by the government, usually through the PAP. Only groups affiliated with the government have full access to the government's immense resources. PAP control of the media enables the party to trumpet government accomplishments while passing over shortcomings.

PAP dominance comes from the view that the party was responsible for securing an end to British colonial rule, thereby constituting a part of the nationalist movement rather than a mere political party. The party has worked to be recognized as a national political institution that draws support from all races and different social sectors. For many Singaporeans, it has become unthinkable to imagine a Singapore without PAP in power.[12]

For many Singaporeans, the degree of PAP control is not a major issue because of the government's continued success in meeting the needs of the people. They overwhelmingly support PAP because they believe that continuation of the economic miracle can occur only by retaining the party's preeminence. Because of this dominance, PAP parliamentary members drafted a plan to take effect after the parliamentary elections of 1988 under which three opposition candidates are seated in parliament as nonvoting observers, even if they lose in their districts.

In another ostensible plan to diversify the legislature, parliament amended the electoral law to create a "Team MP" scheme, effective the 1988 elections, whereby voters choose a slate of candidates in certain group representation constituencies (GRCs) rather than just one candidate. At least one of the candidates in a GRC must be of Indian or Malay ancestry.

A third innovation, also intended to bring fresh blood into parliament, was for six distinguished individuals to be selected to serve as nonvoting members of parliament. All these arrangements aim to legitimate PAP rule while broadening parliament's sociopolitical base so that it will be more representative of the population.

Political stability is tested when leaders change. The dominance of the society by Lee Kuan Yew for some forty years led many to believe that his retirement would entail instability. However, the transition in 1990 was remarkably smooth, with the new Prime Minister Goh Chok Tong effectively building on Lee's status, striking out in new directions, and strengthening his own reputation. Lee Hsien Loong's elevation to prime minister in 2004 assures stability.

Political stability, then, has resulted from the view of PAP dominance as legitimate.[13] The legitimacy stems from the fact that PAP takes credit for the country's economic success—not just for the wealthy few, but for most citizens. The government is staffed by highly trained, technologically sophisticated leaders imbued with hard work principles, who are highly paid. The best and the brightest in Singapore go into government service because of PAP's dominance and exceedingly high salaries for officials; in no other Southeast Asian country is that true.[14]

What I call Singapore's "soft authoritarianism" combines a capitalist economic system with a paternalistic authoritarianism that persuades rather than coerces.[15] This kind of government is viewed by some observers as more appropriate for nations in the midst of political and economic development.[16]

Compatibility of Politics and Culture

Prime Minister Lee Kuan Yew and his successors, Goh Chok Tong and Lee Hsien Loong, have rejected Western concepts of human rights and emphasized the need for deference and discipline, arguing that Singaporean traditions and conditions preclude Western individualism, which they equate with decadence. Many ordinary citizens accept Lee's contention that too much liberty equals insecurity. Singapore has the best educated, healthiest, and longest-lived citizens in Southeast Asia. Indeed, in Singapore, education for the individual indicates that Lee Kuan Yew does not reject individualism out of hand. However, he views the development of the individual within the context of the community, which is not necessarily contradictory to entrepreneurship. Japan, for example, has both entrepreneurship and a sense of community.

In Singapore, the streets are immaculate. Public transportation is better than anywhere else in Asia, and the telephones work. For the most part, the politicians are honest. These real benefits go a long way to compensate Singaporeans for the frustration they feel over ubiquitous rules and regulations governing their daily behavior. Lee claims that such vigilance keeps Singapore from sinking to the level of Bangkok, New Delhi, or New York City, with their littered streets, high crime rates, and social alienation.

The view of a unique Asian political system rests on the premise that Asia and the West have fundamentally different traditions, cultures, and values. The core values of Singapore are defined in Confucian terms. The West is viewed as having too much democracy, resulting in chaos, licentiousness, and lack of respect for societal needs. In contrast, Confucian rulers are expected to exercise their power hierarchically, yet with decorum and respect for their followers.

Singapore's leaders preach such Confucian principles as consensus, harmony, reverence for those in power, and stability. Respect for superiors often manifests itself as unquestioning, even obsequious, behavior toward those in authority. Confucius postulated a universal moral order that remains in harmony as long as all persons carry out their duties by fulfilling obligations to inferiors and superiors. Even the ruler must not rule arbitrarily but is bound to rule honestly, and the ruled are bound to follow orders from the ruler. If chaos occurs, the people have the right to overthrow the rulers in order to restore order. Lee Kuan Yew has seen himself as the quintessential Confucian ruler. His leadership was based upon paternal authority; he believed that he had a duty to take care of his people and to lead by moral example. His rewards were high status, political popularity, and subordinates eager to obey him.

Singapore's leaders have argued that there is a congruence between their culture and their authoritarian political system, and that Singapore is far more democratic than one might surmise from a study of the cultural history of the region. That point is made especially regarding a person's duties to his or her group rather than to personal liberty. In many Asian societies, the word "individualism" implies selfishness. Confucianism admonishes individuals to suppress their "selfish" desires and to think of others instead. Singaporeans tend to be bound together in patron-client relationships, the foundation of politics and society. These reciprocal ties are linked with others in a grand pyramid that extends from the lowly peasant to the most exalted personages. These ties integrate the society, fitting into the Singaporean culture with its emphasis on gratitude, hierarchy, personalism, reciprocity, and status.

The rejection of individualism in favor of community is not antithetical to entrepreneurship. Indeed, Singapore's leaders have long promoted values that encourage creativity to make sure that the nation remains in the front line of technology. The government has rewarded talent with better pay and with privileged positions. What the leaders have derided is not individualism per se, but self-centeredness. Lee Kuan Yew, in particular, has argued that community values are not the opposite of creative individual pursuits. It is "rampant individualism" that Singapore officials denounce.[17]

In a study of cultures, business administrators in both Asian and non-Asian societies were asked to rank countries on a spectrum of individualism to communalism.[18] The majority of Asians consistently ranked social stability as more important than personal liberty. Asians regarded "personal freedom" and "the rights of individuals" as less important to people in their own societies than did Americans. Singaporeans scored especially high on the value of order, and the data suggest that ordinary Singaporeans thought that they were less capable of handling personal freedom than elites in the country. This view is a variation on the notion that susceptibility of everyone is exaggerated except for themselves. Hence, many Singaporeans believe that they can handle morally or politically sensitive information, but their neighbors cannot.

Singaporeans read about the decadence of the West in their controlled press. Lee Kuan Yew has been particularly critical of the lack of freedom to walk the streets at night in the United States, comparing that with Singapore's very low crime rate.[19] He also scorns the "coddling" of habitual criminals in Western countries. He believes that the safety of the community must take precedence over Western notions of due process of law.

Lee denounces the U.S. penchant for citing human rights violations in Asian societies. For example, he rejects criticisms of his administration's censorship of foreign newspaper and journal publications, claiming that the government has the right and responsibility to limit information that enters the country and to keep inflammatory and destabilizing materials from creating chaos and undermining public morality. The media's role is "to inform people of government policies" rather than to question these policies.[20]

Singapore, then, has been forthright about admitting that it lacks a free and unrestricted press. But government leaders argue that an unfettered press can lead to civil commotion, an especially unacceptable state of affairs in a small, vulnerable island state. Moreover, officials have argued that cuts in the circulation of Western journals and newspapers are not so much censorship as they are a restriction on profits from news media that meddle in domestic politics.[21] The prevailing governmental view has been that journalists have a responsibility to help, not hinder, national solidarity and unity. Moreover, Singapore leaders believe that the country is not amenable to the democratic traditions of other societies because of ethnic, cultural, and geographic considerations.

Lee has also spoken forcefully about the importance of discipline, arguing that discipline rather than democracy leads to development: "The exuberance of democracy leads to undisciplined and disorderly conditions."[22] Lee's critics have responded by arguing that economic development has already been achieved and that the government's severe security measures are out of proportion to recent risks to public order. The critics say restrictions on press freedom and other human rights protect the powerful from embarrassment and inconvenience more than Singapore's citizens from harm.

The ideology of an "Asian democracy," based on the Singapore model, is a coherent and serious challenge to Western liberal democracy because it appears to be appropriate to both economically advanced nations and Third World countries. Singapore's leaders are eloquent spokespersons for the view that the West is not necessarily a good political model for Asia. They reject the view that there are universal civil and political rights which must be adhered to in all conditions. They say that economic development must take precedence over such rights, and that discipline and conformity to group values are more desirable than freedom and individualism.

Lee Kuan Yew's ideas strike a responsive chord with leaders of other Third World nations who are trying to reach a balance between authority and freedom. This is not mere sophistry. In fact, some of Lee's ideas seem attractive to those in the West who believe that their own societies are in the process of decaying while Asian countries flourish. Surrounded by societal ills, many Americans are beguiled by the message of the Asian democracies. The liberal traditions of the United States have never been so vilified as at in the 1990s. Widespread U.S. public approval for the caning of the young American who allegedly vandalized cars in Singapore during 1993 reflects the anti-liberal stance of many. Of course, Americans who favor the caning are not likely to discern the implications of such an extreme action on the broader landscape of American politics.

International Relations

In the 1950s, a Communist insurgency in Malaya threatened Singapore. In the 1960s, survival was a key issue in Singapore when Indonesia launched its "konfrontasi" policy against the formation of Malaysia. In the 1970s, China and Vietnam were viewed as potential aggressors, particularly after Vietnam's entry into Cambodia in 1978. Although Singapore's leaders eschewed the term "neutrality," they joined the nonaligned movement and established diplomatic relations with China while supporting the United States vis-à-vis Vietnam and U.S. military bases in Southeast Asia during the Cold War. Today, however, there are no direct foreign threats to Singapore from external powers. Nevertheless, as a small city-state with only minimal military capacity, Singapore's sovereignty is intact and invulnerable.

Singapore is no longer threatened by internal insurgency. As the Cold War diminished, and as regional and international ties have improved, Singapore's security has been assured. Singapore's security now rests on its ability to survive in the global economy. By instituting an export-oriented economy, economics came into command, overwhelming all other considerations.

Singapore has heightened its international involvement through its close regional ties, specifically its active participation in the Association of South-East Asian Nations (ASEAN) and related regional groupings. Singapore moved to a foreign policy of "economic diplomacy" in order to ensure positive relations with Indonesia, Malaysia, Thailand, and other neighbors, with which the island republic has important trade ties.

Singapore's most difficult ally is the United States because of tensions arising between the two nations over human rights issues. From time to time, Singaporean leaders have accused the United States of meddling in Singapore's internal affairs. Nevertheless, the Singaporean economy is highly dependent on trade, and the United States is one of its largest trading partners. Hence, neither country desires to inflame the relationship.

Conclusion

No one claims that Singapore is a Western-style democracy, except in terms of a narrow definition that requires free elections. In fact, many Singaporeans do not covet Western-style democracy, fearing that it could jeopardize their stability and threaten their affluent living standards. Overwhelmingly middle class, and dependent on foreign capital, Singaporeans do not want to compromise their entitlements and high living standards. Even those who vote for opposition (non-PAP) party candidates do not desire a major change; they want even more entitlements. Singaporeans perceive that they have a dichotomous choice between continuing their present rule and changing to opposition rule, which might undo the nation's achievements.

When asked what kind of government they have, most Singaporeans respond with the term "democracy," reflecting the procedural components of elections, a functioning parliament, and a modicum of civil liberties. The dominance of the PAP in every aspect of the society is viewed as peripheral as long as decisions are made that do not negatively affect self-interests. Complaints about lack of democracy emerge when the government practices cruelty or favoritism. Thus far, the number of complaints is fewer than the number of approbations.

In many respects, Singapore does enjoy substantive democracy. There are regular and free elections, unencumbered by massive fraud or vote buying. Laws may limit some individual rights, but there is due process of law in many respects. There is equality of opportunity. Singaporeans are free to travel anywhere and to own property anywhere. Singaporeans are educated all over the world. Despite ex-cesses of the island republic that are played up in the Western press, about 95 percent of these students return voluntarily to Singapore.

The rise of efficient, pragmatic, and strong leaders in Singapore, committed to a post-industrial economy, is a factor of immense importance in stating the case for Singapore. The degree of economic and political success was unimaginable just a few decades ago. The high quality of life, political stability, social cohesion, and international standing and security far exceed what anyone predicted, so it is unfortunate when the leaders jeopardize that reputation from time to time by conducting vendettas against critics who might otherwise not be taken very seriously. A primary aspect of good government is the capacity to bring about change before crises emerge. The success of Singapore's technocratic meritocracy in coping with changing demands has been remarkable. That capacity is the essence of the case for Singapore.

Epilog (by Michael Haas)

Singapore remains an admirable country in economic and technocratic terms. Nevertheless, the less developed economies have higher growth rates today: Singapore's current growth rate (4.4 percent) compares with Malaysia (5.0), Indonesia (5.6), and the Philippines (7.0).[23] The local manufacturing percentage has declined from 30 percent to 24 percent.[24]

Singapore prides itself on superior educational opportunities. In 2000, the Wharton School of Finance of the University of Pennsylvania partnered with the Singapore Management University. On the other hand, in 2005, the University of Warwick decided not to establish a campus in Singapore, citing costs and lack of academic freedom.[25]

In 2002, under Prime Minister Goh Chok Tong, the ban on chewing gum was lifted. Goh also allowed dissident Chee Soon Juan to host the International Youth Conference on Democracy that year.[26] Goh was trying to bring about a "kindler, gentler" Singapore, borrowing a phrase once used by former President George H. W. Bush.

When Lee Hsieng Loong became prime minister in 2004, the world wondered whether he would bring a fresh outlook. One early pronouncement was "our society must open up."[27] Loosening of controls, however, was immediately limited to no longer requiring licenses for indoor talks with the stipulation that "criticism that scores political points and undermines the government's standing" and "crusading journalism" would not be tolerated.

Perhaps the most extraordinary sign of a new era was the decision by current Prime Minister Lee Hsien Loong to revoke the public sector ban on hiring gays and lesbians.[28] In 2007, the government decided not to prosecute consenting sex between gays and lesbians, though there was no legal decriminalization as a sop to conservative Singaporeans.[29]

Notes

1. *Fortune* (13 November 1995) named Singapore the world's number one city for business based on afforda-

bility, entrepreneurial opportunities, lifestyle, and standard of living. No other Southeast Asian city made the top ten. The top ten cities in order are as follows: (1) Singapore, (2) San Francisco Bay Area, (3) London, (4) New York, (5) Frankfurt, (6) Hongkong, (7) Atlanta, (8) Toronto, (9) Paris, (10) Tokyo.

2. *Gross domestic product* (GDP) is the value of all goods and services produced in one year. *Infant mortality* is the number of babies per 1,000 live births who die before reaching one year of age. *Literacy* generally means the ability to read and write a short, simple statement about everyday life.

3. In 1996, the *Far Eastern Economic Review* and the *Asian Wall Street Journal* published articles stating that Senior Minister Lee Kuan Yew and Deputy Prime Minister Lee Hsien Loong (Lee Kuan Yew's son) were given "favors" in the purchase of a condominium. Lee's response was "I am me. Life is not fair." He pointed out that the owner desired to sell him the condominium at a less expensive price. The incident raised questions about the "incorruptibility" of Singapore's leadership. Nevertheless, for many years, world business executives have voted Singapore one of the least corrupt societies in the world for doing business. The amount of money involved in the condominium incident was negligible relative to that of most other nations.

4. Algeria is higher in gross savings per gross domestic product, according to the World Bank.

5. Ibid., 53.

6. Clark D. Neher, *Southeast Asia in the New International Era* (Boulder, CO: Westview, 1994), 150. Figures for 2014 are from The Observatory of Economic Complexity at the Massachusetts Institute of Technology.

7. Linda Low, "The Public Sector in Contemporary Singapore: In Retreat?" in *Singapore Changes Guard: Social, Political and Economic Directions in the 1990s*, ed. Garry Rodan (Melbourne: Longman Cheshire, 1993), 175.

8. *Ibid.*, 180.

9. Singapore is consistently voted the world's least corrupt society by international business executives. The reasons are as follows: (1) the senior leadership's commitment to the eradication of corruption; (2) stringent anti-corruption laws; (3) a functioning anti-corruption agency, with powers to prosecute; (4) salaries and fringe benefits competitive with the private sector. See Jon S. T. Quah, "Controlling Corruption in City States: A Comparative Study of Hongkong and Singapore," *Crime, Law and Social Change*, XXII (1995): 391-414.

10. The following paragraphs are taken from Clark D. Neher and Ross Marlay, *Democracy and Development in Southeast Asia: The Winds of Change* (Boulder, CO: Westview, 1995).

11. Jose Manuel Tesoro and Santha Oorjitham, "Testing Times," *Asiaweek*, 6 September 1996.

12. Bilver Singh, *Whither PAP's Dominance? An Analysis of Singapore's 1991 General Elections*, (Petaling Jaya, Malaysia: Pelanduk, 1992), 38-39.

13. Taiwan and South Korea, both Confucian-oriented societies, approximate the Anglo-American model of government. If it is conceded that there is the institutionalization of Anglo-American democracy in these two countries, one reason lies in the fact that both South Korea and Taiwan need to define their identities against Communist regimes, their significant opposites. Both are highly dependent on U.S. support to maintain their identities and sovereignty. There are strong reasons why their political elites would want to move their poli-

tics toward democracy and rein in the natural cultural reflexes. In both cases, now and again the reflexes of a strong authoritarian leader do emerge.

14. Civil servants in Singapore earn the highest salaries in the world. The Chief Justice in Singapore makes a higher salary than the persons holding that position in the United States, Great Britain, and Germany combined. Civil servants are provided competitive salaries and fringe benefits to reduce the gap between the public and private sectors. See Quah, "Controlling Corruption in City-States," 398.

15. See Denny Roy, "Singapore, China, and the 'Soft Authoritarian' Challenge," *Asian Survey*, XXXIV (1994): 231.

16. Samuel P. Huntington, *Political Order in Changing Societies* (New Haven, CT: Yale University Press, 1968).

17. See Tham Seong Chee, *Values and Development in Singapore*, (Singapore: Department of Malay Studies, National University of Singapore, 1994), 16.

18. Donald K. Emmerson, "Singapore and the 'Asian Values' Debate," *Journal of Democracy*, VI (1995): 102-105.

19. Singapore's crime rate is low although it is not lower than that of Seoul and Tokyo which is almost minimal, according to George Thomas Kurian, *World Encyclopedia of Police Forces and Penal Systems* (New York: Facts on File, 1989); cf. Hernando Gomez Buendia, ed., *Urban Crime: Global Trends and Policies* (Tokyo: United Nations University, 1989). Still, Singapore's crime rate is low when compared globally and even regionally.

20. Lee Hsien Loong, "Media's Role 'To Inform People of Govt Policies'," *Straits Times* (overseas edition), 16 June 1990, 2.

21. Michael Haas, "The Politics of Singapore in the 1980s," *Journal of Contemporary Asia*, XIX (1989): 55.

22. *Manila Chronicle*, 19 November 1992, 10.

23. Data are from *tradingeconomics.com*, accessed 15 January 2013.

24. Ministry of International Trade and Industry, "Productivity Spillover to Local Manufacturing Firms from Foreign Direct Investment." July 17, 2013.

25. Jospeh B. Tammey, *The Struggles over Singapore's Soul: Western Modernization and Asian Culture* (Berlin: de Gruyter, 1996); Garry Rodan, "'Vibrant and Cosmopolitan' Without Political Pluralism," *Asian Survey*, XLVI (2006): 185.

26. William Case, "Singapore in 2003: Another Tough Year," *Asian Survey*, XLIV (2004): 117.

27. Garry Rodan, "Singapore in 2004: Long-Awaited Leadership Transition," *Asian Survey*, XLV (2005): 140-141.

28. Ibid., 142.

29. Chua Beng Huat, "Singapore in 2007: High Wage Ministers and the Management of Gays and the Elderly," *Asian Survey*, XLVIII (2008): 59-60.

4

Political Economy
Christopher Lingle and Kurt Wickman

Singapore's Economic "Miracle"

From 1960 to 1991, Singapore's economy grew faster than any other country in the region except for South Korea.[1] The annual rate of growth of real gross domestic product (GDP)[2] in Singapore was 8 percent, and per capita GDP growth rate was above 6 percent. With the exception of recessions in 1964 and 1985, Singapore's GDP was on a long-run growth path of about 8.5 percent in 1998,[3] which is impressive because annual growth of only 7 percent means the doubling of GDP in a decade. In comparison, Germany and the United States have exhibited real GDP growth of 2-3 percent over the same period. However, the growth rate slowed to 4.4 percent by 2012.[4]

In absolute terms, Singapore's per capita income rose from less than US$2,000 in the early 1960s to about US$25,000 in 1995 and $60,900 by 2012 (Table 3.1). As a result, the island republic's per capita income has surpassed that of several European countries, including its former colonial master, Great Britain, which Singapore outstripped in 1994.

Singapore now boasts a highly skilled and technologically sophisticated labor force.

Since labor demand and real wages have grown rapidly, there is little unemployment (less than 2 percent), and poverty has been largely eliminated.[5] Despite a labor market characterized by excess demand for practically all types of skills, not just advanced skills, Singpore's average inflation rate of 3-4 percent per annum, is well below the world average. This is noteworthy, since excess demand for labor normally pushes up inflation.

The economy was able generate a foreign exchange surplus of nearly $100 billion in 1990 and $273 billion in 2013.[6] Singapore's international competitiveness is constantly rated near the top. In 1996, it was in first place and second place in two international surveys; as of 2012, Singapore remained the world's second most competitive economy.[7]

Singapore's hard-working laborers and managers can take considerable pride in their efforts to achieve such excellent economic results. Singapore's economy has shifted from low-wage, labor-intensive production to high-wage, capital-intensive production of high-tech goods. GDP has risen from S$39 billion in 1985 to S$109 billion in 1994 to S$126 billion in 2012 (Table 3.1). International investors have given Singapore a vote of confidence by increasing foreign direct investment from S$2.5 billion in 1985 to S$4.3 billion in 1994 and S$57 trillion in 2012.[8]

On the basis of these impressive results, Singapore was included among an elite group of East Asian countries identified as "miracle" economies in a World Bank report of 1993.[9] Independent surveys by free-market think tanks have suggested that Singapore's economy should be regarded as one of the most free in the world.[10]

Several social policy innovations have been undertaken by the People's Action Party (PAP), the party that has run Singapore's government since independence. Perhaps the most noteworthy initiative is the transformation of inner-city slums into government-built tower blocks of apartments. Today, most Singaporeans live in owner-occupied housing units. Improvements in the quality and availability of schooling have led to dramatic increases in literacy (Table 3.1). Infant mortality fell sharply and remains about half the rate of the United States.

Singapore's traffic control policy also has sparked considerable outside interest. Rising incomes could be expected to exacerbate enormous problems of vehicular traffic congestion. However, several market-based schemes have been implemented to reduce the number of vehicles on the road. One is "peak-load pricing," where road users pay higher fees for using certain arteries during periods of high-peak usage. Although Singapore is known as a free port, high tariffs on imported cars and an auction of "certificates of entitlement" (COEs) price cars out of the reach of most citizens. Further, a fixed quota on the number of COEs, valid for only ten years, places a limit on the numbers of vehicles sold.

Following success in developing industrial townships at home, Singapore's government is offering expertise to its neighbors and is expanding business opportunities beyond the confines of its borders. In an ambitious program involving "software transfer" of development skills, Singaporean technocrats oversaw the opening of an industrial township in Suzhou, China. Singapore Technologies Industrial Corporation, a government-linked company (GLC), has undertaken a project in Wuxi, China, as well as industrial parks in India (Bangalore) and Indonesia, and now has a presence in 41 cities within 23 countries.[11]

Several forces have defined the economic logic behind Singapore's development and modernization. From its inception as an independent political entity, Singapore has coped with economic conditions that arise out of the essential nature of a city-state, while confronting the new structural changes in the global economy. Viewed in this light, Singapore's experience seems less miraculous and lacking in mystery. Indeed, the role of Singapore's government is often exaggerated in different studies. In this chapter, we argue that the role of the government in promoting Singapore's economic "miracle" has been more passive than active, that more of Singapore's economic success occurred because of the economic imperatives of a city-state in today's world economy than due to the meddling of the government in the economy.

Economics of a City-State

The Republic of Singapore is a city-state detached from or, at least, not directly connected to a self-supporting countryside that provides an agricultural base. Although Singapore had some of the properties of a city-state for a long time, formal recognition of this fact first occurred in 1965, when Singapore left the Federation of Malaysia.

Surprisingly little research has examined the economics of city-states. Our objective here, in the absence of robust research results, is to lay out some observations and to formulate some hypotheses about city-states. In sum, we offer a sketch of Singapore's political economy as a case study that might serve to build a general economic theory of the city-state.

Observations based on European economic history suggest a scenario in which an urban organization (town or city) develops successively from the economic resources of an adjoining countryside, provided that certain favorable conditions are present.[12] If individuals are attracted to move from the countryside to town, urban centers emerge, prompting a major change in a regional economy, which shifts from (mainly) self-supporting activities to (mainly) market-based activities. The lower productivity of the self-supporting economies is the source of lower living standards and slower economic growth. As differences in living standards between urban and rural areas widen, more immigrants are drawn from the countryside into the town. Those with the greatest mobility, usually the young and potentially high-productive workers, move toward better-paid positions. At the same time, the amenities of a more varied and interesting social life encourage even more migration to urban centers.

The making of modern Singapore generally followed the above urban development scenario. The migration process involved large numbers of Chinese immigrants, who arrived over an extended period, joined by smaller numbers of Indian and Malay immigrants, into a well-run British-controlled port city that served as an entrepôt for the India and China-Japan sea trade. Most early immigrants were young men with little formal education, with skills generally limited to agricultural production.

After the first waves of immigrants settled in Singapore, later waves of individuals with different backgrounds arrived. Some present-day workers from Bangladesh, India, Myanmar, the Philippines, and Thailand—and to some extent Malaysia—tend to be sojourners who readily move on to other jobs in the fast-growing Southeast Asian markets. Singapore's immigration policy has also contributed to the high mobility rate of workers.

Thus, Singapore's labor market has an unusually high proportion of workers in their most productive ages. Skill differences between local and immigrant labor have widened over time. The transition process can go on smoothly, as long as productivity differences are reflected in wage differentials. Accordingly, proposals for an egalitarian distribution of income, either through strong trade unions or an interventionist government wage policy, will lack support. It is not surprising that trade unions in Singapore are weak, and the PAP government has not offset this weakness with an explicit wage policy. Indeed, one of the criticisms of "Western" development raised by Singapore's leaders is that the welfare state results in a loss of labor market flexibility and national competitiveness.

To continue to explicate the urban development scenario, the most productive segments of the population in the surrounding regions are attracted to urban entities, such as a city-state, due to the different sophistication levels that can be observed between the self-sufficient (underdeveloped) and market-based (emerging or developed) economies. In essence, the range in compensation between higher and lower productive positions in the city-state is wide. Those in rural areas who are able (or have the potential) to secure employment in high-wage jobs will have a strong incentive to migrate to a city in order to receive higher incomes. The tendency of the city-state to attract workers with higher productivity will result in the classical precondition for the establishment of an exchange relationship that allows all parties to gain and leads to the formation of markets.

The inflow of people to a city-state increases the population or, alternatively, tends to increase the population density (number of persons per square mile). Thus, Hongkong and Singapore exhibit the highest population densities in Asia. The labor force of a city-state is highly mobile due to its skill levels, and there is high potential or actual mobility between different jobs within the borders of the city-state. That is, individuals can target a "long-term income level path" by moving through a hierarchy of jobs and by acquiring new skills through education and on-the-job training. Three important consequences follow from this analysis.

First of all, the labor market in a city-state provides clear signals to all market participants. Individuals can more readily find a job that matches their productivity. The normally high costs of job switching are relatively low in city-states. Since there is an efficient use of labor power, economic growth is maximized. High job mobility means that labor market adjustments to changes in productivity and demand for skills are continuous. A continual upgrading of workers' skills, accompanied by high labor mobility, allows new technology to be more readily integrated into the economy. In turn, growth occurs from increases in productivity levels, leading directly to higher wages.

Secondly, both a flexible labor market and rapid economic growth allow individuals to influence their own income path in a direct way that is not possible in other systems. For example, a rigid European-style politicized labor market is characterized by restrictive job definitions imposed by centralized trade unions, which bargain for wages collectively. Such practices, along with regulations and wage legislation, obstruct the "matching" of jobseekers with jobs. A politicized approach to income distribution is less attractive to workers in a city-state than elsewhere. Leaders of a mature city-state, in which wages rise with productivity, are less likely to be pressured to develop an advanced income distribution policy, and so this source of social tension is eliminated.

Thirdly, a city-state will accumulate "middle class" citizens from its wider regional economy. Apart from assuring political stability, a concentration of relatively high-income earners will also promote "middle-class values" that promote hard work, honesty in contract fulfillment, life-long learning, and savings habits. The importance of establishing a "contract culture," though rather intangible, cuts deep. Indeed, in a categorization of explanations for European economic growth, Douglass North identifies "public attitudes" as among of the most important.[13]

Impact of Singapore within Southeast Asia

The establishment and growth of a city-state also has regional economic consequences, as a city-state must trade with its neighbors. Singapore's economy, for example, is self-sufficient only in egg and poultry production, and there are no raw material deposits within its borders. Consequently, it must trade for most foodstuffs and for all its industrial inputs. Even water is traded, with Singapore relying upon imported technology to purify water that is brought in by pipeline from Malaysia and then re-exported back as partial payment.

The high volume of foreign trade of a city-state will draw parts of the countryside economy into market relations, resulting in the introduction of a new division of labor into the more backward parts of the regional economy. Doubtless, such Asian city-states as Hongkong and Singapore have contributed to the economic modernization and subsequent higher growth of the economies of the surrounding hinterland. In modern Asian economic history, such symbiotic relations between advanced and backward regions have enjoyed "success." Japan's long-term development is sometimes described as "growth without domestic raw material sources," and Hongkong, another city-state, has neither a source of domestic raw materials nor sufficient food production. In promoting the demand for interregional trade a foreign-oriented "trading class" has emerged in Asia, composed mainly of expatriate Chinese in East Asia. The oft-quoted cliché that Chinese are "natural-born capitalists" has, of course, no roots in genetics, but apparently results from this peculiarity in the development of Asian economic relations.

Successively, various Chinese trading groups have prospered in East Asian countries within non-Chinese environments, notably Indonesia, Malaysia, Thailand, and Vietnam. Since most Chinese trading houses in East Asia would prefer to base their interregional business activity in a Chinese social environment with a basic tolerance and infrastructure for capitalist trading practice, the most successful Chinese trading families took up residence in Hongkong and Singapore. The attraction of these city-states as "free ports" was enhanced by China's political disintegration and subsequent transformation into a Communist country in the 1940s and early 1950s.

The industrial structure of a city-state best thrives under maximum openness in international relations. Accordingly, the Singapore government has been especially active in trying to guide and to maintain a common Asian trade policy. The demand for and scope of such policies are already present through the economic structure of the city-states and their networks over Asia.[14] Although Malaysia once promoted the formation of an East Asian Economic Council (EAEC) that would exclude non-Asian countries, especially the United States, Singapore has never clearly endorsed such suggestions, in spite of strong anti-American sentiments often expressed in government circles of the island republic. The fact that the United States is one of Singapore's largest trade partners has effectively stopped such sentiments from being translated into policy.

In 1989, Singapore took a leadership role in the formation of the Asia-Pacific Economic Cooperation (APEC) and the establishment of a "growth triangle" with Indonesia and Malaysia. This latter growth arrangement, known as "Sijori," encompasses the Riau Islands of Indonesia, the Malaysian state of Johore Bahru, and the entire territory of Singapore. The basic advantage is that Singapore contributes capital, transport and logistic facilities, whereas Indonesia and Malaysia contribute abundant and cheap labor and land.

Economic Policy

Perhaps it is most transparent in the city-state that economic structure guides economic policy. Hongkong was the pioneer of economic policies suited to a modern city-state. The most comprehensive way to characterize the economic policy of Hongkong is as a "Ricardian free port." Nineteenth century British economist David Ricardo showed that, in normal circumstances, any country or region allowing unrestricted international trade would prosper more than under any other approach to trade policy.[15] Ricardo's studies are among the most durable observations in economics. His ideas are taught and widely treated as a cornerstone of international economics.

Nevertheless, few countries have followed Ricardian policies. One explanation, offered by public choice theorists, is that a protectionist trade policy emerges when domestic producers seek restricted competition to the advantage of their own businesses. Producer groups are easy to organize, and the costs of protectionism can be shifted to consumers and taxpayers, who are seldom well organized.[16] Since the pressure on policy formulation is asymmetrical, protectionist measures tend to be implemented, and special interest groups benefit, while costs are imposed on the rest of the population.

Hongkong's organization as a Ricardian free port was a novelty that created a competitive advantage for that city-state. In 1965, after leaving of the Federation of Malaysia, Singapore "emulated" Hong-kong's economic policies because this fundamental political change forced the PAP government to rethink its entire policy. Establishment of a noninterventionist trade policy required that general economic policy should also be market-based, resulting in few government interventions, low public expenditures, and minimal tax rates.

The policy choice in Singapore after 1965 can be described as the successive introduction of a supply-side economic policy. Central elements have been to offer businesses certain advantageous conditions, especially but in no way restricted to export-oriented activities. Low-interest credit for such investments was the most important single element in this particular policy in Japan, South Korea, and Taiwan, but it was less important in Singapore. In general, city-states develop their competitive advantage by eliminating subsidies, taxes, and regulations that distort business decisions. The two major types of government intervention in Singapore's economy were quite straightforward, with few distortions.

First of all, high priority was given to modernizing the educational system, as elsewhere in East Asia. When the World Bank released its first major study of East Asia in 1993, education was identified as an important explanation for high growth in the region.[17] Interestingly, considerably more benefit was derived by enhancing quality at the lower levels of education than by developing college education. The primary benefit from the educational system in Singapore is apparently in the provision of a stock of loyal workers with good literacy, well prepared to follow and interpret instructions, even complicated instructions. At higher levels of the educational system, Singapore does not produce innovators. There are some innovative homegrown businesses, the best example being Creative Labs, whose Sound Blaster has set the standard for computer audio components. However, the contribution to such innovations from Singapore universities is negligible. American universities have played a considerably more important role in providing higher education for Singaporeans. Applied research and development in business corporations that market and directly profit from the results of such innovations account for the rest of the educational impact on high growth in Singapore.[18]

The second high-priority area for government involvement has been in the provision of infrastructure, which has focused on transportation. The government-run Keppel Corporation organized Singapore's basic economic activity—the port infrastructure. On the basis of a well-managed comprehensive infrastructure for the port, thousands of private companies could trade with the rest of the world. Trading houses, of course, demanded improvements in port facilities.

With the rising importance of air freight, Singapore's government also invested heavily in airport facilities. Changi airport, often described as a "state-of-the-art" airport, acquired the same central role in facilitating air freight as Singapore's harbor has played in sea freight.[19] Government-run Singapore Airlines has benefited from the exploding demand for passenger transport in Asia, where there are long distances between the region's central trading cities.

In the few instances when the Singapore government intervened directly into the economy outside these narrow areas, results have been mixed. One example is the introduction of a new wage policy in 1980-1981, wherein wages were generally raised, based on the assumption that higher wages would force the economy into more productive activities at a faster pace. But in 1985-1986, Singapore's economy was hit by a deep recession; real GNP growth fell almost to zero while private investments declined by about 50 percent. In 1988, after the PAP government withdrew the high-wage policy, the economy returned to its former high growth path.[20]

The innovative development of market-oriented economic policies in Asian city-states was out of step with general strategies promoted by international bureaucrats and development economists in the United Nations from the late 1950s to the mid-1980s. UN officials proposed three strategies for developing countries. One strategy was to encourage a relatively closed economy and a low level of foreign trade; supported partly by the so-called "infant industry" argument, nascent domestic industries were portrayed as requiring protection, since they could not compete with well-established world corporations during their initial build-up phase. A second UN-backed strategy was to promote an extensive worldwide policy of aid to developing countries; a transfer of savings from rich to poor countries was expected to provide access to the hard currency lost by not trading. The third strategy was for developing countries to place severe limits upon the activities of international multinational corporations within their borders.

City-states were unable to follow the threefold UN approach, since their economies require maximum openness to international trade. The same logic led them to reject the dependence upon aid for development and to repudiate the exclusion of international corporations. The difference in results was striking. Firms established in the city-states were able to compete internationally because of full exposure to world markets. No country with heavy dependence upon aid and exclusion of multinationals was able to do the same. For example, in Tanzania annual aid transfers in 1996 were more than 50 percent of GDP in 1996, almost three times the government budget, while aid transfers to the city-states were no more than around 1 percent of GDP.[21]

One crucial problem in supporting the growth process in underdeveloped countries, the transfer of technology, was solved by welcoming multinational corporations into the city-states. Access to the high technology used by multinational corporations contributed to the growth of domestic high technology industries in the city-states. No comparable arrangement was observed in countries that followed the UN strategy. Instead, government hostility toward foreign companies in underdeveloped countries encouraged multinational corporations to focus mainly upon short-term, usually low-level trading activities, possibly out of fear of being nationalized.

Internationalization of Capital and City-States

The benefits of the market-based policy of city-states were intensified by their access to the expansion of international financial markets, which occurred due to the two "oil crises" in the 1970s and the deregulation of national capital markets in Europe and the United States in the 1980s. In the former case, an enormous stock of dollars was transferred to governments in oil-producing countries. Because the amounts were so large that they could not be absorbed by most oil-exporting countries, either as domestic or regional investments, they were deposited in Western financial institutions. In turn, these "Petrodollars" were used for different international projects, with a disproportionately large share going to Latin American governments. By the early 1980s, this loan structure threatened the survival of several large American and European banks when Latin American governments ran into problems in servicing the loans.

The combined effect of large international capital flows and international loan crisis management paved the way in the 1980s for a wave of national deregulation of capital markets.[22] With the volume of world trade growing rapidly from the 1950s, the world economy had already changed in several important aspects. An international capital market had emerged, a new situation that has been described as the "globalization" of national economies. In the 1980s, international considerations became so important that it became widely accepted that the future course of the world economy (and politics) would be influenced more heavily by international than traditional national conditions.

The open trading structure of the Asian city-states, with open connections to their respective "hinterland economies," put them in a favorable position to compete in the worldwide competition to attract capital and investments, in what has been called "the new institutional competition."[24] Following legislation that had already been in effect in Hongkong for some time, Singapore's parliament adopted new laws in June 1978 aimed at facilitating the internationalization of its economy.[25]

All restrictions on Singapore's capital flows—in all currencies—were abolished, as were capital gains taxes, inheritance taxes, and wealth taxes. Foreign companies operating in Singapore were granted major tax relief. The government issued a solemn promise that no foreign company, under any pretext, would be nationalized. At the same time, the educational system was further reformed to insure that laborers would better fit into the industries that started to move into the region in the 1970s.

The logic of Singapore's economic liberalization is straightforward. Due to the free movement of capital, governments are obliged to compete with one another regarding such institutional arrangements as subsidies, tax policies, and access to a well-educated labor force. What is happening is a new form of competition in which national economic policies, long thought to be sheltered from international market forces, are now subjected to international comparison by global corporations. In the long run, there will be a harmonization of economic policy across countries regarding institutional arrangements. Success will greet countries that provide policy packages that encourage the development of a productive labor force while having few restrictions on international investment.

The change in economic policy by Singapore's government in the late 1970s proved successful in attracting foreign investment, particularly since 1978, when Singapore's liberalization legislation was adopted. Before 1978, Singapore's participation in the international economy was mostly in the area of trade. The upswing that began in 1978 was a major turning point. The trend line, estimated as an exponential function of time, indicates that foreign investment became a leading factor in the progress of Singapore's economy from the late 1970s.

The change in direction was very swift and well-timed to match the enormous success of Japan's export drive. Indeed, some researchers portray the emergence of Singapore and the other Asian "tiger economies" as a response to the recycling of Japan's trade surplus.[26] However, closer inspection suggests that this conclusion has little merit: American and European capital flows to Singapore and other parts of Asia have been as, or more, important than Japanese investments.

The statistics on foreign investment in Singapore show that the domestically oriented wage regulation policy of the early 1980s was associated with a withdrawal of international capital. Indeed, international investments fell by one-half from 1981 to 1986. After the sharp economic recession in 1985-1986 induced the government to withdraw this policy, Singapore returned to the "natural" economic policy dictated by its international character as a city-state. This experience offers a partial explanation for the peculiar mix of Singapore's policy, in which the international sector is regulated by free trade politics, but domestic policies are guided by a form of Chinese authoritarianism.[27]

In general, foreign investment statistics suggest that Singapore, as an internationally-oriented city-state, experienced notable gains from widening its "Ricardian free port" approach to include unencumbered capital flows. Most of the economic growth from the 1980s can be explained by direct and indirect effects of huge capital flows into Singapore.

Hence, Singapore was well-prepared for the new institutional competition emerging in the 1980s. As a consequence of Japan's and the Asian city-states' long-term growth, East Asia emerged as a new world economic center.[28] Today, East Asia ha become the world center for light industry production, especially in electronics. Asian city-states can also be considered as gateways to the Asian "hinterland economies." Singapore's leaders prefer the description "hub" for the city, a metaphor with the same meaning.

"Asian Values" & Corporatist Singapore

Singapore's PAP government was an especially ardent defender of the concept of "Asian Values" during the 1990s. The ideas behind the concept are not always very clear, but we note that five assertions are repeatedly made by its proponents:

- Asians are said to put "society before self," thus suggesting that "extreme individualism" in the West is to be avoided.

- Asian society is portrayed as being based on the "family network," wherein low divorce rates and care for the elderly guarantee family stability. These networks form the basis of independent family business and, at the same time, promote an interest in advanced education among the younger generation.

- The stability of Asian societies is seen as the outcome of cooperation among different social groups, making it possible to avoid high-level social tensions. The resulting stable social environment is cited as an explanation of high levels of savings and investment as well as the ethic of hard work.

- The social contract in the "Asian Values" context is a basically a "trust contract" between the government and the citizens, wherein "virtuous" governments guarantee that only fair rules are applied, and the citizenry follows these laws. One cornerstone of this philosophy is that only government officials are able to have a balanced view of the entire social process. Individual citizens are mistrusted, since are assumed to act on special interests that may not promote the general welfare of society.

- The wider commitment of the government is to guard citizens from information that can destabilize society and contribute to social tension. Hence, curbs on press freedom are to insure that the press behaves responsibly, and access to information is limited so that citizens will not form bad attitudes or habits (e.g., Western liberalism, pornography).

The "Asian Values" formulation, which former Prime Minister Lee Kuan Yew associated with Confucianism, is uniquely "Singaporean." Other defenders of Asian special characteristics, such as Malaysian Prime Minister, Mohamad Mahathir, stress other aspects. Yet the Confucian-oriented societies of Hongkong, South Korea, and Taiwan already embrace "Western" and "liberal" influences associated with popular democracy.

Although one scholar characterizes Singapore as "communitarian,"[29] the most precise way to categorize Singapore's political economy is in terms of the "corporatist" arrangements that guide politics, sometimes called "Singapore, Inc." Corporatist systems tend to mix market and planned elements together, such that market aspects will dominate planned aspects as the complexity of contracts become greater.

Singapore is often described as a "meritocratic" society, implying the positive characteristic that talents can always find a suitable career. The reality is much more complicated. Economic growth and rising incomes in Singapore are based on the success of its business elites, who find success in the financial, industrial, and trading sectors by entering into a number of accords with customers, producers, and one another. These agreements involve an enormous skein of contracts and "understandings," which are guaranteed by the force of law and a set of implicit values that are likewise enforced by the government. Governments always occupy an important position in such a system by overseeing the formal institutions that hold the web together and by guaranteeing the social cost-benefit advantages of the entire fabric.

A public choice theoretical interpretation of the social contract inherent in the five "Asian Values" suggests a set of arrangements reminiscent of contracts in feudal Europe. Under these conditions, the feudal lord (government) provides safe shelter and infrastructure for the economy in return for loyalty, subordination, and tax payments from the serfs (citizens). Such modern political concepts as "consent," "reciprocity," and "mutuality" between the government and the governed are as absent from the "Asian Values" model as they were under feudal arrangements.

To better understand Singapore's political economy, one must realize that government expenditures averaged about 20 percent of GDP from 1985 until 1998, but today are half that percentage.[30] Perhaps the greatest element of government control over the economy is in the mandatory pension scheme, the Central Provident Fund (CPF), which serves as a substitute for a social security system. CPF places about 40 percent of total labor earnings into the hands of PAP-appointed government managers of GIC Private Limited, formerly known as the Government of Singapore Investment Corporation. CPF contributes are held as government securities, but the earnings are invested mostly in overseas ventures.[31]

In addition, several state-owned enterprises operate outside of the government budget. At the beginning of the twenty-first century, there were nearly seventy statutory boards (SBs) and five hundred government-linked companies (GLCs). SBs operate in a range of areas often associated with government activity, such as infrastructure, public utilities, and regulatory bodies. GLCs, which are managed by able corporate executives, are involved in activities that are more often associated with the private sector.

Little information is available about the individual size and financial results of these state-owned enterprises, but their existence clearly suggests that they exert an influence over Singapore's domestic economy that is not negligible. Some of the large domestic players in the stock market are enterprises that are either owned or controlled by the government (e.g., Temasek Holdings). Although the government owns the bulk of the developed and undeveloped property, it has been successively privatized.

Thus, there is a "dualism" in the economy—a division between sectors of the economy that face differential levels of government intervention. In the sector identified by the presence of elites and foreign companies, including the government-run corporations, there is little government intervention. In contrast, the domestic sector is characterized by massive government intervention. The implementation of educational and social policies in domestic politics, in addition, relies upon a politically compliant judiciary that does not contradict policies made by the other branches of government (see Chapter 6 herein).

The explanation for Singapore's high score on various economic freedom ratings, thus, is simply a reading of its elite/foreign sector. Few controls over the domestic economy are evaluated in these studies, even though they limit economic freedom in very real ways. For example, the requirement for annual renewal of business licenses places subtle pressures upon business owners to support PAP in the normal and long political tradition of "Oriental despotism."[32]

Singapore's elites believe that their city-state is plagued with a risk of instability, based on at least three hypothetical factors. One factor is that Singapore is sandwiched between Malaysia and Indonesia, Islamic countries with a combined population of nearly three hundred million. This geopolitical positioning implies a potential military threat, especially if militant Islamic fundamentalists were to come to power in either country. Consequently, Singapore's military strategy is based on a variant of the Israeli strategy of total command in the air. Unsurprisingly, Singapore's Muslims are barred from frontline military service, especially in the air force.

A second potential source of instability arises from a combination of the probable track of long-term development in the "hinterland economy" that may be combined with the idea that capital flows in the world markets operate in a "random" manner. The hinterland economy around Singapore is developing rapidly and competing directly with Singapore in manufacturing. In Singapore, manufacturing labor costs grew by 10.8 percent a year from 1985 to 1995, but slowed to 2 percent thereafter, despite an increase in while unit labor costs to about US$22 per hour by 2012.[33] By comparison, the average hourly wage in Taiwan is $9, in the Philippines $2, while in both China and India is less than US$2. Since not all wage differences are compensated by higher productivity in Singapore, investment has shifted from Singapore to all these countries in recent years. As a partial response, Singapore has moved to upgrade the offering of financial services, a "normal" adjustment for a city-state in response to a more fierce competition from the hinterland economy, reflecting the nature of the comparative advantages of the city-state, such as higher quality education and better access to

companies investing in the region. However, a problem may arise if the financial flows by-
pass Singapore and go elsewhere, as this would cause a major contraction of its economy.

A third possible source of instability in Singapore is derived from the view, bordering on
a strong conviction, that only the judgments of the elite groups can be trusted. Those outside
the elites are assumed to espouse policies based upon shortsighted, irrational group interests
that would cause irreparable damage to the economic and social structures. The PAP government interprets political opposition in the context of the long tradition of political struggle
against Communist insurgencies in the region. In the 1950s and 1960s, Communist groups in
Singapore jeopardized the city-state's business structure and threatened to subvert the political structure, while elsewhere in East Asia Communists seized power and waged civil wars.

Where the most influential groups of society feel that they are facing the equivalent of a
state of siege, demanding that the population must rally around the leadership as the only
way to guarantee stability, they are unlikely to allow full-blown democracy. The general response to the perceived threats of instability has been to make politics ultrastable. Political
opposition is punished in subtle and not so subtle ways. Freedom of speech, especially in the
media, is severely curtailed. Domestic media are edited with a keen eye on consistency and
agreement with government policy. More ominously, the judiciary has been politicized to the
point that it is hard to imagine any Singapore court that would pass a sentence that would not
meet the approval of the government.

With a belief in imminent danger, PAP makes few democratic concessions. Political
rights of citizens are restricted, though the general public participates in elections. Since political rights in Singapore are not grounded in civil rights, as they were in the politics of British Hongkong, opposition political parties in Singapore encounter many obstacles, and reporting on election campaigns is seldom balanced in the state-controlled media.

Outcomes of elections in Singapore have been landslides in favor of the PAP because the
government enjoys deep popular support. But that support is deeply contingent upon a continuation of economic success. Democratization in Singapore is unlikely to result from political demonstrations or labor disputes, as in the Philippines during 1986 and Eastern Europe
after the Cold War.

The "Asian Values" concept of Singapore, in our opinion, served as nothing more or less
than an ideological justification for an approach to provide ultrastable economic, political,

and social structures. The ruling party seeks to control the public by depicting a sense of national insecurity and a dread of the unknown based upon a fear of government retribution. The government seeks legitimacy by judiciously marrying a Western democratic vocabulary with a particular set of traditional values that it claims are uniquely Asian.

Problems Facing Singapore

Three major problems face Singapore today, all derived from the logic of the development of the city-state. The economically successful city-state tends to develop a larger middle class than other countries. A key element of PAP's continued political role requires that this emergent middle class, which arises through independent initiatives, be co-opted by the regime. A natural tendency for successful individuals in the middle class, apart from traditional elites, is to demand a voice in politics. In particular, middle class employers will seek to participate in the formulation of labor market regulations. Similarly, as they are also major taxpayers, they will seek influence over the extent of taxes collected and how they are spent by the government.

As an independent middle class emerges, they can move politically in a direction that may challenge policies of the government. Support for PAP is not what it used to be. In the 1993 elections, the PAP candidate for president won only 58 percent of the vote, despite the fact that the opposing candidate had no previous political experience. To avoid a similar surprise, only one candidate was certified to run for president in 1999 and 2005; S. R. Nathan has remained in office until 2011, when Dr. Tony Tan was elected in a split vote without a majority. PAP support has declined in each parliamentary election of the twenty-first century, with the increased presence of foreign workers a major campaign issue because of dissatisfaction with such problems as overcrowded streets, increasing prices for property, suppressed wage levels, and increased competition for jobs and education.

Even if the emergent middle class accepts PAP's vision of a need for ultrastability, there are pragmatic arguments for easing restrictions that emasculate the public politically. PAP would have their citizens believe that a small group of enlightened politicians, advised by skilled technocrats, are sufficient to run the country. However, any system that engages more of the electorate in decision making will have more information to guide the system. Any system that can handle more information will be able to make more enlightened decisions. Institutions that can facilitate the processing of more information from different walks of social life should be encouraged, especially if the general feeling is that present stability may not last.

The rise of Singapore's "new" middle class, then, points in the direction of democratization of political life, once the arguments are generalized. The monopoly on power of traditional business elites is under attack, even if the forms of the opposition are peaceful and visible mainly in breaches of the domestic political discussion. Overreactions to the domestic opposition (e.g., against Singapore Democratic Party leaders) and the international media (*The Economist, International Herald Tribune*, etc.) is probably a sign of deeper political conflict going on behind the scene.

The second major problem is that Singapore's "dualism" leads to problems of economic policy that must be resolved. As the logic of the city-state unfolds in Singapore, the more unsustainable is its "dualism" in economic policy. A small domestic firm that delivers input materials for some international corporation can easily argue that taxes and restrictions on local businesses should be no more than on businesses operating in export industries. Today, when overlapping of business activities in both sectors is widespread, appeals for domestic restraint in the name of "Asian Values" are no longer credible.

The third problem is quite recent. The manufacturing structure of Singapore is vulnerable both to regional competition and to changes in the world market. For example, large parts of the strategic computer-assembly industry have moved from Singapore to the island of Penang in Malaysia, and the glut of microchips in the world market in the 1990s contributed to a contraction of the growth potential in Singapore's economy, appearing to signal a long-term downward trend in Singapore's economy.

Blindness to the shortcomings of the intricate and extensive elements of development strategies leaves the government open to a potentially serious crisis. The forces of modernization, per se, may not prompt political change in Singapore. A failure in the economy may come first. The stability of Singapore's economy might be undermined by the classic symptoms of a property and stock market "bubble," as has been manifested in many countries for centuries.[34]

Conclusion

Singapore may have one of the world's highest rates of consumption of Mercedes or French cognac, but the legitimacy of the system depends upon maintaining a high level of prosperity. A downturn in the economy may result in a more active civil society. The driving forces behind Singapore's continued success will be the youngest, the best educated, and therefore most flexible and potentially productive persons in the private sector, not a government with old-fashioned ideas about how to overregulate the lives of its citizens.

There is no doubt that Singapore's post-independence leaders in the People's Action Party have contributed to the remarkable transformation of an underdeveloped economy, even though the role of political factors is often overstated. In discussing Singapore's economic success story, we feel that the current set of economic relationships is only one phase in a dynamic and evolving order. Singapore's political leaders may deserve credit for having implemented a set of "capital friendly" institutions. But that was yesterday. The policy of "Asian Values" posed a strategic problem for the future development of Singapore, since it excluded too many from the political decision-making process. Events are likely to weaken the iron grip of the PAP government. Either PAP leaders will allow more political space to unleash the creative, entrepreneurial spirit or an economic crisis will herald their fall from grace.

Epilog (by Michael Haas)

Although Singapore's economy remains strong, growth has slowed down in recent years. The stock market index of 1996, as noted above, was about 2,000 but has averaged 2,720 from 1999 to 2014. After plunging to 1,457 in March 2009, the index rebounded fairly steadily to a high of almost 3,400 in mid-2013 and has remained at amount 3,200 ever since. The prediction of steady decline, in other words, has not been borne out. Singapore emerged from the financial crisis of 2008-2009 relatively unscathed, though wages were cut and programs were initiated for job retraining.[35]

A debate on the explanation for the rise of Singapore has continued over the years. In contrast with city-state theory of the authors of the present chapter, some Singaporean economists believe that five factors are responsible: (1) a free market orientation, (2) reliance on foreign trade, (3) high savings and high investment, (4) macroeconomic stability without inflation, and (5) sound and stable public administration.[36]

For Paul Krugman, the key factor is human resource development, not productivity,[37] as the educational system stresses engineering and sciences, and in 2005 the government announced the goal of having every Singaporean get post-secondary education. However, much of the workforce consists of semiskilled foreigners, whose minimum wage keeps Singapore competitive with developing countries.

Another economist currently diagnoses Singapore as having a "bubble" economy with ultra-low interest rates encouraging too much growth in mortgage and commercial loan borrowing, a high ratio of household debt to gross domestic product, and astronomic property prices.[38] There is a potential banking crisis if non-performing loans increase once interest rates normalize. The government's responses is that the banking sector is well managed, Singapore has a large current account surplus, property values have stabilized, and action has been taken to ease household debt by an increase in wages.

Singapore relies heavily on multinational corporations to set up branch offices with special tax rates. Local businesses are considered unprofitable, and opportunities to develop local entrepreneurship are neglected. Many government-linked corporations, which compete with some local businesses, have yet to be privatized. In other words, the government plays the role of economic manager with little diversity in economic decision making.[39]

While the debate continues, Singapore's economy roars on, with the government gloating about lack of corruption. Yet during 1996, Temasek Holdings, the government's investment country bought 46.6 percent of the shares in a corporation owned by Prime Minister Taksin Shinawatra, who then raked in nearly $2 billion. However, the sale came after Thailand's law had just been changed to exempt him from paying taxes on the sale. Protests over the move ultimately resulted in a coup that ousted him.[40] What was clearly a shady deal, a sale that was held up until the Thai law changed, was the last straw of corruption for the Thai people.

In 1997, as noted above, Temasek was implicated in drug smuggling. In 2005, a China Aviation oil executive in Singapore was charged with insider trading.[41] Such indiscretions are rare, however.

High salaries of top government employees, criticized for being excessive, have been justified as a way to ensure continuity of employment in a highly competitive global job market. However, in the case of the National Kidney Foundation, a *Straits Times* article in 2005 reported that the executive officer had a salary over S$360,000, whereupon an outcry forced his resignation as well as the entire board of directors.[42]

The government continues to control worker organizations under the framework of the National Trades Union Congress (NTUC),[43] which also operates the largest retail grocery store chain. In 2003, the Congress sponsored a conference in which speakers criticized management for cutting wages, laying off workers, and holding back contributions to the Central Provident Fund. NTUC encourages firms to use local workers rather than foreign workers, and the government since 2007 has provided an income supplement program with an 8 percent bonus to local workers to encourage full employment. Singapore encourages workfare more than welfare.

Central Provident Fund contributions have fluctuated over the years. As of 2010, employers contributed 15.5 percent and employees 20 percent. Older workers must contribute a larger percentage of their salaries,[44] which are regulated by the semiofficial National Wages Council.

In 2004, Singapore Airlines proposed to cut the pay of pilots, whereupon pilots objected and voted out the leaders of the union. In response, newly appointed Prime Minister Lee Hsien Loong threatened "broken heads" and then revoked the permanent status of the organizer of the protest; he had held that status for twenty-six years.[45]

Most foreign investment, however, goes to Singapore companies that operate overseas, though their profitability is disputed.[46] In 2012, out of S$460 billion invested overseas, the largest chunk went to China (20 percent); other recipients were Britain (10 percent), Hongkong and Australia (8 percent each). Singapore's investment in the United States (2 percent) is overshadowed by Indonesia, Malaysia, Thailand, India, and even the Cayman Islands. Of S$732 billion investments coming from abroad, the United States accounted for 15 percent; next came the Netherlands (9 percent), Japan (8 percent), Britain (7 percent), and the rest was a diversified mixture.[47]

In 2006, reflecting on the fact that S$720 million were spent by Singaporeans on casinos in neighboring countries, the government granted the first license to a casino to operate in Singapore despite a petition opposing the proposal signed by 29,000 names.[48] Although Singapore granted licenses in out-of-the-way resort locations, and the first casino opened only in

2010, the country's casinos now boast that they exceed the business of Macao.[49]

With reserve capital on hand, the government has always been quick to make adjustments during ups and downs in the economy. During the 1997 Asian financial crisis, the currency was downgraded, compulsory retirement amounts were cut in half, and worker bonuses were reduced.[50] In 2003, responding to competition from other countries in Asia, the government decided to shift government investment from electronics production to medical technology manufacturing.[51] Thus, the economy has remained investment-driven as the world economy increasingly becomes innovation-driven.

The beginnings of a welfare state have emerged in recent years.[52] In 2005, the Com Care Fund was established to provide support for the disabled, elderly poor, unemployed breadwinners, and so that low-income parents could afford fees for kindergarten. During 2007, other changes were made in the social safety net: One announcement was that the compulsory retirement age would be raised from age 62 to 65 and later to 67. Upon retirement, the elderly would be permitted to sell back their investments in the 99-year leases on their apartment units, similar to the American concept of the reverse mortgage. In addition, persons aged 50 are now required to contribute to an annuity fund before retirement. One problem is that the government had been assuming that younger members of Singapore families would take care of their elders, but there is no medical coverage after retirement, so low-income families are unable to afford their medical bills.

When the two authors of the present chapter referred to increasing restrictions on immigration in their original essay, they were referring to the government's measures to limit the import of skilled (called "foreign talents") and semiskilled workers (called "foreign workers") in a country with a low birthrate as well as an out-migration of many Singapore citizens and noncitizens. In April 1987, to limit the foreign worker inflow, a twofold policy was adopted: Employers must pay a "levy" monthly for each foreign worker employed, and a "dependency ceiling" limits the proportion of foreign workers in an employer's workforce. The levy has occasionally increased in economic downturns.[53] Because Singapore has a shortage of workers in the manufacturing sector, such limits serve as signals to the local population annoyed by the presence of so many noncitizens.

Singapore continues to have the highest percentage of foreigners in Asia (28 percent of the population).[54] To fill increasing demand for workers, Singapore has even given university scholarships to promising students from poorer countries, enraging local students. As result of the decreasing support for PAP in the 2011 election, levies and dependency ceilings were increased, wages paid by the government increased, and priority has been given to Singapore citizens in primary education.

Singapore offers an unusual model of how to marry free market capitalism with state control of the economy. China, which has benefited from Singapore investments, has its eyes on Singapore as a model.

Notes

1. Kenneth Bercuson, ed., *Singapore: A Case Study in Rapid Development*. (Washington, DC: International Monetary Fund, 1995).
2. "Real GDP" is the output of final goods and services adjusted for price level changes.
3. International Bank for Reconstruction and Development, *World Tables 1996: Data on Diskette* (Washington, DC: International Bank for Reconstruction and Development, 1996). This institution is called the "World Bank."
4. "GDP Annual Growth Rate-Countries-List," *tradingeconomics.com*, accessed 18 February 2014.
5. "Unemployment Rate-Countries-List," *tradingeconomics.com*, accessed 18 February 2014; United States, Central Intelligence Agency, "Inflation Rate (Consumer Prices)," *World Factbook*, *www.cia.gov/library/-publications*, accessed 18 February 2014.
6. Singapore, *Economic and Social Statistics of Singapore* (Singapore: Department of Statistics, 1996); "List of Countries by Foreign-Exchange Reserves," *wikipedia.com*, accessed 18 February 2014.
7. *World Competitiveness Yearbook, 1996* (Lausanne: International Institute for Management Development, 1996) and *Global Competitiveness Report, 1996* (Davos: World Economic Forum, 1996, 2012).
8. "Foreign Direct Investment, Net Inflows," *data.worldbank.org*, accessed 18 February 2014.
9. World Bank, *The East Asian Miracle* (New York: Oxford University Press, 1993).
10. Recent figures are from the Fraser Institute (*fraserinstitute.org*) and the Heritage Foundation (*heritage.org*).
11. *stengg.com*, accessed 15 January 2014.
12. Without defining (and discussing) these "favorable circumstances," our proposition is close to a tautology, but we advance it, since it has a guiding value. Not every collection of countryside villages has historically produced an urban, market-based organization.
13. Douglass North, *Institutions, Institutional Change and Economic Performance* (New York: Cambridge University Press, 1990).
14. In spite of smallness, city-states have been "leading links" in the reshaping of East Asia during the last quarter-century. They have played an important role in forming long-term East Asian planning, which is probably

reflected in the fact that Lee Kuan Yew has been a political advisor to the governments of China and Vietnam. Obviously, both China and Vietnam strive to move from a planned economy to a market economy and from politics based on Communist one-party rule to some kind of authoritarianism wherein the Communist Party will retain the commanding heights. To these governments, Singapore seems to be one possible role model.

15. David Ricardo, *The Principles of Political Economy and Taxation* (London: Dent, 1911). Originally published in 1817.

16. The distributive effects of unobstructed international trade are such that although the community as a whole is better off, individual losses to the "losers" are greater than are individual gains for the "winners."

17. World Bank, *The East Asian Miracle*.

18. Of course, a case can be made that this is a general, worldwide phenomenon. During the 1990s, normal business corporations produced new knowledge at various (and numerous) research frontiers. One illustration is Microsoft's $2 billion budget for research and development in 1997, which is more than the budgets of all the universities for many countries, such as Sweden, a country with an advanced industrial economy and several world-recognized universities. The point is that the Western tradition of independent research institutions has been an important source for societal innovation in a very broad sense, but there is no such tradition in Singapore or elsewhere in Asia.

19. The cowardly behavior of international media (*Asian Wall Street Journal, The Economist, Far Eastern Economic Review, International Herald Tribune*, and *Time*) in accepting restricted circulation, heavy fines, and demands to publish unedited official government responses is possible because Changi airport plays a key role in their Asian transport logistics.

20. Singapore, *Economic and Social Statistics of Singapore* (1996).

21. International Bank for Reconstruction and Development, *World Tables 1996: Data on Diskette*.

22. Doubtless, there are other and more specific factors behind the internationalization of capital. However, we point to what we feel are the most important trigger factors.

23. In his studies of the interaction of the European economies in the European Community, German economist Horst Siebert has developed a partially new concept of competition, which he termed "institutional competition." See Horst Siebert, *The New Economic Landscape of Europe* (London: Basil Blackwell, 1991); Horst Siebert and M. J. Koop, "Institutional Competition: A Concept for Europe?," *Aussenwirtschaft*, XLV (1990): 439-462.

24. The combination of British colonial rule, well-established civil rights, but an underdeveloped domestic political system probably allowed the internationally-oriented Hongkong business community to serve as central agents in the formulation of new economic legislation and thereby to lead the Asian movement towards internationalization.

25. For a more complete presentation of this legislation, see The Hongkong and Shanghai Banking Corporation, *Business Profile Series: Republic of Singapore* (August 1987), 22ff.

26. For example, Walden F. Bello and Stephanie Rosenfeld, *Dragons in Distress: Asia's Miracle Economies in*

Crisis (Washington, DC: Institute for Food and Development, 1990).

27. Lingle, *Singapore's Authoritarian Capitalism.*

28. The last time this was observed was after the American Civil War, when the United States emerged as a second world center alongside Europe. At that time, the outside challenge led to the "long recession" from 1873 to 1896 in Europe. In turn, strong protectionist movements and the introduction of a higher level of technology also emerged. All these new traits can be summarized as the foundation of modern capitalism. It is probably no exaggeration to expect that the emergence of East Asia will have similar far-reaching economic consequences.

29. Chua Beng Huat, *Communitarian Ideology and Democracy in Singapore* (London: Routledge, 1995). However, his use of the term is at variance with the meaning in the philosophies of Michael J. Sandel, *Liberalism and the Limits of Justice* (New York: Cambridge University Press, 1998) and many others.

30. "General Government Final Consumption Expenditure (% of GDP)," *data.workbank.org*, accessed 18 February 2014.

31. Central Provident Fund contributions have fluctuated over the years. On average, employers contribute 15.5 percent and employees 20 percent today. Older workers must contribute a larger percentage of their salaries, which are regulated by the semiofficial National Wages Council. "Central Provident Fund," *wikipedia.com*, accessed 14 January 2014.

32. Karl A. Wittfogel, *Oriental Despotism: A Comparative Study of Total Power* (New Haven, CT: Yale University Press, 1957).

33. *Asiaweek*, 7 July 1995; U.S. Department of Labor, *Charting International Labor Comparison* (Washington, DC: U.S. Department of Labor Statistics, 2012).

34. Rosalind Chew, "Global Financial Tsunami: Can the Industrial Relations Mechanism Save Singapore This Time Around?" In *Singapore and Asia: Impact of the Global Financial Tsunami and Other Economic Issues*, eds. Sng Hui Ying and Chia Wai Mun (Singapore: World Scientific Publishing, 2010), chap. 4. For an exposé on the Japanese bubble economy, see Christopher Wood, *The Bubble Economy: The Japanese Economic Collapse* (London: Sidgwick & Jackson, 1992).

35. Chew Soon Beng and Rosalind Chew, "The Current Productivity Drive and Singapore and Labour Market Policies." In *Challenges for the Singapore Economic After the Global Financial Crisis*, ed. Peter Wilson (Singapore: World Scientific Publishing, 2011), chap. 5.

36. Lim Chong Yah, "Singapore Growth Model: Its Strengths and Weaknesses." In *Singapore and Asia: Impact of the Global Financial Tsunami, and Other Economic Issues*, eds. Sng Hui Ying and Chia Wai Mun (Singapore: World Scientific Publishing, 2010), chap. 7.

37. Paul Krugman, "The Myth of Asia's Miracle," *Foreign Affairs*, 73 (6): 62-78; Sunny Kai-Sun Kwong, "Singapore: Dominance of Multinational Corporations." In *Industrial Development in Singapore, Taiwan, and South Korea* (Singapore: World Scientific Publishing, 2001), 52.

38. Katie Holiday, "Is Singapore Set for an Icelandic-Style Crash," *cnbc.com*, 15 January 2014, accessed 15 January 2014.

39. Manu Bhaskaran, *Re-Inventing the Asian Model: The Case of Singapore* (Singapore: Eastern Universities Press, 2003); Singapore Institute of Policy Analysis, *The IFER Report: Restructing Singapore's Economy* (Singapore: Times Academic Press, 2002).
40. Chua Beng Huat, "Singapore in 2006: An Irritating and Irritated ASEAN Neighbor," *Asian Survey*, XLVII (2007): 209.
41. Garry Rodan, "Singapore in 2005: 'Vibrant and Cosmopolitan' Without Political Pluralism," *Asian Survey*, XLVI (2006): 184.
42. Ibid., 183.
43. Case, "Singapore in 2003: Another Tough Year," 118; Chew, "Global Financial Tsunami: Can the Industrial Relations Mchanism Save Singapore This Time Around?," 74; Kampon Adireksombat, "Workfare, Not Welfare: An Exploration on International Experiences and Policy Implications for Singapore." In *Singapore and Asia: Impact of the Global Financial Tsunami and Other Economic Issues*, eds. Sng Hui Ying and Chia Wai Mun (Singapore: World Scientific Publishing, 2010), chap. 10.
44 "Central Provident Fund," *wikipedia.com*, accessed 14 January 2014.
45. Garry Rodan, "Singapore in 2004: Long-Awaited Leadership Transition," *Asian Survey*, XLV (2005): 142.
46. Kwong, "Singapore: Dominance of Multinational Corporations," 52; Alan Chong, "Singapore's Political Economy, 1997-2007: Strategizing Economic Assurance for Globalization," *Asian Survey*, XLVII (2007): 955; Garry Rodan, "Singapore in 2004: Long-Awaited Leadership Transition," *Asian Survey*, XLV (2005): 142.
47. Singapore Department of Statistics, "Investment," *singstat.gov.sg*. Accessed 14 February 2014.
48. Rodan, "Singapore in 2005: 'Vibrant and Cosmopolitan' Without Political Pluralism," 181.
49. Rodan, "Singapore in 2004: Long-Awaited Leadership Transition," 143-144; Anshuman Daga and Kevin Lim, "Singapore Casinos Trump Macao with Tourism Aces," *Reuters*, September 23, 2013, accessed 14 February 2014.
50. Case, "Singapore in 2003: Another Tough Year," 119.
51. Chong, "Singapore's Political Economy, 1997-2007," 956; Chua Beng Huat, "Singapore in 2007: High Wage Ministers and the Management of Gays and the Elderly," *Asian Survey*, XLVIII (2008): 60-61; Rodan, "Singapore in 2005: 'Vibrant and Cosmopolitan' Without Political Pluralism," 184.
52. Tilak ASbeysinghe, Himani, and Jeremy Lim, "Equity in Singapore's Healthcare Financing." In *Challenges for the Singapore Economy After the Global Financial Crisis*, ed. Peter Wilson (Singapore: World Scientific Publishing, 2011), chap. 7.
53. Chew and Chew, "The Current Productivity Drive in Singapore and Labour Market Policies."
54. Singapore, *Population Trends*, and other references cited in "Immigration to Singapore," *wikipedia.com*, accessed 17 January 2014.

5

The Press
Derek Davies

Lee Kuan Yew's opinion of journalists and journalism became perfectly clear to me during an 1985 interview. If the *Far Eastern Economic Review*, of which I was then editor, wanted to continue maintaining a correspondent in Singapore, he said, then "Send me a clerk; send me an amanuensis." So much for intelligent, in-depth reporting for the demanding readers of an up-market weekly. So much for the cherished journalistic aims of objectivity and balance. He saw the correspondent's function as the passive recording of government statistics and announcements, just as the duties of an amanuensis consisted of copying documents.

Lee went on to claim that he did not see the necessity of a business/economic weekly that covered Asia to maintain a resident correspondent at all, suggesting instead that, from time to time, I should

> Send in teams of editorial writers. Say what you like about me or my country. I don't care. I just don't want them in Singapore.

I demurred: Singapore's importance demanded continuity of coverage. Anyway, was not such "parachute journalism" one of the developing world's major objections to the Western media?

Lee, thus, poured scorn on journalists' lack of professional training and qualifications, without acknowledging that politicians needed no qualifications, that many of his PAP colleagues were poorly educated, that other regional leaders who won his support (from Burma's Ne Win to Indonesia's Suharto) rose through army hierarchies without other distinctions and indeed that many journalists had academic qualifications rivaling his double first-class Cambridge degree.

It had not been an easy conversation. Lee, having failed to stop the foreign media from "meddling in Singapore's domestic affairs," told me that instead of attempting to control editors and journalists, he would target instead the pockets of owners and publishers. "I will hit you where it hurts. Then we will see your commitment to a free press." Anyway, he enjoyed a confrontation with the media: "Don't forget, I can hurt you more than you can hurt me." A bill was then being prepared with the aim of giving the government powers to limit the sales of foreign publications in Singapore, thereby reducing their revenues from circulation and advertisements. That would bring direct and more effective pressure to bear on editors. Privately, I felt that foreign publications would hardly submit to such pressures, but I was wholly wrong and Lee largely right.

Lee's view of the press in 1985 and today is radically different from his commitment to a free press earlier in his career. In this chapter, I will trace some of the events that lead to the decline and extinction of press freedom in Singapore, querying why such a staunch defender of Western democracy in his youth has become an opponent of press freedom in the name of "Asian Values."

Early Commitment to Press Freedom

In his early days as a lawyer and leader of Singapore's independence movement, Lee Kuan Yew sung the praises of a free press as an integral part of an open, democratic society. He made effective use of the media to further his cause, praising those who subjected the colonial authorities to critical examination and criticizing the British establishment press, such as the *Straits Times*, for failing to give adequate coverage to his People's Action Party (PAP). In opposition, Lee was a strong advocate of Western-style democracy and human rights. In 1955, he attacked Singapore Chief Minister David Marshall for proposing a Preservation of Public Security Bill. He asked:

> If it is not totalitarian to arrest a man and detain him when you cannot charge him with any offense against any written law—if that is not what we have always cried out against in fascist states—then what is it?[1]

In later years, as prime minister, Lee detained many men and women without trial. In 1987, after his security police had arrested and detained a group of Catholic church workers alleged to be part of a "Marxist conspiracy," the Archbishop of Singapore asked Lee for proof that the detainees were really engaged in subversive activities. Lee angrily replied:

> It is not our practice, nor will I allow subversives to get away by insisting that I've got to prove everything against them in a court of law on evidence that will stand up to the strict rules of evidence of a court of law.[2]

By his own earlier definition, it would seem that Lee had become either totalitarian or fascist, or both.

In 1955, he defended Western—or global—concepts of freedom and human rights, as follows:

> These are fundamental beliefs. They may or may not work in Asia, that no one can say. But one can say this: one must have the courage to make it work, to try it; for if it cannot work, then the alternative is one of constant suppression, the end of which no one knows.[3]

Lee, however, did have a very good idea of the results of suppression. In 1956, he outlined what happened when a leader repressed the media and voices of dissent:

> Then an intimidated press and the government-controlled radio together can regularly sing your praises, and slowly and steadily the people are made to forget the evil things that have already been done, or if those things are referred to again they are conveniently distorted and distorted with impunity because

there will be no opposition to contradict.[4]

These words are an impressively accurate description of the situation in Singapore today.

Lee may have simply changed his mind. (Even politicians should be allowed that freedom.) But it may also be that he has succumbed to the tendency of power to corrupt and that, back in the eighteenth century, Dr. Samuel Johnson got it right when he commented: "It has been observed that they who most loudly clamor for liberty do not most liberally grant it."

Despite Lee's championing of such freedoms when in opposition, the People's Action Party's relations with the local press were extremely strained when, in 1959, it won the election and took over the internal self-government of Singapore. During the election campaign, PAP candidates accused the press of maligning them, their chief anger being directed at the principal English-language newspaper, the *Straits Times*, which they excoriated as a colonial mouthpiece under largely British ownership and management. The fiercest critic, ironically enough, was Sinnathamby Rajaratnam, who had worked as a journalist for four years on the *Straits Times*, had been president of the Singapore Union of Journalists and who, as Minister for Culture, was later used as one of Lee's main weapons against the local press. "Raja" poured scorn on the newspaper's worries about the fate of press freedom under a PAP government, which were to prove absolutely justified. Already, Lee appeared to have dumped his regard for justice, the independence of the judiciary, and press freedom, since he threatened imprisonment for any journalist who tried to sour relations with Malaya: "We shall put him in and keep him in."[5]

Commenting acidly that Rajaratnam had not been considered a stooge of the white man when he worked for the *Straits Times*, Lesley Hoffman, the paper's Eurasian editor, saw the way things were going. As soon as the PAP was elected, he moved the newspaper's head office to Malaysia, where it eventually became the *New Straits Times*, whereupon a new publication by the name of the *Straits Times* was reconstituted in Singapore. Lee commented:

> We of the PAP believe just as zealously in the freedom of the press. If locally owned newspapers criticize us, we know that their criticism, however wrong or right, is bona fide criticism because they must stay and take the consequences. . . . Not so the birds of passage who run the *[New] Straits Times*. They have run to the Federation [of Malaya] from whose safety they boldly proclaim they will die for the freedom of Singapore.[6]

Lee took up the cudgels for a free press once again when Singapore merged with Malaya to become a state in the Federation of Malaysia in 1963, as the Singapore media became a valuable outlet for Singapore's views within the enlarged country. The press across the Causeway, according to Lee, cast "a shroud of silence" over PAP and Singapore.[7] It was in this context that in December 1964 Lee made an eloquent speech in favor of press freedom which has often to come back to haunt him:

> Let us get down to fundamentals. Is this an open, or is this a closed society? Is it a society where men can preach ideas [,] . . . where there is a constant contest for men's hearts and minds on the basis of what is right, of what is just, of what is in the national interest, or is it a closed society [in which] men's minds are fed with a constant drone of sycophantic support for a particular orthodox political philosophy? . . . . It is not only in communist countries where the mass media is used to produce the closed mind. . . . If your ideas, your views cannot stand the challenge of criticism then they are too fragile and not sturdy enough to last. . . . I am talking of the principle of the open society, open debate; ideas, not intimidation; persuasion not coercion. . . . It is not possible because whatever the faults of the colonial system, and there are many, . . . [T]hey generated the open mind, the inquiring mind.[8]

During this period, PAP's main ire was aroused by the main Singapore-based Malay language newspaper, *Utusan Melayu*, which circulated throughout Malaysia. It backed Lee and the PAP during the campaign for independence, but thereafter increasingly reflected Malay attitudes—an editorial line that became increasingly irritating to PAP in the years leading up to and after Singapore's expulsion from Malaysia. Under increasing threats that legal action would be taken against articles deemed to be prejudicial to the peace and security of Singapore, *Utusan Melayu* followed the example of the *New Straits Times* and shifted its headquarters to Kuala Lumpur, ceasing to circulate in Singapore in 1969. The gap in the Malay vernacular press was filled by *Berita Harian*, a member of what was to become the all-powerful Straits Times Group.

Press Shutdowns by Intimidation

During the 1960s, Lee raised the Cold War bogey of Communism to defeat his domestic enemies, in particular to harass and imprison the former left-wing, Marxist members of PAP who had hived off to form the Barisan Socialist Party. As he intensified his campaign to bring his domestic press to heel, he raised a second, more immediate bogey—communalism. In April 1971, speaking to a student seminar, he accused Malay-language newspapers of taking a narrow, ethnic perspective, pushing for policies and measures that would benefit the bumiputra (i.e. the Malays, or "sons of the soil"). Similarly, he accused Chinese-language newspapers of playing up Chinese interests, not only on cultural/linguistic matters, but with a Communist, pro-Beijing slant. He also damned elements of the English-language press for advocating Western decadent lifestyles, a permissive society, and tolerant attitudes to drink, drugs, and sex. He spoke darkly of foreign influences on and financing of local newspapers.[9]

That speech proved to be the first trumpet blast launching Lee's massive and protracted campaign to destroy Singapore's independent media. Although he has accused the foreign press of judging Singapore by irrelevant Western standards and ignoring "Asian Values," many Asians, presumably properly imbued with "Asian Values," have been imprisoned, tortured, ruined, and denied the right to write or to publish articles that were insufficiently respectful towards the ultrasensitive Lee and his PAP colleagues.

After the speech, Lee's first target was the Chinese-language newspaper, *Nanyang Siang Pau*, which was never within shouting distance of being Marxist or pro-Beijing in any political sense, but generally rejoiced in a pan-Sinic welcome to the China that was gradually emerging from the chaos and cruelties of the Cultural Revolution via some pingpong diplomatic initiatives leading up to the Nixon visit that resulted in the Shanghai Communiqué, both in 1972. The assault was clumsy. In the early hours of May 2, 1971, officers of Singapore's Internal Security Department (ISD) broke into the houses of three of the papers' executives and took them into detention. Those arrested were Lee Mau Seng, a former general manager who was about to emigrate to Canada with his family, having already sold his interest in the newspaper to his brother, Lee Eu Seng; Shamsuddin Tung, the editor, a Chinese Muslim, son of a Kuomintang (KMT) diplomat, and a prominent anti-Communist writer; and Ly Singko, a senior editorial writer, a Catholic also with KMT connections, well-known for his anti-Communist articles. A fourth employee, Kerk Loong Seng, of the paper's public relations staff, who had no connection with editorial policies, was picked up and detained the next day.

The quartet was denounced in a government statement for "glamorizing Communism and stirring up communal and chauvinistic sentiments over language and culture [with] all the signs of what in Special Branch is called a `black operation'." The authorities even went on to squeeze some capital out of the well-known anti-Communist, pro-KMT opinions of Shamsuddin and Ly, stating blandly that their views made their "glamorizing of the Communist way of life all the more sinister."[10]

The spirited defenses put up by Lee Mau Seng's elder brother, Eu Seng, and by the newspaper itself were more convincing than the fantastic official allegations. Lee Eu Seng, chairman and chief executive of the newspaper group, pointed out that he had always been responsible for its policies; that he had always opposed racism and had never supported Communism; that he had been responsible for hiring Shamsuddin and Ly; that Nanyang was a multimillion dollar organization with no need of foreign capital, and that he had published the public's letters of complaint "since there is no opposition in Parliament to do so."[11] (The government riposted ominously that it had taken notice of this admission.) As for his brother, Mau Seng had been absent from Singapore for long periods during his wife's fatal illness. Eu Seng only sat in for his brother while the latter took a year's break; indeed, his brother did not read or write Chinese, which would have made it difficult for him to have been in day-to-day command of editorial policies and presentation of news. Anyway, most of the articles that the government found objectionable had been published long after his brother sold all his interests in the paper, prior to his planned departure for Canada.

In June, the detainees applied for writs of habeas corpus, based on the denial of the right of access to their lawyers. (They had been held incommunicado for three weeks undergoing interrogation, for sessions lasting up to forty hours.) The judge refused to rule on the applications, and the four remained behind bars. Ultimately, Lee Mau Seng was detained for two and a half years; he was released in December 1973 after signing what he later characterized as a "Russian confession."[12]

Soon after the detention of the three, Lee Kuan Yew's vengeance fell upon Lee Eu Seng, whose courageous demonstration of the anomalies in the government's case had embarrassed Lee and even given rise to public suspicion that Mau Seng had been arrested by an incompetent ISD in mistake for Eu Seng. On this occasion, Eu Seng was accused under the Internal Security Act of "using his newspaper to incite the people against the Government over issues of culture."[13] Eu Seng was not to be released until another five years had passed, during which the government passed legislation that stripped him of his shares in the *Nanyang Siang*

Pau.

Lee Kuan Yew gave the *Eastern Sun*, largely staffed by expatriates, much shorter shrift. *Eastern Sun* was founded in 1966 by its owner and publisher, Dato Aw Kow, who was the managing director of Sin Pau, a large newspaper publishing group, and a scion of the distinguished Aw family, makers of the famous Tiger Balm ointment and founders of a phantasmagoric garden, one of Singapore's main tourist attractions. On May 15, 1971, two weeks after the assault on the *Nanyang Siang Pau*, a government statement alleged that Aw had received three low-interest loans from Chinese Communist intelligence officers in Hongkong (in fact the loans were made by the Bank of China, which maintained a branch in Singapore itself) on condition that the *Sun* adopted a neutral or sympathetic stand on issues involving China. It was further alleged that, as part of the price for these loans, Aw had agreed to infiltrate a Chinese agent into Singapore who would feed news items into the Sin Pau group, a plan that the government had frustrated.

Minister of Culture Rajaratnam admitted that the paper had consistently and responsibly supported the government. However, its alleged acceptance of funds from Communist sources "did not involve freedom of the press, but the freedom of Singapore," since foreign interests would use the newspaper for their own ends "when the time came."[14]

Accordingly, the editor and six senior expatriate staff gave a month's notice of resignation. They stated that they had discussed the source of the funds with the paper's management and they were completely satisfied that these sources had not influenced editorial policy "for which only we are responsible."[15] Although assured by government officials that they were "in the clear" and that the paper's policies were "acceptable and positive," and although it had been pointed out by management that their departure would regrettably precipitate the paper's closure, they announced that they would quit within a month unless vindicated by Lee himself, for they stood "accused of being part of a black operation" and were unwilling to work under a pall of mistrust. The editor added that neither Dato Aw nor his wife had ever given him any editorial direction since he had joined the *Sun* two years previously. No official vindication was forthcoming. Shortly thereafter, the *Eastern Sun* sank.

Many questions remained. The matter of the loans was never clarified (overseas investment was welcomed by Singapore), nor was the identification of Bank of China officials as agents of Beijing's intelligence service ever justified. And, in view of the harsh treatment of the *Nanyang Siang Pau* executives, it must be said that Dato Aw got off very lightly. According to the government, he had been directly involved in a "black operation" and had knowingly agreed to help infiltrate a Chinese propaganda agent, but he was neither arrested nor even hauled in for interrogation.

Another member of the Aw family was embroiled in the death of the lively tabloid, the *Singapore Herald*, which began publication in 1970. The brainchild of Francis Wong, its founding editor who had once edited the *Sunday Mail*, and Jimmy Hahn, a former regional manager of Reuters, its main original financial backer was Tan Sri Donald Stephens, a former journalist who had risen within Malaysia's hierarchy to become Chief Minister of Sabah and thereafter Malaysian High Commissioner to Australia. Stephens put up money that he made in the timber business. Francis Wong, a close friend, fully briefed Rajaratnam that the start-up capital would be channeled through Heeda Company, a Hongkong nominee firm, though the authorities claimed later that they had been kept ignorant of the investment.

The *Herald*'s founders believed that a space in the market existed for a lively challenge to the gray sycophancy of the *Straits Times*. Lee regarded them, and particularly Francis Wong, with suspicion, but Rajaratnam gave them the go-ahead, telling Wong: "Once I am convinced that you are 100% for Singapore, you can be as critical as you like" and he welcomed the appearance of a new newspaper.[16]

However, it was not long before the paper, with its lively coverage, cheeky cartoons by Morgan Chua (later to join the *Far Eastern Economic Review*) and particularly its spirited Letters to the Editor column, aroused the prime minister's fury. The failure to follow official "guidance" in presenting the news was described by Lee as "taking on" the government, and he ordained that the *Herald* would forfeit government support. The newspaper was boycotted; all official advertising was withdrawn; its reporters were denied access to press conferences and briefings; reader's letters were ignored; and subscriptions were canceled. The tactic of hitting an undercapitalized newspaper in the pocketbook, reducing its revenues and placing obstacles in the way of news gathering, was to prove effective. Once again, the government muttered darkly about the motives of foreign investors. Since Lee Kuan Yew still harbored dislike and mistrust of Wong, the *Herald* offered him up as a sacrificial lamb: Wong retired to Kuala Lumpur, to be replaced by Ambrose Khaw, a former senior editorial member of the *Straits Times*. But the gods remained unpropitiated.

Help, however, seemed to be at hand. The government's bully-boy tactics had aroused widespread resentment in publishing circles outside Singapore, and many offered financial support. Chief among them was another scion of the Aw/Tiger Balm empire, Sally Aw Sian, proprietor of a large Hongkong newspaper group, generally regarded as pro-Taiwan.

The harassment continued. In May 1971 the *Herald*'s foreign editor (an Australian, Bob Reece) and its features editor (Reece's wife, Australian-born Adele Koh) were ordered to quit Singapore within forty-eight hours, and a subeditor, M. G. G. Pillai, was told that his visit pass would not be renewed. On the same day, a series of meetings, evidently designed to cut off all further funds from the paper, were held between Lee, Rajaratnam, Sally Aw Sian (summoned from Hongkong), Jimmy Hahn, Ambrose Khaw, and Hendrik Kwant, the local manager of the *Herald*'s bank, Chase Manhattan.

Two days later, Prime Minister Lee held an extraordinary press conference. Flanked by all the major players except for Sally Aw Sian, who had returned in disgust to Hongkong after being persuaded to sign a piece of paper stating that she would put no further money into the *Herald*, Lee used direct accusation, innuendo, and heavy sarcasm to characterize the *Herald* as an unsavory plot to undermine Singapore. He said he was very puzzled by Sally Aw's investment: How could she have parted with her money without wanting to know more about the paper's financial standing? "She looked a bit unhappy when I pressed her but, her being a lady, I thought, well, that's about as much as we could ask her."[17] Lee threw doubt on the original source of the money, although Aw Sian was wealthy, saying he had no idea where the start-up capital had come from: "I pressed Miss Aw Sian very hard, and she was very hard put to say that it was her money."

Although he found it difficult to believe that Communists were subsidizing the *Herald*, Lee claimed that "it had all the hallmarks of a hasty 'op.'" Suspicious that the *Herald* was a "black operation," he was puzzled by the funding from a Malaysian timber company owned by Stephens "without them telling us that it was their money." But Wong had fully briefed Rajaratnam, and Stephens had written personally to Lee. Repeatedly saying that the newspaper was losing money, struggling to get into the black, Lee asked "What sane person would have invested in it?" So the investments must have been made with ulterior motives, Lee reasoned, and such funds could be used to finance "operations for more than just commercial returns."

Things would have been different if the *Herald* had been financed from local sources, according to Lee: "Not only would Singaporeans have the right to make money, they would have a right to make politics." Of course, Singapore proprietors had been denied this right, so Singaporean publications looked overseas for funding. Lee then turned to browbeat the perspiring banker Kwant. Quite careless of any damage he might be causing to Singapore's reputation as a business and finance center, Lee improperly pushed him to disclose details about a client's account. Kwant duly revealed that the *Herald* owed Chase Manhattan S$850,000 and even promised in front of the gathered journalists that he would honor no further of its checks.

The doomed *Herald* took a long time to die, as its plight stimulated press organizations and publications around the world to bombard Singapore with protests. Chase Manhattan had second thoughts, announcing from New York that a senior official would investigate the *Herald*'s finances, giving the newspaper a breathing space by indicating that it would await the findings before taking any further action, such as foreclosing its loan.

Perhaps encouraged by this international support, protests were even heard within Singapore itself, not only from the Barisan Sosialist Party but from such normally passive organizations as the Industrial Workers Union, the National Union of Students, and the Singapore Polytechnic Students' Union. The National Union of Journalists launched a fundraising campaign to "Save the *Herald*," the staff of which volunteered to go on working without pay. Thousands of well-wishers contributed to the fund or went to the *Herald* offices to volunteer their services. The newspaper's circulation rose steeply from about 13,400 to 30,000 and to over 50,000 by the time it finally succumbed.

Faced with so much foreign criticism and disquieting support for the *Herald* within Singapore, Lee staged a cruel charade to bring the drama to an end. The government announced that an unnamed local financier was willing to save the *Herald*. If negotiations were satisfactorily concluded within five days, the government would issue a temporary printing license to the new owner; otherwise, the license would be withdrawn and a receiver would be appointed to close down the *Herald*.

In due course, the unnamed financier, who later turned out to be an obscure banker and industrialist (Wee Cho Yaw), announced on the eve of the deadline that the receiver's valuation was far in excess of the figure he and a group of local business executives had in mind.[18]

The government promptly carried out its threat, revoking the printing permit, and the *Herald* folded.

The Chase Manhattan's undistinguished role in this affair closed with a statement by David Rockefeller that, unfortunately, Hendrik Kwant did not know of the bank's policy of not investing in newspapers, since they do become involved in politics. Rockefeller was also quoted as stating that he had learned that Lee would withdraw the bank's license to do business in Singapore unless it foreclosed on the *Herald*.[19]

Lee Kuan Yew, while addressing the International Press Institute's Annual Assembly in Helsinki the following month (June 1971), met a hostile reception. He said that the media's duty in Singapore was to reinforce, not to undermine, Singapore's cultural values. It was his duty to prevent the fads and fetishes of the West from weakening the ethics of discipline, hard work, and thrift. Singapore was very exposed: "With parts of our population, it has been wiser to inoculate them from these maladies."[20] After claiming that violence could be inspired in multiracial Singapore by the printed word, radio, or television," he stated, "In such a situation freedom of the press . . . must be subordinated to the overriding needs of Singapore, and to the primacy of purpose of an elected Government."

Under questioning from the delegates, Lee repeated his line that Stephens's investment in the *Herald* had been "discovered" (when he had known about it from the beginning); that he believed that American intelligence had some involvement in the *Herald*; and that he did not believe that Sally Aw Sian's investment was her own money ("Either I am lying—or, well, I never like to call a lady a liar").

Sally Aw Sian soon called her own press conference to state that it was her own money. She added: "No paper only seven months old can be expected to be in the black. It was a simple commercial venture. If it had been making money, they would not have needed more capital. I came in because I thought it was a good long-range investment."[21]

The *Herald* was finally wound up in August 1972 at the request of Chase Manhattan. The affair cost Lee greatly in terms of his international reputation. By choosing to make unproven accusations against respected individuals, blackening them as channels for unidentified forces that for unstated reasons were attempting to bring about the downfall of the Singapore government, Lee reduced his credibility. And there was an unwelcome message for the business community, which was otherwise happy to overlook the short shrift given to democracy and human rights in the cause of stability and prosperity, as Lee had demonstrated no respect for the confidentiality of banking transactions.

Press Shutdowns by Legislative Sanction

After Singapore's expulsion from Malaysia, Lee Kuan Yew worked to build up a sense of Singaporean identity in order to unite its multiethnic community. To this end he deliberately created a "garrison mentality," painting Singapore as a tiny beleaguered island of stability in a region of comparative poverty wracked by wars and ruled by unstable regimes that were envious of the island state and, for unstated reasons, anxious to encompass its downfall, as were—for equally unstated reasons—certain countries of the West.

Foreign threats, especially within the context of the Cold War, were useful to Lee in providing excuses for measures to strengthen his power, and he invoked them to justify a series of draconian measures that ended all shreds of media independence. The first, the Newspaper and Printing Presses Act of 1974, effectively ended the private ownership of any newspaper by requiring all newspaper companies to go public with two types of shares—ordinary and management. The latter could only be issued to selected Singapore citizens and to government-approved organizations. Both shares were equal in power for votes on financial and administrative matters, but management shares had 200 times the voting power of ordinary shares on matters of editorial policy and staffing. The Act also forbade newspapers from receiving any foreign funds without government approval. Further, the government acquired management shares in the Straits Times Group and in the two main Chinese-language newspapers, enabling government nominees to sit on the company and editorial boards, together with PAP members already in place. Thus, Lee effectively placed most of Singapore's newspapers under direct surveillance.

In 1977, an amendment to the Newspaper and Printing Presses Act forbade any individual from holding more than 3 per cent of a newspaper's ordinary shares. Although such shares had already been shorn of management power, and the newspaper market was still highly competitive, the government blandly stated that it was desirable to break the monopolistic hold over newspapers by individuals and families. Lee also expressed the pious hope that the measure would result in "a free, healthy and responsible press" with editors and journalists unafraid of owners "breathing down their necks."[22] Most editors and journalists at the time felt that a more powerful force was breathing down their necks.

In fact, the 1977 amendment was the instrument by which Lee Eu Seng, the owner/publisher of the *Nanyang Siang Pau*, still in jail for his insolence in defending the freedom of the press, was divested of his newspaper. Upon his release in 1978 after five years of detention, the Home Affairs Ministry commented tartly that, having in the interim forfeited his ownership, he "can no longer make use of the *Nanyang Siang Pau* against the public interest."[23]

Having killed off the *Herald*, leaving the *Straits Times* and its evening tabloid sister paper, the *New Nation*, alone in the English-language newspaper market, Lee began to fret about the low quality of the local press, which he attributed not to Big Brother's surveillance and bullying, but to the lack of competition. He decided to ordain the creation of a second English-language daily; to this end, Rajaratnam was ordered to organize financial backing. Major Singapore banks were recruited, together with the publishers of the rival Chinese newspapers, *Nanyang Siang Pau* and *Sin Chew Jit Poh*, which were forced into a shotgun wedding to produce what was to be a new daily broadsheet challenge to the *Straits Times*, known as the *Singapore Monitor*. The two Chinese rival newspapers were forced to "restructure" into subsidiaries of one holding company, Singapore News and Publications Ltd. (SNPL), sharing one management team and one financial administration. SNPL took a 52 percent share of the Monitor, and the banks 48 percent.[24]

In October 1981, when the *Monitor* was preparing for its launch, opposition leader J. B. Jeyaratnam defeated a PAP candidate in a by-election in the Anson constituency, becoming the sole non-PAP member of parliament. He was to suffer dearly for his effrontery. But, for the moment, an infuriated Lee exacted revenge on the ungrateful electorate when the Housing Development Board announced that, apart from emergencies, it would give priority to upgrading amenities in loyal constituencies that returned PAP candidates. He then turned on the supine press for failing to put the PAP's case. Under attack from Lee, PAP officials accused the *New Nation* of running a story about an impending rise in bus fares—a story those involved in always maintained was correct, but which brought about a last-minute change in policy, leaving the newspaper defenseless.

In yet another rethink, Lee now believed that competition was the last thing he wanted: Newspapers engaged in circulation wars might be tempted to adopt less sycophantic attitudes. Consequently, the *Monitor* was denied a daily morning license and was forced into becoming an evening tabloid; to make room, the Straits Times Group was "persuaded" to close down the *New Nation* (a nice vengeful touch by Lee) in exchange for a three-year guarantee of a monopoly of the morning daily market. The group was also given permission to acquire a controlling interest in the Chinese afternoon daily, *Shin Min Daily News*. The reasons given for these measures were blandly unconvincing: The object was to establish two economically viable and competitive publishing houses, each capable of producing English- and Chinese-language papers.

After the Anson by-election, controls were tightened. Editors were instructed not to cover the activities of opposition parties (shades of the days when Lee had complained that the *Straits Times* gave PAP in opposition no coverage!), and Lee threatened to place government officials or PAP party cadres permanently on the *Straits Times* board of directors and inside its editorial departments to monitor their workings.

The Straits Times Group wriggled, but could not escape. The formidable figure of S. R. Nathan, former boss of the Security and Intelligence Division of the Ministry of Defense, was appointed Executive Chairman of the entire group. Nathan, of course, had been previously responsible for the monitoring of dissent; he had ordered the arrest and detention of journalists and other citizens put in jail under the Internal Security Act. In his new role, he had an understandably dampening effect, not only on the management but also on the staff. Nathan, later to be Singapore's ambassador to Washington and later president of Singapore, was in due course replaced as *Straits Times* watchdog by one of Lee's political cronies, former cabinet Minister Lim Kim San.

In early 1983, Lee ordained more deaths and reincarnations. The *Nanyang Siang Pau* and the *Sin Chew Jit Poh* closed, and in their place appeared the *Lianhe Zao Bao* and the *Lianhe Wan Bao* (Mandarin Chinese titles meaning the "United Morning New" and the "United Evening News"). The disappearance of the old, proud *Nanyang Siang Pau* was Lee's final act of petty revenge against the defiant Lee Eu Seng, who had been released from detention five years previously. Another Chinese afternoon newspaper, the *Kuai Bao*, launched in 1980, discontinued publication in 1983 and was absorbed by the *Lianhe Wan Bao*.

The final coup de grace to any remaining pretence that the Singapore press enjoyed any degree of freedom or independence was administered in 1984. Astonishingly, the rival Straits

Times Group and the Singapore News and Publications Ltd., which had been gearing up for intense competition between their newspapers, announced that they would merge. The government denied any hand in the move, but allowed that it approved. In fact, its views had been made plain to both groups. The merger was regarded as a breaking of previous pledges that the two major publishing houses would be allowed to compete.

By the end of the decade, Singapore Press Holdings was a huge, all-powerful monopoly, owning every newspaper of any significance, only excepting a few small vernacular publications aimed at ethnic minorities. It controlled Singapore News and Publications Limited, the Straits Times Press Limited, and the Times Publishing Company. It owned the *Straits Times* and its Sunday edition, the *Sunday Times*; the *New Paper* (an afternoon tabloid launched in 1989, offering stories that were "fun" to read); the major Malay-language daily, *Berita Harian*, and its Sunday edition the *Berita Minggu*; and its empire included the three surviving Chinese newspapers, the *Lianhe Zao Bao*, the *Lianhe Wan Bao*, and the *Shin Min Daily News*. With government nominees on their boards, with official watchdogs in their editorial offices, and with PAP members occupying senior editorial positions, Singapore's newspapers by the end of the 1980s were less free and independent than those in China.

Taming the Foreign Press

While the process of taming the media of Singapore was well under way, Lee did not overlook the foreign press. In 1971, a *New York Times* stringer, the late Anthony Polsky, was expelled for making inquiries about Singapore's political prisoners. Three years later, *Newsweek* and its Singaporean correspondent Pang Cheng Lian were found guilty of libel because her article on an unsuccessful defamation case brought against a PAP Member of Parliament commented that the verdict "did little to dispel the notion long charged by critics that the courts of this country are little more than extensions of the one-party system."[25]

With these early warning shots and Singapore's mounting complaints against the foreign media in mind, I made an appointment in March 1976 to see Lee while on my way, via Singapore and Kuala Lumpur, to London for some leave. I found naught for my comfort. Lee was critical of the coverage of the *Far Eastern Economic Review*. Dismissing my arguments that nearly all articles were properly positive, he predicted trouble for the *Review* if we persisted in our "attacks." He then launched into an ad hominem attack on our Singapore correspondents, Arun Senkuttuvan and Ho Kwon Ping, both Singaporeans with university educations—in Madras and California, respectively. Lee had fewer reservations about Ho, who would as a Chinese readjust, but he threw grave doubt on Senkuttuvan's loyalty. "Why did he choose to go to Madras University?" Lee asked, unmindful of his own years at Cambridge. Senkuttuvan had not served his national military service, he sneered. I pointed out that Senkuttuvan had been too old to be included in the draft law when it was passed. My nostrils picked up more than a whiff of racism in these remarks, an impression more than borne out by subsequent events.

Lee then gave me a short lecture on Confucianism (à la the twentieth century) and its social virtues: If a leader did his duties (preserved peace, appointed uncorrupted officials, eschewed overtaxation, etc.), he earned the Mandate of Heaven and the total loyalty of his subjects. "What you do not realize, Mr. Davies," he said, "is that in a Confucian society, the phrase `loyal opposition' is a contradiction in terms." He then expatiated, off the record, on regional matters, particularly on the future Malaysian leadership. (I should note here, despite extreme provocation, that I kept these remarks off the record, until they became public knowledge when adduced as evidence in a subsequent suit for libel.) He said that a Malaysian leader had to be an "ultra" (an intensely committed adherent of Islam) in order to rise to the top of the Malaysian ruling party, but intelligent enough to jettison any extremism (which would take the economy into disaster) once power had been achieved. A man who fitted such a description? Lee cynically and insultingly mentioned Datuk Haroun Idris, who as Selangor Chief Minister, had recently been convicted on charges of massive corruption.

After Lee repeated his warnings of trouble to come, I returned to my hotel. As it was obviously important that Russell Spurr, the *Review*'s acting editor during my absence, should know of Lee's remarks, I dictated an account of the conversation onto a tape cassette in my room in the presence of Arun Senkuttuvan and my family. Handing the tape to Senkuttuvan, I stressed its confidentiality and asked him to dispatch it to Spurr, for his ears only, so that he could brief the other three responsible editors on the gist of Lee's comments of immediate relevance to the *Review*.

In January 1977, Ho Kwon Ping, then the *Review*'s Singapore correspondent, was arrested and charged with disseminating state secrets in an article on Singapore's defense industries and arms purchases from the United States and for having in his possession notes about the Singaporean armed forces. Admitting one charge, he pointed out that most of the information in the notes was general knowledge and had been published elsewhere. Nevertheless, after being fined S$7,500, he tendered his resignation. The *Review* covered his legal expenses and the fine, accepting his resignation with genuine regret.

In February 1977, almost a year after my chat with Lee and five months after he had left the *Review*'s employ, Senkuttuvan was arrested under the Internal Security Act. After three and a half weeks' interrogation, during which he was stripped of Singaporean citizenship, his "confession" was published, and he gave a televised press conference in which he admitted deliberately slanting articles in both the *Review* and the *London Financial Times* (for which he also wrote) to discredit the Singapore authorities and had "gone to the extent of supporting the Communist cause."[26]

Early that morning, I received a telephone call from a *Straits Times* reporter, asking my reaction to the accusation by the Singapore Ministry of Home Affairs that I had "violated the ethics of [my] own profession" by taping my account of my conversation with Lee "for a wide and indeterminate audience" in order to "cause mischief between the leaders of Malaysia and Singapore." My response was that if copies of the tape other than that locked in my desk at the *Review* office existed, "a gross breach of confidence" had been perpetrated. (Sadly, Senkuttuvan, worried about Lee's remarks about himself, had given several copies of the tape to certain of his friends before dispatching it to Hongkong.) I pointed out that, far from the tape being made for a large, indeterminate audience, it was recorded as a confidential briefing for the *Review*'s senior editors, that Senkuttavan himself had described it as "private and confidential"; and that the Singapore government had been the only party to have caused "mischief" between Singapore and Malaysia by publicizing its existence. I also (a little disingenuously, in view of Lee's championing of the corrupt Haroun for the leadership of Malaysia) added that there was nothing on the tape to cause dissension between the two governments, and I suggested that the text of the tape should be published in toto, a proposal that received no response.

One amusing footnote to the tape affair: While Lee was giving evidence in a subsequent libel lawsuit, he described the text of the tape as a transcript, adding "I thought he had no tape recorder." When it was pointed out to him that the tape was made after, not during, the conversation, Lee commented that I must have total recall—the first and last compliment from Lee on my journalistic abilities.

The *Review* stood by the accuracy and balance of Senkuttuvan's coverage of Singapore affairs from May 1975 and September 1976, when he had left its employ. The texts of the articles show conclusively that they were overwhelmingly confined to business and economic subjects, with little or no political or social content or comment. The *London Times*, similarly, stated that his articles were published "because we believed that at the time that they were accurate as to fact and fair comment. Nothing which has occurred since then has caused us to change this view."[27]

Shortly after these rebuttals, which apparently annoyed the Singapore authorities, Ho Kwon Ping was arrested again. Within a month, he made a televised confession, stating that he had treated the *Review* as a vehicle for propagating "pro-Communist ideas," using his articles to discredit the Singapore government internationally as an "elitist, racist, fascist, oppressive and dictatorial regime."[28] The government cited two articles to support this confession, neither of which were Marxist in tone or critical of the Singapore government.[29] Released after seven weeks, Ho decided to give up journalism. Interestingly, he told his former colleagues that, while being interviewed by PAP officials with a view to joining the party, nothing would convince them that he did not regularly receive instructions from the *Review*'s editorial offices on what to write and how to write it, or that his copy was not heavily edited or slanted in Hongkong.

Similarly, opposition parliamentarian Jeyaratnam paid for his courage. He was accused of breaching parliamentary privileges, of mishandling his party's funds, and was denied the right to practice as a lawyer. Editorializing on what "many Singaporeans believe is official harassment" of Jeyaratnam, the Hongkong-based *Asian Wall Street Journal* commented in October 1985: "The problem here is government credibility. We don't know if Mr. Jeyaratnam is guilty. But even if he were, many Singaporeans wouldn't believe it because court actions, and especially libel suits, have long been used in Singapore against opposition politicians."[30] In response, the government charged the newspaper's executives with criminal contempt. The *Journal* apologized and pleaded guilty. All those charged were fined, as were the newspaper's feature page editor and the writer of the leader, although neither of them had even been charged.

Singapore's leaders were apparently under the completely false impression that the international press was singling them out for special criticism. They asked why journalists did not turn their guns on corrupt neighboring regimes. But when such attitudes were reported, they were denied, and the writers accused of sewing doubts between Southeast Asian leaders. Lee himself gave the game away when, during a 1985 Singapore Parliamentary Committee Meeting, he argued that the *Asian Wall Street Journal*'s remarks about the credibility of Singapore justice had to be tackled head on; otherwise, he confided, other foreign publications would assume "that we are another Marcos-like regime—that we fix our judges."[31]

My last conversation with Lee, which took place in September 1985, is summarized in the first few paragraphs of this chapter. The legislation he then adumbrated was a further amendment to the Newspaper and Printing Presses Act, which passed in May 1986. The act empowers the government to restrict sales of foreign publications ("gazetting") if any relevant minister declares that it is "engaging in the domestic policies of Singapore."

Singapore leaders made two main points in justifying the measure. The access of correspondents to Singapore and the access of their publications to the Singapore market are seen as privileges and thus are withdrawable. Secondly, the Singapore government demanded a "right of reply," which means that editors are required to print an official letter to correct any alleged mistake, incorrect conclusion, or wrongheaded view that has appeared in print. After the act passed, any article published almost anywhere was likely to attract such a corrective penned by a press officer attached to a Singapore ministry, government office, or a Singaporean mission abroad. The texts of these letters, however long, lamentably drafted, or boring, were considered sacrosanct. An enthusiastic subeditor who tried to liven up or tighten up the bureaucratic prose could easily bring about a ban on his employers' paper. The single-minded insistence on the right to reply gave editors many headaches, for Singapore did not hesitate to demand the publication of letters commenting on matters sub judice, making scurrilous accusations of spite or incompetence against the publications' own correspondents or libelous allegations against third parties. Lee's press officer James Fu, a former journalist who was detained by the British in 1963, wrote to the *Review* in 1988:

> When you receive letters to correct errors and misrepresentation, it means we believe you can and will
> learn how your paper can report without distortion and be gazetted. When you receive no more letters—

whatever your misrepresentations—it means we have given you up.[32]

The Singapore government's argument—that it had a right to reply to mistakes of fact, or what it regarded as biased comment—did have a certain force. I decided to print its letters in full. It would also deny Singapore a pretext for gazetting the *Review*, as Lee's son, Brig. Gen. (Ret.) Lee Hsien Loong, had assured international publications that they would be allowed to circulate freely, provided that they granted the "right of reply." I took him at his word. Throughout 1987, few editions of the magazine were without such a letter, mostly a turgid, self-righteous, nitpicking missive from Fu that was seldom worth the space they took up. Our readers felt the same, and many protested. I tried to explain: "We did this only partly because we believe the government has a right of reply; we printed them partly also because their content and tone revealed more about the mentality of Singapore officialdom than could the most gifted journalist."[33] When in due course the Brigadier-General's promise was broken, and the *Review* was gazetted, my first reaction on hearing the news was: "Thank God we won't have to publish any more of James Fu's rubbish."

The first publication to be gazetted was *Time*, which ran a piece in 1986 describing the vicious harassment of Jeyaratnam.[34] When James Fu wrote a letter, which *Time* did not publish in full,[35] Singaporean officials concluded that the magazine was engaging in domestic politics. *Time*'s circulation was then cut by 50 percent to 9,000 copies and, in January 1987, to 2,000 copies. In the end, *Time* printed the full text,[36] despite its reservations about Fu's accusations, but had to wait nine months before it was allowed to circulate freely again.

Then came the turn of the *Asian Wall Street Journal*. In December 1986, an article reported possible weaknesses in a proposed second securities market. In response, the Director of the Monetary Authority of Singapore wrote a letter, alleging that the article was biased and inaccurate and that its author (the Singapore correspondent, Stephen Duthie) was unprofessional.[37] Fred Zimmerman, editor and publisher, refused to publish the "unwarranted" attacks on his correspondent and allegations of what he viewed as nonexistent errors. Nevertheless, he offered to publish a letter putting forth the Singapore government's points. On February 9, 1987, the *Asian Wall Street Journal* was gazetted, and its Singapore sales were reduced from 5,100 to 400 copies. The newspaper then launched a lawsuit in Singapore, claiming that the right to gazette was illegal.

From Washington, the American Society of Newspaper Editors protested, while the State Department expressed its regret, incurring criticism by Singapore for a lack of impartiality. The American Business Council in Singapore itself commented that American businesses would carefully consider investing in Singapore in view of the restrictions placed on the free flow of business and economic information. Singapore justified its actions with a familiar repetition of arguments: No foreign publication had a right to sell in Singapore, which was a removable privilege; no foreign publication could meddle in the internal politics of Singapore; official letters correcting errors had to published; gazetted publications were not banned (they were still available in some public libraries for photocopying); ergo, gazetting did not restrict the flow of information![38]

Then followed a farcical dance that was to be repeated with variations with other publications. The *Asian Wall Street Journal* requested permission to supply free copies to all its subscribers. Singapore agreed, but only if the newspaper deleted all its advertisements. The paper said this would be too expensive, and that, anyway, advertisements were an integral part of a newspaper. Singapore then offered to share the additional costs, and the paper refused to accept any government subsidy.

Lee Kuan Yew went to Washington in 1988 to defend his actions in a speech before the American Society of Newspaper Editors. Singapore, he said, refused to allow foreign correspondents to act as journalists did in America, taking sides as adversaries of the establishment and influencing the outcome of issues under debate. He doubted whether Singapore's "social glue" was strong enough to stand such treatment. Foreign publications, he admitted, "have become the domestic Singapore press based offshore."[39] Unfortunately, no one made the obvious riposte: That he himself had brought this about by repression. The dull and lifeless Singaporean media rarely debated important issues, as he alleged, but reproduced official handouts. The sad fact was that foreign publications sold well in Singapore because Singaporeans read them not merely to know what was going on in the world or the region, but also to find out what was really happening in Singapore itself.

The next gazetting was of *Asiaweek*, a midmarket weekly originally backed by Marcos money, then taken over by the *Reader's Digest* group and thereafter by *Time*. In 1987, *Asiaweek*'s Singapore correspondent, Lisa Beyer, reported the arrest and detention of twenty-two young persons, mostly Catholic churchworkers, who were, almost incredibly, accused of belonging to a Marxist plot to overthrow the Singapore government. Beyer annoyed Singaporean leaders by reporting statements by the released detainees of how their "confessions" had been extracted from them by abuse, lack of sleep, prolonged interrogation, threats, and torture.[40] The magazine's circulation was then cut from about 10,000 to 500. Later in mid-1988, after the editor of *Asiaweek* lunched with James Fu, Beyer was posted from Singapore to Hongkong, whereupon she handed in her resignation. Although the editor denied any deal with Fu, a few months later *Asiaweek*'s officially licensed circulation in Singapore rose from 500 to 5,000 and a year later rose again to 7,500.

The arrests of the churchworkers had been partially inspired by the part that the Catholic Church played in overthrowing the Marcos regime in the Philippines. Lee was later to describe how the spectacle of nuns and priests taking part in a "people's power" demonstration in Manila had determined him to restrict the church's role in Singapore to religious matters, free from any social and political activity.[41] Lee warned Singapore Catholic Archbishop Gregory Yong not to involve the church in a long list of social issues, ranging from the problems of the aged to the status of Filipina maids. Lee condemned the publication *Catholic News*, then edited by Father Edgar D'Souza, for criticizing increases in bus fares and changes in education policy. Lee even warned the Pope, when he visited Singapore, that problems were emanating from the Church.

Lee won adverse publicity in the world press from the arrests and ill-treatment of the Catholic layworkers in Singapore in May and June 1987 and the claim that they were involved in a Marxist plot. Counterattacking in parliament, Home Minister Shanmugam Jayakumar castigated Father D'Souza, who had fled to Australia shortly after the arrests, accusing him of taking part in a campaign to discredit the government, instigating foreigners to interfere in the country's internal affairs, and of carrying on an "illicit" affair with a woman.[42] In fact, D'Souza had fallen in love and was on the point of resigning his priesthood in order to marry.

On December 17, 1987, I wrongly assumed that Lee would be the first to agree that Edgar D'Souza also had a "right to reply" to an attack from the safety of parliamentary privilege. Accordingly, the *Review* reported Jayakumar's speech and D'Souza's response from his exile in Australia. The article, entitled "New Light on Detentions," and written by *Review* staffer Michael Malik, quoted D'Souza on the arrests and treatment of the detainees and about events leading up to a press conference at which Archbishop Yong, flanked by Lee and Jayakumar, stated that he was satisfied that the arrests were not directed against the Church. In the subsequent action, no fact in the article was disproved. (In fact, there was one immaterial error—the statement that D'Souza left Singapore after the arrests on June 3 instead of June 5.)

Lee Kuan Yew then sued the *Review* for libel and gazetted the magazine, reducing its circulation from well over 9,000 to 500. Similar to the danse macabre performed by the *Asian Wall Street Journal*, I refused to allow the *Review* to circulate in Singapore at all, arguing that the gazetting placed the *Review*'s circulation under Singapore's control and insisting on treating all its subscribers alike. I added that gazetting was in effect "a ban by any other name" that enabled Singapore to claim that it was not. Hilariously, the Singapore government accused the *Review* of impeding the free flow of information into Singapore. Incredibly, and in defiance of all copyright laws, Singapore then licensed a local printer to run off pirate copies of the *Review*, minus the advertisements, for sale locally. The *Review* thereupon counter-proposed to supply advertisement-free copies for distribution in Singapore, seeking only to recover costs as permitted under the new measure. Even this offer was turned down.

The libel case was remarkable, in that Lee Kuan Yew was forced as the plaintiff to undergo several days of searching cross-examination from Geoffrey Robertson, QC, a new and evidently uncomfortable experience for him. He gave a lamentable performance. As he appealed to the judge for protection against hard questioning, contradicted himself, pleaded ill health, painted himself as a victim of vicious journalists, and caused great amusement in the public gallery, it was hard to recognize the first-class Cambridge law graduate. But the judge, somehow persuaded that the *Review* had maliciously libeled him, awarded Lee costs plus a fine of S$230,000 in aggravated damages on the grounds that Robertson's cross-examination had introduced irrelevant issues and was intended to hurt Lee's feelings.

Shortly after the case, I ceased being editor of the *Review*. (To use the American euphemism, Dow Jones, which had a few years previously acquired 100 percent ownership of the magazine, had decided to "let me go.") Meanwhile, the *Review* applied—vainly—for an agreement to appeal against the verdict to the Privy Council, but anyway entered an appeal in Singapore's courts. Lee cross-appealed, asking for larger damages.

In New York, Peter Kann, President and Publisher of Dow Jones, commented on the "unwarranted determination" of the court against an "essentially accurate" article "solely because it was read to be critical of Mr. Lee."[43] Kann was then charged with contempt of court, and Lee instituted libel proceedings against him in both Singapore and Malaysia, although not, of course, in the United States. Eventually, Dow Jones threw in the towel (to use the *New York Times*' expression):[44] The *Review* abandoned its appeal and paid all Lee's costs, stating that it had never intended to libel Lee or imply that he had improperly influenced the judge, while Lee dropped his cross-appeals and libel suits.

Since then, the *Review*'s coverage of Singapore affairs has been such as to keep Singapore's feathers relatively unruffled. But bullies are not easily appeased. The *Asian Wall Street Journal* and the *Review* had to wait as their Singapore sales were very gradually allowed to rise by installments over the years. By June 1996, the former was allowed to sell 9,000 copies, the latter 6,000—just over half what it had been selling nine years previously, prior to gazetting.

Looking back at the trial, the ban, and its consequences, only one person emerged with any credit—Edgar D'Souza, the courageous priest, who witnessed and backed up the *Review*'s account of the archbishop's meeting with his priests after his confrontation with Lee and the subsequent press conference. The part played by the Catholic Church and by its senior representatives in the region was far from admirable.

In June 1989, Bernard Levin, a *London Times* columnist, wrote up the story of the harassment of Ben Jeyaratnam,[45] as recounted in more detail in the chapter by Francis Seow in this book. Levin commented: "The misuse of law here has been gross. . . . Legality has been twisted into a hideous shape." The *Times* duly received from Abdul Aziz Mahmood, the Singapore High Commissioner in London, a long letter of complaint, which the *Times* refused to publish in full. (It contained a paragraph claiming that Jeyaratnam was "after all, a criminal.") Incredibly, the commissioner then asked the *Times* to publish the defamatory material with a Singapore government indemnity for fines and costs should its publication lead to libel proceedings. As Levin pointed out, apart from anything else, publication would probably have constituted a contempt of court. Denied access to the letters column of the *Times*, the High Commissioner published his letter as advertisements in the *Guardian* and the *Financial Times*.

In 1989, while a verdict was pending on the challenge in the Singaporean courts by the

Asian Wall Street Journal to the legality of gazetting, Singapore's parliament abolished the right to appeal to the Privy Council in civil cases, unless both the defendant and the plaintiff agreed. After the bill passed, the newspaper appealed to the Singapore courts to render judgment before the new law took effect. The Court of Appeal refused and later upheld the gazetting order. A final appeal to the Privy Council was then dismissed "for want of jurisdiction."

As in China, an official secret in Singapore can be anything that has not been officially announced. In 1993, the editor of the *Business Times*, Patrick Daniel, and some of his colleagues were prosecuted for publishing an estimate of Singapore's gross domestic product before its official release.[46] In an article entitled "Pssst, Wanna See a Statistic?," *The Economist* expressed dismay that a GDP figure should prove so sensitive.[47] Citing the case of a doctor fired from the National University of Singapore after standing as an opposition candidate in a by-election, the magazine said that hopes that Singapore's new Prime Minister, Goh Chok Tong, would lead a "kinder, gentler" regime seemed to have been blighted.

Again, Mahmood duly penned a response, which *The Economist* was reluctant to publish in full. This led to a bitter exchange of letters, with the magazine finally agreeing to publish the offensive missive.[48] But the editor, Bill Emmott, was still reluctant to publish another letter, replying to one from Jeyeratnam,[49] which had merely set out the points of law that prevented him from appealing to the Privy Council against his criminal convictions, as opposed to his illegal disbarment from the roll.

The government promptly gazetted *The Economist* in August 1993, capping its Singapore sales at 7,500. The reply to Jeyeratnam was finally published,[50] and in January 1994 *The Economist* was degazetted, and the ceiling on its circulation was removed, but the magazine was required to post a S$200,000 bond. *The Economist* editor explained to his readers why he had "capitulated:" A publication must try to obey the laws of the countries in which it circulates, while seeking to ensure that its readers are not misled by government propaganda.[51] Despite his assurance that *The Economist*'s coverage would remain "critical or complimentary, whichever is appropriate," his explanation was regarded as a copout and a considerable victory for Lee Kuan Yew, as *The Economist* is a rich and powerful publication whose Singapore sales account for a tiny fraction of its global circulation.

The requirement that *The Economist* should post a large bond was made under further amendments to the Printing and Publications Act, adopted in 1990, requiring all foreign newspapers with sales of over 300 in Singapore to apply each year for permits to circulate; the permits were to be revocable at any time. The government reserved the power to specify the maximum copies allowed to circulate. At the same time, each newspaper had to nominate a representative who would be able to accept legal notices or writs on its behalf and had to post a bond of up to S$292,000 to meet any fines or costs imposed by the courts. The government blandly claimed that the measure was designed to ensure fair, objective, and responsible reporting, not to curb the sales of any newspaper.

Perhaps Singapore took note of the widespread criticism that this measure inspired or wanted to use its new powers to reward amenable publications and punish the recalcitrant. Anyway, it backtracked, announcing in November 1990 that fourteen publications were exempted from the requirement to apply for permits. This list included *Time, Newsweek, The Economist*, and the *International Herald Tribune* (IHT). It did not include the *Asian Wall Street Journal* or the *Review*, both anyway being pirated in Singapore with official approval.

Lee's approval, however, could not be taken for granted. IHT, a newspaper published in Paris and jointly owned by the *New York Times* and the *Washington Post*, which sold about 7,000 copies in Singapore where 17,000 of its Asian edition was printed, had long maintained Michael Richardson as a senior correspondent in Singapore—its "Asian Editor." Richardson's articles on his host country were rarely critical, although his judgments on neighboring countries tended to be more trenchant. In August 1994, the IHT ran an article by Philip Bowring, whom Dow Jones had recently relieved of his duties as *Review* editor. Bowring argued that "Asian Values" rarely bore scrutiny, that "dynastic politics" were practiced in both China and Singapore, for example, despite official devotion to "bureaucratic meritocracy."[52]

Senior Minister Lee Kuan Yew, Prime Minister Goh, and Deputy Prime Minister Lee Hsien Loong (the "Holy Trinity," as they were then known in Singapore, being the Father, the Son and the Holy Goh) claimed that the article defamed them, that Lee Hsien Loong's swift rise through the army's ranks and subsequently through the ranks of politicians had nothing to do with his being his father's son, but was entirely on merit. The IHT hardly hesitated. Apparently with no prior attempt to ensure via lawyers that a climbdown would call off the Singaporean dogs, the paper published a groveling apology that effectively denied it any defense against the libel suit which nonetheless followed. Record damages were awarded—the equivalent of US$250,000 to Goh and US$214,000 to Lee and Lee, plus costs.

Two months later, the IHT was again inadvertently to puncture the thin skins of the Singaporean leaders by publishing an op-ed commentary written by an American political economist, then teaching at the National University of Singapore. His essay dealt with the various ways in which unnamed Asian regimes suppressed dissent, from the use of imprisonment and tanks to "relying upon a compliant judiciary to bankrupt politicians or by buying out enough of the opposition to take control 'democratically'."[53] "If the cap fits, wear it," goes the old refrain. Evidently, Lee realized that sufficient readers of the IHT would recognize some his own methods of squashing opposition, although the author of the article, Christoper Lingle, had not mentioned Singapore in his article at all. Accordingly, Lingle was interrogated twice, and his rooms were searched in an effort to prove contacts with the opposition. Once again, the *International Herald Tribune* crumbled prematurely, apologizing unreservedly to Lee and the judiciary. The government soon brought a suit alleging contempt of court, Lee himself alleging libel.

Michael Richardson's title of Asian Editor was to prove an embarrassment, for it transpired that his duties involved checking articles on Asia, including Lingle's piece, as fit for publication. With a credibility that the prosecution dubbed worthy of Alice in Wonderland, he had assumed that Lingle had been referring to such countries such as Burma, China, and North Korea.[54] Nevertheless, in proving that Lingle had Singapore in mind, the prosecution was constrained to admit that members of the opposition had indeed been bankrupted. The court, duly proclaiming that Lingle meant Singapore, fined Lingle, Richardson, and the paper's publisher, printers, and distributors. Lingle understandably had already left Singapore's shores for home, but Lee was not to be denied. Despite laws protecting pension funds, the National University of Singapore was constrained to carry Lingle's salary and savings into court, and a ruling that the fine would be paid out of these funds duly followed.

Curiously, although the IHT was hammered in the courts, its Singapore sales never suffered gazetting. Perhaps even Lee had recognized that he overreacted to a couple of comments which, if tactless within the acquiescent political environment that he had imposed, were hardly damaging (certainly no other Asian regime had objected to the writers' views). Perhaps, too, he realized that he was harming Singapore's efforts to become the region's premier communications and information center.

Ludicrously contradictory as it may seem, despite Lee's crushing of the domestic press, his hounding of foreign publications, and his steps to deny Singaporeans access to the Internet and to satellite television programs, restricting them to censurable cable sources, Singapore still nurtured ambitions to become a major junction in the publications network and on the information superhighway. In many speeches and private briefings, Lee has predicted that an increasing number of publications would find Singapore attractive as a editing, publishing, printing, and distribution center. He particularly had set his hopes on a publishing migration from Hongkong (which had for many years been home to the region's only free press) as the June 30, 1997, deadline for its handover to China approached. Generous incentives, including long-term tax holidays, were offered to owners and publishers. Unsurprisingly, there were few takers.

Conclusion

I have presented a selective and incomplete account of Lee's relations with the press. I have failed to recount many acts of spite and tyranny—arrests and detentions, tortures and "confessions," broken lives and careers, canceled work permits, refusals of visas, closures and eviscerations of publications large and small, shattered hopes and businesses, lies and libel lawsuits, long imprisonments, and exiles. Lee would have us believe that Singapore's stability and prosperity are the fruits of his repression, but the argument that the island's "social glue" would have crumbled into unrest and riots if the newspapers had been free to inform and comment is hardly tenable.

Although Lee often sees plots within the Western media, he has successfully restricted world press freedom. The media have themselves to blame, as well as Lee's power complex. Their dedication to their central values—the freedom of the press and the duty to tell it like it is—have proved fragile under pressure. Lee was right to assume that money would win the day over high ideals. Never, at any point, has Lee faced a united front from the press. The so-called solidarity of the press has proved a chimera. The banning of a publication has been cynically regarded as a gap in the market to be exploited by competitors. Nor can the lack of solidarity be blamed solely on the profit motive. Journalists are always in competition for a story and, regrettably, some take pleasure in their fellows' troubles. Journalists often deserve the sobriquet of "hacks."

Singapore is a frightened community, where people nervously glance over their shoulders and lower their voices. Compared to another Chinese enclave that matched its economic progress, colonial Hongkong was free to nurture its ethnic richness. Not only are the newspapers gray in Singapore, but little of note has been produced in the worlds of literature and poetry, drama and theater, painting and sculpture, while in industry and technology, Singapore has proved remarkably non-innovative. It may be a green city-state, but all color has been leeched out of the cultural landscape.

Lee has always reserved a special spite for the press which, on the whole, has praised him and his economic achievements. Perhaps he identified himself too closely with Singapore, and the thinness of his skin was a symptom of "garrison mentality." He identified his leadership with all hopes for Singapore's future, so any dissent was viewed as a threat both to his preeminence and to the nation's prospects—in other words, treason. Something beyond the usual amour propre of tyrants seems to be driving him.

Lee is determined that history should judge him well, and that his shade will be venerated in Singapore's Confucian shrines, if not further afield. It is no accident that an officially-approved CD-ROM disc already exists to record for posterity the authorized version of his life and achievements. But he is uncomfortably conscious that the transitory reports and views of media men are stored in libraries as reference materials for future historians writing their definitive volumes; that other, harsher judgments will contribute to the verdict of history. In the obituary columns, on radio and television programs assessing the impact of his death, in the works of scholars, his shade will be praised for his economic achievements, but his inhumanity will be excoriated. One of the few laws he cannot alter or amend is that it is impossible to libel a dead man. That thought must rankle.

Epilog (by Michael Haas)

In 2013, Singapore ranked 149 out of 179 countries in the Press Freedom Index, making it the worst country among all developed economies.[55] Rather than improving, the ranking was lower than in the previous year. The government still maintains the "right of reply" but does not apply that right to its own statements. In 2004, *The Economist* agreed to an out-of-court settlement including an apology and payment of a S$210,000 fine for comments on the actions of the spouse of newly installed Prime Minister Lee Hsien Loong as executive director of Tomasek Holdings.[56] The *Far Eastern Economic Review* was banned in 2006 for publishing an interview with Chee Soon Juan. During 2009, the *Far Eastern Economic Review* and the *Wall Street Journal* encountered unfavorable judicial outcomes; the former lost an appeal for allegedly defaming Lee Kuan Yew and his spouse, the latter for an article questioning the independence of the judiciary.[57]

Websites have tried to offer alternative but acceptable platforms. The Singapore Internet Community (*sintercom*) was launched by Dr. Tan Chong Kee in 1994 as a forum open to all, but in 2001 he was required by the Singapore Broadcasting Corporation to sign a license agreement that made him technically liable for any defamatory comments made by anyone who might post them without his knowledge. Accordingly, he shut down the website, whereupon an anonymous person opened a bland newsintercom.org.[58]

However, ThinkCentre (*thinkcentre.org*) began as a registered business in 1999, signed the license in 2001, and remains alive despite combining advocacy—but not criticism—with journalism. The website, nevertheless, now protests media censorship and human rights problems. Other blogs and websites flourish today, including *theonlinecitizen.com*.

In 2005, a student studying in the United States on a government scholarship, having started a blog, criticized the terms of the financial grant in terms that so angered the government that he was threatened with a defamation suit, so he then shut down his blog.[59] Blogs insulting teachers have also been shut down.

The Newspaper and Printing Presses Act is still in force.[60] In 2002, the Act was amended to increase the penalty for violations from S$10,000 to S$50,000, and a provision was added to give the government more power to restrict ownership. No major publications have been shut down in recent years, so the Chinese and Malay communities still have their own news media, both in print and online. In 2003, Internet website developers were required to obtain government permits or they would be shut down.

The Undesirable Publications Act of 1967, as amended, includes CD-ROMs, sound recordings, and computer-generated drawings on the list of material subject to censorship. Nevertheless, the Internet gives power to individuals to start blogs, make comments on blogs, and access information of all sorts, thus complicating the government's ability to regulate the flow of information.

Parallel to the Newspaper and Printing Presses Act, the Films Act authorizes the Ministry of Communication and the Arts to ban, seize, censor, or restrict written, visual, and musical offerings if the content is believed to threaten stability, offend morality, or further racial or religious animosity.

As a possible sign of loosening of restrictions under the newly appointed Prime Minister Lee Hsien Loong in 2004, circulation of *Cosmopolitan* was allowed; in the past, the magazine had been considered too pornographic. In addition, the television series *Sex and the City* was allowed to be broadcast.[61]

In 2004 and 2005, however, three films were dropped from the Singapore International Film Festival. In 2004, *Formula 17* (a film deemed too pro-gay rights) and *Destiny's Children* (on China's treatment of Tibetans) were rejected for inclusion. The following year, *Singapore Rebel*, a biography of Chee Soon Juan, was withdrawn from the Singapore International Film Festival. That same year, a program featuring members of the Cabinet, including the prime minister, was deemed a violation, but no prosecution occurred.

The same law permits the police to search homes for unlicensed materials and arrest alleged offenders. All films must be approved by the Board of Film Censors. An amendment adopted in 2009 allows endorsement of a political party or politician and on-line undramatized election advertising, provided that the narrative is considered factual by the government.

In July 2009, Martyn See was informed that *One Nation Under Lee* was refused permission to be distributed unless scenes were deleted. In July 2010, See was ordered to remove a video from the YouTube website and his blogsite. The video, *Ex-Political Prisoner Speaks out in Singapore*, alternately titled *Dr. Lim Hock Siew*, had a November 2008 speech by Dr. Lim regarding his detention in 1963. The reason given was that the video would "undermine public confidence in the government." In 2012, the attorney general wrote to Alex Au, with a demand that he apologize and remove a post in his Yawning Bread blogsite that criticized the judiciary for showing deference to the executive.

Singapore also has an Internet Code of Practice, which requires Internet Service Providers, all of which are government owned or linked, and internet content providers to "ensure that prohibited material is not broadcast." Any such efforts may require licensees to deny access to sites or refrain from a relationship with selected newsgroups.

In addition, the Official Secrets Act and Sedition Act limit free expression. The Sedition Act is concerned with race and class disharmony and incitement to "disaffection" with the Singapore government. In 2005,[62] a speaker on nonviolent protest was barred entry to the country, Amnesty Interntional was banned from a rally protesting the death penalty, and the police cleared four persons protesting lack of accountability from the Central Provident Fund building. In 2010, Vincent Cheng, who had been held under the Internal Security Act in 1987, was invited by the National University of Singapore History Project to speak about his detention, but the National Library Board, the venue operator, soon withdrew the invitation.

In 2010, Singapore's attorney general cited fourteen statements in the book by Alan Shadrake, the British author of *Once a Jolly Hangman: Singapore Justice in the Dock*, for "scandalizing the judiciary" for alleging that court decisions may have been affected by political and economic pressures, biases against the "weak," "poor," or "less educated," and PAP interference. The attorney general, charging Shadrake with "contempt," argued that the accusations and insinuations tended to "muzzle confidence in the courts' impartiality, integrity and independence." The prosecution warned any media publicizing Shadrake's remarks could also be charged. In 2010, Australian author James Minchin was refused entry into Singapore for statements he earlier made on television.

Singapore, thus, remains guilty of the same charges that Lee Kuan Yew once leveled at British colonial authorities. Why there is such a need to control information remains a habit as well as a puzzle. For the Singapore government, criticism is seen as delegitimation and disrespect, so government replies are framed in that context. Instead of conceding some truth in what might be perceived as a constructive comment, Singapore rejoinders do not apply the same standards to themselves and tend to be disrespectful.

Nevertheless, as noted in Chapter 2, social media operate under the radar and seemed to have engineered victories for opposition candidates in the 2011 election. *Facebook* and similar platforms may erode the monopoly of information that Singapore leaders so desperately covet because "tweets" and other forms of communication are too numerous to monitor. Therein lies some optimism for the future.

Notes

1. *Hansard*, Legislative Assembly Debates, 1955. Quoted in "An Interview with the Young Mr Lee," *Far Eastern Economic Review*, 2 June 1988, 40.
2. Quoted in Francis T. Seow, *To Catch a Tartar: A Dissident in Lee Kuan Yew's Prison* (New Haven, CT: Yale University Southeast Asia Studies, 1994), 71.
3. *Hansard*, Legislative Assembly Debates, 1955. Quoted in "An Interview with the Young Mr Lee," *Far Eastern Economic Review*, 2 June 1988, 40.
4. *Hansard*, Legislative Assembly Debates, 4 October 1956, cols. 322-323.
5. *Straits Times*, 19 May 1959.
6. Straits Times, 22 May 1959 (letter).
7. *Hansard*, Malaysian Parliamentary Debates, 18 December 1964, cols. 5075-5083.
8. Quoted in Seow, *To Catch a Tartar*, 174.
9. *Straits Times*, 29 April 1971.
10. *Straits Times*, 3 May 1971. A "black operation" is also known as a "covert operation."
11. *Straits Times*, 3 May 1971; 4 May 1971.
12. Quoted in Francis T. Seow, *The Media Enthralled: Singapore Revisited* (Boulder, CO: Rienner, 1997), 51.
13. *Sunday Times* (Singapore), 25 May 1971.
14. *Sunday Times* (Singapore), 16 May 1971.
15. Quoted in Seow, *The Media Enthralled*, 54.
16. *Straits Times*, 21 May 1971.
17. Quoted in Seow, *The Media Enthralled*, 67.
18. *Straits Times*, 28 May 1971.
19. *New York Times*, 29 May 1971.
20. Quoted in Seow, *The Media Enthralled*, 92.
21. *Straits Times*, 11 June 1971.
22. *Hansard*, Parliamentary Debates, 26 March 1981, col. 1284.
23. *Straits Times*, 2 February 1978.
24. Seow, *The Media Enthralled*, 119.
25. Pang Cheng Lian, "Singapore—Selective Justice," *Newsweek* (Asia edition), 11 November 1974.
26. Quoted in Seow, *The Media Enthralled*, 113.
27. *London Times*, 18 March 1977.
28. Quoted in Seow, *The Media Enthralled*, 114.
29. "Union Chief Sides with the State," *Far Eastern Economic Review*, 7 May 1976; "Countering the Communist Sinister Conspiracy," *Far Eastern Economic Review*, 7 May 1976.
30. "Jeyaratnam's Challenge," *Asian Wall Street Journal*, 17 October 1985.
31. *First Report of the Committee of Privileges, Complaints of Allegations of Executive Interference in the Judi-*

ciary, Parliamentary No. 3 of 1987, 21 January 1987, D483 et seq.

32. *Far Eastern Economic Review*, 4 February 1988 (letter).
33. Derek Davies, "A Ban by Any Other Name," *Far Eastern Economic Review*, 7 January 1988, 10 (editorial).
34. "Silencing the Dissenters: Prime Minister Lee Restricts the Opposition's Maneuvering Room," *Time* (Asia edition), 8 September 1986.
35. *Time*, 15 September 1986.
36. *Time*, 27 October 1986.
37. Stephen Duthie, "Singapore Exchange Puzzles Financiers: Mixed Signals Cloud Proposed Bourse's Aim of Spurring Small Firms," *Asian Wall Street Journal*, 12-13 December 1986, 1, 6.
38. Quoted in Seow, *The Media Enthralled*, 149.
39. Quoted in ibid., 155.
40. Lisa Beyer, "A Distortion of Facts, You Say," *Asiaweek*, 27 September 1987.
41. "Govt Must Defends Its Turf When Religion Intrudes," *Straits Times*, 17 August 1987, 15; "Lee States His Case," *Far Eastern Economic Review*, 12 October 1989, 15-17.
42. Michael Malik, "New Light on Detentions," *Far Eastern Economic Review*, 17 December 1987, 28.
43. *Wall Street Journal*, 11 February 1991; 27 March 1991.
44. *New York Times*, 31 March 1991 (editorial).
45. Bernard Levin, "The Law Grossly Misused," *London Times*, 19 June 1989, 16. Levin followed up this article with two more—"A Lively Trade in Vilification," *London Times*, 24 August 1989, and "New Martyrs to Lee's Tyranny," *London Times*, 12 April 1990.
46. *Business Times* (Singapore), 29 June 1993.
47. "Pssst, Wanna See a Statistic?," *The Economist*, 20 June 1993.
48. "Singapore Prosecutions," *The Economist*, 10 July 1993 (Abdul Aziz Mahmood letter), 6.
49. "Singapore Prosecutions," *The Economist*, 10 July 1993 (Jeyaretnam letter), 6.
50. "Singapore, cont," *The Economist*, 7 August 1993, 34 (Abdul Aziz Mahmood letter).
51. "A Singapore Saga," *The Economist*, 7 August 1993, 34.
52. Philip Bowring, "The Claims About `Asian Values' Don't Usually Bear Scrutiny," *International Herald Tribune*, 2 August 1994.
53. Christopher Lingle, "The Smoke over Parts of Asia Obscures Some Profound Concerns," *International Herald Tribune*, 7 October 1994.
54 Quoted in Seow, *The Media Enthralled*, 174.
55. Reporters Without Borders does the rating. See "Press Freedom Index," *wikipedia.com*. Accessed 18 January 2014.
56. Garry Rodan, "Singapore in 2004: Long-Awaited Leadership Transition," *Asian Survey*, XLV (2005): 141.
57. Tan Chong Kee. "The Canary and the Crow: Sintercom and the State Tolerability Index." In *Renaissance Singapore? Economy, Culture, and Politics*, ed. Kenneth Paul Tan (Singapore: Singapore University Press, 2007).

58. Cherian George, *Contentious Journalism: Towards Democratic Discourse in Malaysia and Singapore* (Seattle: University of Washington Press, 2006).
59. Garry Rodan, "'Vibrant and Cosmopolitan' Without Political Pluralism," *Asian Survey*, XLVI (2006): 181.
60. The following paragraphs are mainly based on Human Rights Watch, "Singapore UPR Submission," 18 October 2010. See also Narayanan Ganesan, "Singapore in 2009: Structuring Politics, Priming the Economy, and Working the Neighborhood," *Asian Survey*, L (2010): 253-289.
61. Rodan, "Singapore in 2004: Long-Awaited Leadership Transition," *Asian Survey*, XLV (2005): 142; Rodan, "'Vibrant and Cosmopolitan' Without Political Pluralism," 182.
62. Ibid.

6

The Judiciary
Francis T. Seow

In the waning days of the Lim Yew Hock government (1956-1959), the usual Friday morning crush of lawyers milled outside the chief justice's chambers, awaiting their turn to appear on their respective motions before the chief justice, an expatriate. Standing aloof from the chattering crowd was "Harry" Lee Kuan Yew, secretary-general of the increasingly vociferous left-wing People's Action Party (PAP), whose political fortunes brooked fair at the forthcoming watershed general elections. When a lawyer approached him, fawning upon Lee that he would fain be the next chief justice when Singapore attained self-government, he was rebuffed with the chilly reply that the next chief justice would be appointed by him. As events turned out, it was no idle boast, for he became prime minister[1] of the new—and durable—PAP government, whose prerogative powers included advising Singapore's president on appointments of the chief justice and other judges.

One of Lee's first official acts was the designation of Justice Wee Chong Jin, a relatively recent recruit from the bar to the high court bench, as chief justice. Wee's industry and political acuity had recommended themselves to Lee. In so doing, he ignored the claims of seniority and experience, and set in train the gradual investment of the Singapore judiciary.

The judiciary, a bulwark between citizen and state that can play a consequential role in the affairs of a nation, often sets the ultimate seal of legitimacy on controversial policies and actions of the state by its decisions. Governments, therefore, try to ensure that persons who are called upon to make these weighty decisions understand the purpose of controverted legislative acts and policies. The PAP government is no exception, also trying to ensure that judicial aspirants, who are screened for loyalty and political correctness, are not unmindful of the honor which has been bestowed on them. Although the PAP government recognizes the role of the judiciary in the body politic, it no longer sees the courts as a check on the balance of power in the traditional sense but rather as an important instrument for the prolongation of PAP's political longevity. In the present chapter, I intend to document the thesis that the courts, in serving political objectives, are no longer independent organs of government in Singapore.

The Jury Is Hung

The century-old jury system was decidedly in the way. In the words of David Saul Marshall, Singapore's first chief minister, a panel of seven men and women—good and true—could be "an obstruction to the exercise of absolute power by the executive."[2] Jurors, at best an unknown quantity by their uncertain composition, could not be relied upon for predictability. Therefore, the jury system had to go, even though—as the prime minister himself conceded—it had worked "reasonably well."[3] Juries had withstood the test of time since they were introduced into Singapore as early as 1823, consisting of "either five Europeans, or four Europeans and three respectable natives."[4]

In 1963, using merger with Malaya as a pretext, Prime Minister Lee Kuan Yew claimed that the partial abolition of juries brought Singapore into line with the Malayan judicial system.[5] Notwithstanding, Marshall led the objections from the bar, whose strenuous opposition was carefully muted in the nation's news media. The minister for law assured the legislative assembly that there was no intention to abolish the jury system completely.[6] As a sop to the bar, jury trials were retained for capital offenses only.

In 1969, Lee decided that it was time to abolish the jury system altogether. The same pretext, however, could not be used, as Singapore was no longer a state within the Federation of Malaysia and, furthermore, the jury system was still in vogue there. The gravamen of the charge against the jury system on this occasion was that it was an "Anglo-Saxon concept which had no relevance to Asia," and "completely alien to Asians." By the same token, Singapore's entire legal system was, to borrow the prime minister's words, a "foreign implantation."[7] Once again, Marshall spearheaded the Law Society's opposition, labeling the final abolition as "the last nail being driven into the coffin of our basic freedoms."[8] It was essentially a legal storm in PAP's teacup. The mass media, cowed by the Essential Information (Control of Publications and Safeguarding of Information) Regulations of 1966, did not engage in any serious debate. Thus, a judicial system in good working order for nearly 150 years was unceremoniously consigned into legal history.[9]

The prime minister proposed that jury trials be replaced by trials by three judges, an innovation that would be more efficient and would better serve the interests of justice, as issues of law and fact would be sifted and determined by trained legal professionals, not easily influenced by extraneous considerations. But, because of the shortage of judicial manpower, the proposed number was eventually reduced to two judges, who, if they were unable to reach a unanimous decision as to the guilt of an accused person, might acquit or discharge or order a retrial before another court; or, if they agreed, convict on any lesser offense on the same facts. In proposing the abolition of trial by jury, the personable minister for law, E. W. Barker, tried to allay public fears, by stressing that it was "inconceivable that the government would 'stoop so low' as to influence the judges, who by virtue of our constitution are in fact fully independent."[10]

Even this minimal safeguard of two judges was removed in April 1992, when a change in the law whittled trials down to a single judge. Borrowing the words of his predecessor that it was a "logical conclusion" to amendments begun in 1960, Shanmugam Jayakumar, then minister for law, explained that the change was being brought about at the instance of the new chief justice with the concurrence of the other judges "to reduce delays and avoid 'the ugly and unacceptable risk' that an innocent person might spend several years in prison before he was *acquitted* by the court" (emphasis added).[11] As a result of the change, it was claimed that the backlog of cases had been drastically reduced—"doubling the rate of disposal of capital trials."[12] Another procedural right of an accused person was lost under the guise of speedy justice and efficiency. Thus, at the ceremonial opening of the 1995 new legal year, the chief justice perorated:

> We now have reached the stage when criminal cases can be disposed by the high court in about six months. Criminal appeals are disposed of by the court of appeal in about six months. And condemned prisoners can be disposed of by the prison authorities in about six months.[13]

At this point in his peroration, the audience of lawyers hissed, which startled him, who belatedly realized that his audience was furious. When does efficiency end and callousness begin?

Sanctions for Judicial Independence

The PAP government inherited from the colonial administration a legal and judicial service that was responsible, inter alia, for appointments, promotions, and transfers of legal and judicial officers inter se. But somehow the word "judicial" was lost in the shuffle of the pack. Be that as it may, although legal and subordinate judicial officers were interchangeable, the British administrators were slow in transferring officers across the legal spectrum, a convention that they observed with their customary finesse, evoking no outcry or resentment whenever transfers were effected.

This convention was, however, brought into sharp relief in 1986, with the sudden transfer of Senior District Judge Michael Khoo, one of the ablest and intellectually honest judges to grace the bench, to the attorney general's chambers. The transfer followed his acquittal of Joshua Benjamin Jeyaretnam, the abrasive opposition Workers' Party member of parliament, and, more significantly, Lee Kuan Yew's political bête noire,[14] on all charges save one—financial impropriety. From being the respected head of the subordinate judiciary, Khoo overnight became a mere digit within the attorney general's chambers. The prosecution appealed the decision of acquittal, and Chief Justice Wee allowed the appeal, with the unusual direction for it to be heard before another district judge.[15] Jeyaretnam's application for the retrial to be heard before a high court judge, which would have enabled him in law to pursue the anticipated adverse decision up to the British Privy Council, was pointedly refused.[16] At the re-hearing, Jeyaretnam was predictably found guilty and convicted. He appealed against the conviction and sentence to the high court, which dismissed his appeal but varied the sentence of three months' imprisonment to one month plus a fine that was so high as to disqualify him from sitting in parliament.[17] At the appeal, Chief Justice Wee warned Jeyaretnam's counsel against casting "serious imputations of bias against the appellate judge without a supporting affidavit."[18]

Consequent upon the dismissal of Jeyaretnam's appeal against the convictions, the Law Society duly proceeded to disbar him, a decision that was subsequently upheld by the chief justice.[19] It will be seen below that the chief justice featured prominently in the Jeyaretnam epic, a singular fact that later disturbed the Privy Council, Singapore's last court of appeal in London.

Executive Interference

Jeyaretnam, meanwhile, alleged in parliament that Khoo's transfer in the circumstances had caused "public disquiet," implying that it had been motivated by political considerations, which he later expanded to include both the chief justice and the attorney general as being "beholden" to the prime minister for having extended their respective appointments beyond their legal retirement age.[20] In a rancorous parliamentary debate, it emerged that Khoo's transfer was not a "routine departmental transfer," as claimed. The prime minister nevertheless asserted that there were "good grounds" warranting his transfer, for Khoo had allegedly committed several errors—six factual mistakes and two in law—in the questioned judgment.[21] Measured by this strict standard, the chief justice, too, should have been transferred when the Privy Council subsequently found that he had erred badly and reversed his fateful decision.

A commission of inquiry into Jeyaretnam's allegations of executive interference in the subordinate judiciary was set up, with T. Sampanther Sinnathuray as sole commissioner. The latter's notoriety as a pro-establishment judge was further fueled when the attorney general branded him as "Slippery Sam," among other sobriquets.[22] Because of certain procedural disagreements with the commissioner, Jeyaretnam withdrew from participation, but persisted in his allegations elsewhere. Nonetheless, according to Sinnathuray's report, there was no truth in the claims: "The wholly unfounded allegations of Mr. Jeyaretnam were scandalous statements that should never have been made."[23] When Jeyaretnam then filed a motion asking parliament to reject the report, the matter was referred to a parliamentary committee of privileges, where the outcome was never in doubt.[24] Parliament, under the absolute control of PAP, resolved that Jeyaretnam was guilty of contempt of the committee and of parliament, and fined him S$1,000.

In addition, he was found guilty of contempt not only of publishing five offending newsletters relating to the committee proceedings, and fined S$5,000 for each,[25] but also of authoring an article on the same topic in the party newspaper, *The Hammer*, and fined S$5,000 for each, as editor and publisher.[26] Jeyaretnam refused to pay. The attorney general on behalf of the government sued him and obtained summary judgment of the total sum plus costs. Jeyaretnam then appealed to the high court, which dismissed his appeal.[27]

The End of Privy Council Appeal

Meanwhile, Jeyaretnam had appealed the disbarment to the Judicial Committee of the Privy Council, which roundly castigated the chief justice and the Singapore courts for their legal reasoning, and allowed the appeal in resonant terms:

> Their Lordships have to record their deep disquiet that by a series of misjudgments the appellant [Jeyaretnam] and his co-accused Wong [Hong Toy] have suffered a grievous injustice. They have been fined, imprisoned and publicly disgraced for offences of which they were not guilty. The appellant, in addition, had been deprived of his seat in Parliament and disqualified for a year from practicing his profession.[28]

This was the selfsame Judicial Committee of the Privy Council that Prime Minister Lee in 1967 waxed lyrical as the acme of Singapore's judicial independence, when cautioning successive governments against interfering with its status in the judicial infrastructure:

> I can only express the hope that faith in the judicial system will never be diminished, and I am sure it will not, *so long as we allow a review of the judicial processes that takes place here in some other tribunal where obviously undue influence cannot be brought to bear. As long as governments are wise enough to leave alone the rights of appeal to some superior body outside Singapore, then there must be a higher degree of confidence in the integrity of our judicial process. This is most important.*[29] (emphasis added)

Resort to the Privy Council was also extolled in 1986 by Minister for Law Jayakumar during the debate on Khoo's transfer. In a blunt reference to Jeyaretnam's series of legal failures, Jayakumar dismissed Jeyaretnam's remarks as the "jaundiced view of a person who has not had satisfaction in the courts as he would have liked," with the reminder: "How many countries are there in the world that he can refer to where there are appeals to the Privy Council in criminal and civil cases . . . other than Singapore? That is the litmus test of our judicial system's independence."[30]

The judgment of the Privy Council reflected severely on the integrity of the Singapore judiciary and was seen by many as solemn confirmation of unspoken misgivings about its independence. Any other government, to use an Americanism, would have rolled with the punch; but this is a government whose sensitivity to the slightest criticism is proverbial. As long as the Privy Council handed down judgments supportive of the prime minister and his government, its status at the apex of the judicial infrastructure was inviolable. With the crucial decision regarding Jeyaretnam, the Privy Council sealed its own fate. In 1989, ignoring his previous laudatory rhetoric, Jayakumar moved in parliament at the behest of the prime minister—who in the circumstances assumed an understandably passive posture—for the abolition of appeals to the Privy Council, which he decried as being "interventionist" and "out of touch" with local conditions—a decrial questionable both in law and in taste.[31]

The Law Society met in emergency session, but was precluded by a bizarre law from publicly discussing this momentous change in the legal system.[32] So, the Law Society took out a paid advertisement in the local media, noting its concern at the proposed abolition "as unwarranted and contrary to the interest of justice."[33] The Society's action underscored the depths to which the prime minister and his PAP government had debased the legal profession, and, by necessary extension, the judiciary itself, lest it be overlooked that it is ordinarily from qualified members of the bar that the judicial benches are filled.

Asked about the abolition of the Privy Council during the controversial conferment of academic honors on him at the 1995 convocation ceremony at Williams College, Goh Chok Tong, who had succeeded to the premiership in 1990, responded that, in allowing Jeyaretnam's appeal against his disbarment, the Privy Council had "gone outside its prescribed role" and was "playing politics."[34] It was forsooth a disgrace, as well as a willful contempt of Singapore's own superior court. But, as Juvenal said, "Quis custodiet ipsos custodes?" (Who guards the guardians?) Implicit in Goh's statement was the admission that the PAP government could no longer afford the hard political currency of a free and independent court.

The Jeyaretnam case is perhaps unsurpassed for the pathetic attempts by the Singapore courts to stretch the law to fit the facts—a difficult attempt in the best of times—, highlighting the grotesque contortions that the politically corrupt judiciary went through to rid a political irritant to the prime minister and his government. The case shows the misuse of the law in advancing the agenda and interests of the ruling political party.[35]

In order to assuage a growing public perception that the judiciary was inclined towards the executive, the chief justice was perforce to publicly address this matter:

> It is our responsibility to let there be no shadow of doubt whatsoever that we are committed to these two principles—the total commitment of the judiciary in Singapore to dispensing justice according to law, and to upholding the independence of the judiciary—and to dispel as forcefully as lies within our power any attempt from any quarter to cast doubt that these two principles are being adhered to here.[36]

There was, alas, a vast chasm separating the precept from the practice. Nonetheless, this judicial protestation climaxed the events of the troublous 1970s, from the enforced closure of newspapers to the arbitrary arrests and incarcerations of their owners and practitioners on spurious and questionable grounds, amid mounting allegations of violations of human rights, culminating in the withdrawal of the People's Action Party from the Socialist International (to avoid the indignity of expulsion), segueing into numerous detentions of persons said to be Communists, pro-Communists, or allied with Euro-Communists and other colorful labels—in all of which the courts rendered judgments favorable to the PAP administration.

Similarly, in 1977, Attorney General Tan Boon Teik sought to show that the administration of justice was impartial by stressing the supervisory jurisdiction of the courts:

> Your lordships' impartial and unbiased administration of the law in all matters, particularly in respect of those matters requiring strict observance of the rules of natural justice, and in respect of matters where the exercise of administrative discretion has been challenged, is the cornerstone upon which our system of justice has been constructed. Those charged with the functions of the Government, in all their wide diversity, know full well that ultimately there can be recourse to these courts to correct irregularities and injustices in governmental administration. *As in all countries where the rule of law prevails, it is your*

lordships' exercise of the court's supervisory jurisdiction that provides one of the most important safe-guards against the arbitrary exercise of power.[37] (emphasis added)

Judicial Accommodation to the Executive

In accentuating the supervisory powers of the courts as the capstone of democracy, Attorney General Tan Boon Teik overlooked the egregious fact that in 1971 he argued on behalf of the state in the habeas corpus applications of Lee Mau Seng and three other employees of *Nan Yang Siang* Pau (a privately owned Chinese language newspaper) that orders of detention under the Internal Security Act were not justiciable.[38] Notwithstanding the inconsistencies and contradictions in the official statements, the court could "not look behind the orders," and "inquire into the reasons why and wherefore a detention order is made. This is an executive act." The court willingly abdicated its judicial responsibility in favor of officialdom rather than the aggrieved suppliants, even though the current of legal authorities was beginning to run their way.

Allowing for Tan's remarkable amnesia, the rich situational irony could not possibly have escaped the attorney general when he was later called upon to draft the amending legislation depriving the courts of their supervisory jurisdiction, which was—in his own words— "one of the most important safeguards against the exercise of arbitrary power." A principled attorney general would have resigned his office in protest. But there was not a squeak of protest from him or the complacent judiciary, save for some protesting squeals from a frightened legal profession. As a result, habeas corpus applications are now largely legal history in Singapore.

Yet another instance of judicial accommodation occurred in 1987, when twenty-two young social activists were arrested under the Internal Security Act, which allows preventive detention on grounds of national security. The twenty-two were accused of being involved in a dangerous Marxist conspiracy to subvert the PAP government through violence and to replace it with a Marxist state. They were released only after they made ritualistic television confessions. But eight of them were re-arrested after they alleged that their confessions had been coerced. In the ensuing *habeas corpus* proceedings, they were represented by Anthony Lester, QC (now Lord Lester of Herne Hill), and Geoffrey Robertson, QC. In the face of their arguments, supported by compelling modern English and other legal authorities, Singapore's court of appeal had perforce to allow the appeal, but it did so on procedural rather than substantive grounds, thus enabling the government to hurriedly amend the constitution and the relevant laws, and at the same time re-order their detention.[39]

Supremely confident of the reliability of his judiciary, the prime minister used the courts as a legal weapon to intimidate, bankrupt, or cripple the political opposition, while ventilating his political agenda. Distinguishing himself in a caseful of legal suits commenced against dissidents and detractors for alleged defamation in Singapore courts, he has won them all, as Chapter 5 by Derek Davies so eloquently reports.

Yet another egregious example of judicial accommodation is *Re Dow Jones Publishing Company (Asia) Inc. Application*, wherein the court of appeal deliberately delayed a decision, thereby denying the appellant the opportunity of pursuing an appeal to the Privy Council. Counsel for the appellant pleaded with the court to rule on the application and to give its decision later, but the court could not be hurried. As a result, the appellant lost the right to appeal to the Privy Council. The appellant tried one last desperate course by petitioning the Privy Council in London for special leave to appeal, but their lordships, in dismissing the petition, said,

> Their lordships understand the petitioner's sense of grievance that, after the appeal from the judgment of Sinnathuray, J., had been argued and at a time when it was known that the [Judicial Committee of the Privy Council Amendment] Act of 1989 would shortly come into operation, the court of appeal in Singapore did not accede to an invitation to give their decision promptly, if necessary giving their reasons later, which would have enabled the petitioner to take advantage of the transitional provisions in the Act of 1989.[40]

Those gentle words of reproach spoke volumes for a free and independent judiciary.

"Contract" Judges

High court judges are appointed from within the legal and judicial service and among qualified members of the bar by the president on the advice of the prime minister after consultation with the chief justice. But, under the Presidential Elections Act of 1991, the Singapore president may now veto such key service appointments as judges of the supreme court. In any case, the judges hold their appointment until the age of sixty-five years and thereafter at the will of the president. For many years, retiring high court judges have had their appointments extended on contract for short periods at a time and, in some cases, from year to year because it was said there were no suitably qualified members from the bar.

Needless to say, the practice of judges on contract, renewable at the will of the prime minister, is not conducive to judicial independence. And yet, curiously enough, soon after the retirement of Chief Justice Wee, the courts were filled by judges drawn from the bar—that same talent pool, which he was periodically pleased to complain, was deficient of talents, experience, and/or character.

In 1991, Prime Minister Lee Kuan Yew, who once boasted that the persons he appoints know what is expected of them, selected Yong Pung How, a banker who had not practiced law for close to two decades, as chief justice. Yong's claim to this illustrious position was that he is a loyal crony.[41] During an hour-long defense in parliament, in response to my criticism of the appointment,[42] he delved into bathetic nostalgia—recalling his student's days at Cambridge University when his friend, the future chief justice, lent him lecture notes enabling him, a late arrival at Cambridge, to catch up with his law studies; his co-mate's personal wealth and magnitude of annual income as banker; and his personal attributes, amongst which was a fine judicial temperament that rang somewhat hollow and contrived.[43] Canadian Glen How, a Queen's Counsel who in 1996 argued before the chief justice the appeal against the conviction of his client of being a member of Jehovah Witnesses, a proscribed society, would probably be all amazement to hear of his judicial temperament. The language was crass and the temperament far from fine.[44]

Strategic Case Assignments

Judgments of the appellate court must be unanimous, delivered in a collective judgment on behalf of all other judges by a single judge detailed by the chief justice beforehand. As in the body politic, no dissension is countenanced lest a perception is created of disunity within the judicial ranks. Cases are allocated among the judges by the registrar of the supreme court rather than drawn by lots or channeled to special divisions of the court. Thus, it is not unusual to find a particular judge, such as T. S. Sinnathuray, being commonly assigned to sensitive cases—and with predictable results. Judges known for impartiality, independence, and strength of character have never been assigned to such cases.

The situation is replicated in the subordinate courts. As with his counterpart in the supreme court, the registrar fixes cases and, where specially instructed, ensures that certain cases are directed to selected judges for infallibility of decisions.

My income tax case in 1988 provides a superb illustration. After a date for mention of the case had been fixed in open court, and defense counsel exited the court building, an embarrassed registrar canceled the date on higher instructions. Ignoring the fullness of the court calendar, the case was brought forward for trial over strenuous objections of counsel, who had been summoned to return to court in order to fit into certain plans for the forthcoming general election, the date of which the prime minister had secretly fixed but not yet announced. As the trial would otherwise have taken place long after the general election was over, he decided to use the fact of the trial as critical election fodder in order to put a damper on the growing groundswell of public support for me. Indeed, during the election, voters were warned that it was "useless" to vote me, as, if elected, I would have to vacate my seat in December after my conviction for tax evasion.[45] What an amazing display of the government's faith in the infallibility of their judges!

Nevertheless, counsel applied to the high court for an urgent revision of the registrar's decision. After an incredible reluctance on the part of a scared supreme court registry staff, counsel managed—after much persuasion and reassurance on its legal propriety—to prevail upon them to accept the motion papers. By a strange coincidence, the emergency judge for that day, the ineluctable Sinnathuray, was not available. After waiting an indeterminate length of time within the registry precincts, it became painfully obvious to me that the judge was not overly anxious to hear counsel on the motion. It was suggested that counsel leave the registry and await word elsewhere of the judge's availability. No word came through that whole day. Upon anxious inquiries the next morning, counsel was tersely informed that the ever-reliable Sinnathuray had dismissed the application summarily, even though counsel had indicated readiness to argue it at a moment's notice.[46]

My case illustrates only some of the legal obstacles that beset perceived oppositionists, critics, and dissidents who seek justice in the courts. The manipulation of court diaries to defer or bring forward cases already fixed for mention or hearing in order to suit the prosecution's hidden agenda is well known and is often a matter of dissatisfaction at the bar.

Judicial Salaries or Judicial Bribes?

Adequate economic monthly salaries payable to judges have long been recognized as a condition conducive to a free and independent judiciary. The monthly salary that the PAP government pays its judges has much method in its generosity, what many would well consider astronomical amounts. High court judges receive S$253,000 per annum plus a minimum bonus of three month's salary besides such other perks and privileges as a motor car and a government bungalow at economic rent. The chief justice receives S$347,400 million a year besides an official residence (or an housing allowance in lieu thereof), a chauffeur-driven car, and other handsome perks and privileges.[47] Indeed, the chief justice of Singapore receives more than the combined stipends of the Lord Chancellor of England, the Chief Justice of United States Supreme Court, and the chief justice of Canada. As a Canadian silk (Queen's Counsel) pointedly queried: "Is this kind of money a salary or an income of permanent bribery? How can any of them [the judges] afford to disagree with a government that treats them with such a largesse?"[48]

To ensure that judges appreciate the source of the largesse, the PAP government enacted the Judges' Remuneration Act of 1994, providing that "pensionable salaries of the chief justice, every judge of appeal and every other judge of the supreme court" shall be paid as the minister of finance may from time to time determine. This radical, retrogressive change in the law ensures that such payments would no longer rest on future resolutions of parliament, recalling vividly to mind a popular chestnut, "He who pays the piper calls the tune."

Judges, thus, know on which side their bread is buttered. When the government and/or ministers are concerned in a legal dispute, judges bend themselves backwards to accommodate them. In so-called defamation cases, judges award government officials incredible amounts in damages, as may be seen in the case against the *International Herald Tribune*, in which an unprecedented S$950,000 was awarded in damages against the defendants to three cabinet ministers: S$350,000 to Goh Chok Tong and S$300,000 each to Lee Kuan Yew and his son, excluding costs at S$400,000-S$500,000. The idea that government officials could possibly lose a case is so fanciful that it could be dismissed out of hand. Which judge could be so reckless or foolhardy to award a decision against the top officials of Singapore?

Courts for the Rich

Courts in a democracy, which Singapore professes to be, should be accessible to all litigants—from the rich and powerful to the most indigent of persons. Addressing the subordinate courts' fourth annual workplan seminar in 1995, Chief Justice Yong Pung How stressed that accessibility must be free of "economic or procedural barriers." He declared, "Access to courts should be not only for those who have legal representation but also for all litigants, victims, witnesses and relatives of litigants and the general public"[49] However, in 1993, ostensibly to ensure that trials would not be "unduly long," he introduced a graduated hearing fee scheme beyond the first day of hearing, disavowing it as a "fiscal measure." "The courts," he once said, "will have to be run as efficiently as the best businesses."[50] He considered hearing fees as necessary because "court time is a scarce resource, and others should not be denied early access just because a minority hog to themselves a wholly disproportionate share of the available court time."[51]

As a result, a litigant's day in court has become a more precise metaphor. As of 1998, save for a limited class of actions, a fee of S$1,500 is imposed for the first four hearing days in the high court after the first day, S$2,000 from the sixth to the tenth day, and S$3,000 per day thereafter. A flat rate of S$3,000 is payable after the first day in the court of appeal. In the subordinate courts, it is S$500 for district courts and S$250 for magistrate's courts, respectively, after the first day.[52]

Thus, litigation has become an expensive exercise, open only to those with deep pockets to prosecute or defend their claims in court, in spite of the chief justice's protestation:

> An argument has been made that access to justice may be denied to those who may not have enough means to pay the hearing fees. A review of all cases in the High Court in the past two years which have taken more than two days has shown this argument to be specious.[53]

Except for hearings before the supreme court, where interpreters are now supplied gratis, litigants who use interpreters in lower courts as of 1998 had to pay S$150 for each day of hearing.[54] The registrar explained the fee as necessary to regulate the deployment of interpreters, optimize their usage, and "to stop abuse." Because witnesses, "who are proficient in the English language are known to choose to speak in another language or dialect so as to have more time to contemplate the question and formulate an answer. . . , a trial would take much longer to conclude than it should."[55] Consequently, the use of interpreters is no longer a right but a privilege. In his boundless zeal to keep pace with the PAP government in business efficiency, the chief justice ignored his own words that, "Courts are, after all, meant to serve the public."[56]

Conclusion

One court case illustrates the parlous state of the judiciary in Singapore—*Public Prosecutor v Tan Wah Piow* (1975). Tan, a third-year architectural student and president of the National University of Singapore Students Union (USSU) and the USSU Retrenchment Research Centre, was charged, together with two employees of American Marine (Ng Wah Leng and Yap Kim Hong), with rioting inside the premises of the Pioneer Industries Employees' Union (PIEU), a government-controlled trade union, whose general secretary was Phey Yew Kok, a member of parliament and rising star on the PAP firmament. Phey was also president of the National Trades Union Congress, which had—and has—strong symbiotic ties with the PAP government. The USSU became interested in a labor dispute in a PIEU-member trade union as part of its Retrenchment Research Center project, which gravely upset the PIEU management and, in particular, its general secretary.

The trial was partisan justice at its ugliest before the ambitious T. S. Sinnathuray, who kept Tan and his co-accused on a choke-leash, while he bent over grotesquely backwards in favor of the prosecution. Tan's application for an adjournment to enable John Platts-Mills, QC—who had already been specially admitted to the Singapore bar to represent him at the trial—to travel to Singapore for the purpose was twice denied by the trial judge. Vital defense witnesses were arrested on the morning of the trial and deported.

The defendants claimed that the riot within, and damage to, the premises had been fabricated by Phey Yew Kok, who later absconded from Singapore for criminal breach of trust of a large amount of union funds. But the defendants were not allowed to submit this evidence at the trial, as indeed other matters that they considered crucial to their case, while the solicitor general was free to range over irrelevant matters. Concerned at the judge's selective recordings of the trial, Tan applied for the proceedings to be tape-recorded which, given the outrageous manner in which the trial was being conducted, was understandably denied, for it would have captured unmistakably the Gilbert and Sullivan bathos. The judge for his part made no bones of what the outcome of the proceedings would be. His periodic ejaculations ("Forget about public interest!" "Forget about justice!" "Forget about a fair trial!"), albeit vented in exasperation to Tan's urgent applications or protestations to his rulings, punctuated the proceedings, setting a leitmotif that became a grim reality. All three were assuredly found guilty, and convicted. Tan was sentenced to one year's imprisonment, and his co-accused to one month's imprisonment each. When asked whether he had anything to say in mitigation of sentence, Tan congratulated the judge on his performance and "future promotion to the high court." The judge then threatened him with contempt of court for the nth and last time, and ordered him to be removed from the court immediately. Shortly afterwards, T. S. Sinnathuray was promoted to the high court. Disillusioned at the "brand of justice" they had received, they decided against the futility of "shopping for justice in Singapore."

An Australian Queen's Counsel, Frank Galbally, who observed the trial proceedings at the request of the Australian Union of Students, reported:

> In Australia, the case would be laughed out of court . . . the evidence and procedure . . . would, in my opinion, have aborted any trial in Australia . . . [The three accused] did not get a fair trial. There are no juries in Singapore and this speaks for itself. In my opinion, it is just a political trial.[57]

The experience of an English Queen's Counsel in a 1995 criminal trial in Singapore provides a concluding perspective on the Singapore judiciary. Alun Jones, QC, represented Rajan Pillai, a well-known Indian businessman, who was charged, inter alia, with twenty-nine counts of fraud said to exceed S$13 million in value. After three weeks of conducting his defense, Jones discharged himself from further self-representation, "for the first time in 23 years' practice." He described the judicial proceedings as "a travesty of a trial" and a "perversion of a judicial process." The trial judge did "not have the will, character, or independence to control the court effectively," and displayed a "craven attitude" toward the prosecution. In discharging himself, he explained that he did not wish his presence to be cited by the Singapore government as evidence of the "fairness of the trial," and, leaving the trial "with Pillai's full support, gave him a written statement of his reasons."[58]

The New York City Bar Association, after a fact-finding mission to Singapore led by the late Robert B. McKay, former dean of the New York University Law School, observed in a weighty report, inter alia, that Singapore has

> a government that has been willing to decimate the rule of law for the benefit of its political interests. Lawyers have been cowed to passivity, judges are kept on a short leash, and the law has been manipulated so that gaping holes exist in the system of restraints on government action toward the individual. . . . Any U.S. venture contemplating business in Singapore or with a Singapore company is likely to encounter a wide variety of enterprises in which the government has an economic interest. If a dispute arises with such an enterprise, the U.S. company faces the prospect of a lawsuit before Singapore's judiciary. The same forces which have led that judiciary to be sensitive to the PAP government's political interests would lead it to take account of its economic interests. . . . The only check on the Singapore judiciary is the prospect of ultimate appeal to the Privy Council in London.[59]

That report was published in October 1990. Since then, appeals to the Privy Council have been abolished, and the supervisory powers of the courts have been removed.

In fair conclusion, it should be mentioned that where the government or its ministers are not concerned or interested in disputes before the courts, or where the fair name of Singapore is not besmirched, Singapore judges are free to deliver judgments in accordance with the facts and the justice of the case. If they err in their judgment, the error stems almost entirely from considerations untainted by considerations of national politics.

Epilog (by Michael Haas)

As the last paragraph of Seow's essay indicates, the judicial system works admirably for nonpolitical cases.[60] In 2008, the Political and Economic Risk Consultancy survey rated Hongkong and Singapore as the best judicial systems in Asia. The Rule of Law Index by the World Justice Project gave the top rank in 2010 to Singapore for access to civil justice.

In 2006, "specialist judges" were appointed as judges of the subordinate courts as a pilot project. They are academics and members of the legal profession with specialized knowledge that many judges do not have.

In 2007, Francis Seow published a book-length version of this chapter in *Beyond Suspicion? The Singapore Judiciary.*[61] Very little has changed in the intervening years regarding politically sensitive court actions. The Association for Democracy in Singapore, founded in Melbourne, Australia, has continued to raise consciousness about the defects of the Singapore judiciary since its founding in 2003.

But a new development in criminal justice occurred after the terrorist attacks on the World Trade Center on 9/11/2001. Waves of thirty-six arrests of alleged Muslim terrorists occurred during 2001 and 2002 because Jamaah Islamiyah (JI) was designated as a terrorist organization because its apparent goal is to establish a Java-based Islamic state consisting of the present Brunei, Indonesia, Malaysia, Singapore, and the southern part of the Philippines. Although Muslim leaders in Singapore immediately condemned the 9/11 attack, in 2002 Zulfiker Mohammed Shariff, head of another Islamic organization, questioned on a website whether JI was a terrorist organization. After a week of government denunciations in the press, he was forced to quit the website.[62] Five more JI members were arrested in 2006-2007. In 2010, the government arrested practicioners of Falun Gong, the organization banned in China.

In 2008, true to form, the fine for defamation was upheld by an appeal by the Singapore Democratic Party in a proceeding in which three observers wore T-shirts displaying kangaroos in judicial garb. All three were arrested were fined for defamation as was the defense attorney, Gopalan Nair, for criticizing the ruling.[63]

Twenty-first century "terrorism" replaced twentieth century "communism" as the reason for arrests, preventive detention, and efforts by the government to recreate a siege scenario to justify Internet and press restrictions. In 2008, the Public Order Act empowered courts and the police to ban the appearance of any person in public outside their residence, the most sweeping restriction on individual liberty ever.

Notes

1. Unless otherwise indicated, the expression "prime minister" refers to "Harry" Lee Kuan Yew.
2. *Straits Times*, 16 December 1969.
3. Ibid.

4. C. B. Buckley, *An Anecdotal History of Old Times in Singapore 1819-1867* (Kuala Lumpur: University of Malaya Press, 1965).
5. Christopher Tremewan, *The Political Economy of Social Control in Singapore* (London: Macmillan, 1994).
6. *Hansard*, Legislative Assembly debates, cols. 568-569.
7. Quoted in Andrew Phang Boon Leong, "Jury Trial in Singapore and Malaysia: The Unmaking of a Legal In-stitution," *Malaya Law Review*, XXV (July 1983): 53.
8. *Straits Times*, 16 December 1969.
9. Interestingly enough, reference to the jury system resurfaced briefly in a letter to the editor from Professor Koh Kheng Lian as a result of the case of Ramachandran Suppiah who, after having spent five years in deten-tion, was acquitted of murder by a second court of appeal of five judges. He argued that, "If the clock could be turned back, I would have preferred the jury system. . . . Even though some . . . regarded jurors as incom-petent, what was completely overlooked was the jury system itself." *Straits Times Weekly Edition*, 11 No-vember 1992.
10. For a fuller discussion, see Phang, "Jury Trial in Singapore and Malaysia," 54.
11. *Straits Times Weekly Edition*, 21 March 1992.
12. "Chief Justice's Response: Opening of the Legal Year," 9 January 1993.
13. Quoted in Maggie O'Kane, "Eye of a Tiger," *The Guardian Weekly*, 20 May 1995.
14. Among the many colorful epithets were: "hustler," "skunk," "mangy dog," "charlatan," and "political riff-raff." *Hansard*, Parliamentary Debates, 19 March 1986, cols. 688-689, 720.
15. *Public Prosecutor v Wong Hong Toy & Anor; Wong Hong Toy & Anor v Public Prosecutor* [1986], 1 *Ma-layan Law Journal*, 133.
16. *Wong Hong Toy & Anor v Public Prosecutor* [1986], 1 *Malayan Law Journal*, 336.
17. *Wong Hong Toy & Anor v Public Prosecutor* [1988], 2 *Malayan Law Journal*, 553.
18. *Far Eastern Economic Review*, 28 January 1987.
19. *Wong Hong Toy & Anor v Public Prosecutor* [1988], 2 *Malayan Law Journal*, 553; *Re J. B. Jeyaretnam, An Advocate and Solicitor* [1988], 1 *Malayan Law Journal*, 353.
20. *Far Eastern Economic Review*, 14 August 1986.
21. *Hansard*, Parliamentary Debates, 29 July 1986, cols. 128-181.
22. Christopher Tremewan, *The Political Economy of Social Control in Singapore* (New York: St. Martin's Press, 1994); Tan Wah Piow, *Frame-Up: A Singapore Court on Trial* (Oxford: TWP Publishing, 1987).
23. *Cmd.* 12 (1986).
24. Committee of Privileges (First Report), *Parl.* 3 (1987).
25. Committee of Privileges (Second Report), *Parl.* 4 (1987).
26. Committee of Privileges (Fifth Report), *Parl.* 9 (1987).
27. [1988] 3 *Malayan Law Journal*, 465. Jeyaretnam appealed to the court of appeal, which dismissed the ap-peal. See *J. B. Jeyaretnam v Attorney General of Singapore* [1989], 1 *Malayan Law Journal*, 137.
28. *J. B. Jeyaretnam v Law Society of Singapore* [1988], 3 *Malayan Law Journal*, 425, 434.

29. *Hansard*, Parliamentary Debates, 15 March 1967, cols. 1294-1295.
30. *Hansard*, Parliamentary Debates, 10 January 1986, col. 718.
31. *Hansard*, Parliamentary Debates, 7 April 1989, cols. 24-29.
32. Legal Profession Act, Cap. 161, as amended.
33. *Straits Times*, 25 January 1989.
34. *Straits Times*, 18 September 1995.
35. For more information on the trials of J. B. Jeyaretnam, see Bernard Levin, "The Law Grossly Misused," *London Times*, 19 June 1989; see also John Mortimer, "Our Law in Their Hands: A Misuse of the Legal System in Singapore," *Daily Telegraph* (London), 3 January 1987.
36. [1977] 1 *Malayan Law Journal*, xx.
37. Ibidem.
38. *Lee Mau Seng v Minister for Home Affairs & Anor* [1971], 2 *Malayan Law Journal*, 137.
39. "*Chng Suan Tze v The Minister of Home Affairs & Ors* and Other Appeals," [1989] 1 *Malayan Law Journal*, 69.
40. *Dow Jones Publishing Co (Asia) Inc v Attorney General* [1989], 3 *Malayan Law Journal*, 321, 323-323. See also Francis T. Seow, *The Media Enthralled: Singapore Revisited*, (Boulder, CO: Lynne Rienner, 1997).
41. Upon the expiration of his term, he was reappointed for a five-year term so that "he could bring more changes to the legal system." *Straits Times*, 30 March 1996.
42. "The Rule of Law Is No Cliché in Singapore," *Williams College*, 15 September 1995.
43. *Straits Times*, 3 November 1995.
44. *Law Times*, VII (#26, 29 July—4 August 1996).
45. *Straits Times*, 2 September 1988.
46. Francis T. Seow, *To Catch a Tartar: A Dissident in Lee Kuan Yew's Prison* (New Haven, CT: Yale Southeast Asia Studies, Yale Center for International and Area Studies, 1994).
47. Figures on the current remuneration are from "Judicial Officers of the Republic of Singapore," *wikipedia.com*, accessed 18 January 2014. Higher figures were reported in the *Sunday Times*, 21 July 1996.
48. Personal communication from Glen How, QC.
49. *Straits Times*, 26 February 1995.
50. [1991] 12 *Singapore Law Review*, 16.
51. *Straits Times*, 2 April 1993.
52. The Law Society of Singapore, asked for updated information, has not replied.
53. "Chief Justice's Response: Opening of the Legal Year," 9 January 1993.
54. Information about the supreme court was obtained from its website (*app.supremecourt.gov.sg*), accessed 18 January 2014.
55. *Straits Times Weekly Edition*, 5 June 1993.
56. [1991] 12 *Singapore Law Review*, 18.
57. See Tan Wah Piow, *Frame-Up: A Singapore Court on Trial* (Oxford: TWP Publishing, 1987) and Tan Wah

Piow, *Let the People Judge: Confessions of the Most Wanted Person in Singapore* (Kuala Lumpur: Institute for Social Analysis, 1987).

58. "Who Killed Rajan Pillai?," *The Spectator*, 15 July 1995.
59. Beatrice S. Frank, Joseph C. Markowitz, Robert B. McKay, and Kenneth Roth, *The Decline in the Rule of Law in Singapore and Malaysia* (New York: Lawyers Committee for Human Rights, 1990).
60. The following statements are based on "Judicial System of Singapore," *wikipedia.com*. Accessed 18 January 2014.
61. The book was published by the Southeast Asian Studies unit at Yale University's Center for International and Area Studies.
62. Senia Febrica, "Securitizing Terrorism in Southeast Asia: Accounting for the Varying Responses of Singapore and Indonesia," *Asian Survey*, L (2010): 569-590.
63. Narayan Ganesan, "Singapore in 2008: A Few Highs and Lows While Bracing for the Future," *Asian Survey*, XLIX (2009): 213-219.

7

Foreign Policy
Richard A. Deck

The main objective of Singapore's foreign policy is the achievement of "comprehensive security" through the application of the Total Defense Doctrine. "Comprehensive security" encompasses traditional military security, as well as civil, economic, psychological, and social security. Each corresponding element of the Total Defense Doctrine is the responsibility of a specific ministry—the Ministry of Defence for military defense, the Ministry of Home Affairs for civil defense, the Ministry of Trade and Industry for economic defense, the Ministry of Information and the Arts for psychological defense, and the Ministry of Community Development for social defense. In the present chapter, I will indicate how the desire for comprehensive security arose and how it has been carried out, first in meeting threats from "Communism," then threats from other Southeast Asian countries, and later in lashing out against "the West."

Communist Threats

Singapore's earliest challenge, Communism, arose during the Emergency era (1948-1960), when the Malayan Communist Party (MCP) conducted an armed insurgency against colonial and (later) newly autonomous Singapore. At the apogee of its power, the MCP deployed 9,000 armed guerrillas throughout Malaya, a conflict that littered the peninsula and island with 11,000 dead.[1] Among the most traumatic incidents in Singapore were the labor strike and subsequent riots at the Hock Lee Bus Company in 1955; on three separate occasions, left-wing "mobs," more than 1,000 strong, fought "pitched battles" with the Singaporean police.[2] In October 1956, in a riot inspired by an MCP-influenced student group, some 13 Singaporeans were killed, 127 were injured, and over 1,000 were arrested.[3]

Singapore's attention next turned to the konfrontasi (confrontation) with Indonesia, whose leader Sukarno was under the influence of the Communist Party of Indonesia. In 1963, when the Federation of Malaysia was formed by adding Sabah, Sarawak, and Singapore to the previously independent Federation of Malaya, Indonesia began the "Crush Malaysia Campaign." At the first Malayan Socialist Conference that year, a coalition of six pro-MCP political parties expelled the People's Action Party (PAP) and adopted the following position of *Bintang Timor*, a pro-Communist Indonesian newspaper: "We are more in favor of merger with Indonesia than with Malaya."[4] Some thirty-seven bomb blasts dotted Singapore during 1963-1964, including such targets as water mains and the perimeter of the Istana (i.e., the seat of government, the "Palace").[5] On one occasion, Indonesian marine commandos actually landed in Singapore and committed acts of sabotage; a few of them were captured and subsequently hanged. The konfrontasi ended in 1965, when Sukarno fell from power. One reason why Singapore supported the formation of the Association of South-East Asian Nations (ASEAN) in 1967 was the hope that ASEAN would transform Indonesia into a nonthreatening subregional partner.

In 1975, when Communist movements triumphed in Indochina, Singapore perceived Vietnam as a serious threat. In light of declining American hegemony, Singapore turned to ASEAN as a way to strengthen subregional "resilience."[6] Singapore was less interested in establishing a cooperative relationship with Vietnam than two of its ASEAN partners, Malaysia and Indonesia, and later in 1978 Lee Kuan Yew argued that ASEAN should exploit the growing political rift between Vietnam and the Khmer Rouge government in Cambodia.[7] After Vietnamese troops entered Cambodia in 1978, drove out the Khmer Rouge in 1979, and remained in the country, Singaporean leaders were the most hawkish within ASEAN regarding the "Vietnamese threat,"[8] which they linked to the Soviet Union's invasion of Afghanistan as a forerunner of the Soviet Union's new "empire" in Asia and elsewhere.[9] Singapore also feared the "precedent" established by the Vietnamese for neighboring Indonesia and Malaysia,[10] and was the only ASEAN country that failed to endorse Indonesia's invasion and annexation of the former Portuguese colony of East Timor in 1975-1976.

During the 1980s, Singapore supported of the Coalition Government of Democratic Kampuchea (CGDK), which included the Khmer Rouge, as a bulwark against Vietnam's support for the People's Republic of Kampuchea in Phnom Penh. In 1981, a Working Group was formed, composed of top-echelon officials from the U.S. State Department and the foreign and defense ministries of Singapore, Malaysia, and Thailand. Weapons manufactured in Singapore were then sold to the various CGDK factions under the Working Group's auspices.[11] Michael Haas has asserted that Singapore's "obnoxious rhetoric" partially alienated its ASEAN partners Malaysia and Indonesia, because the continuation of the war increased China's power in Southeast Asia, contrary to the foreign policy objectives of the two Malay nations with substantial Chinese minorities.[12]

The "Threat from the North"

Given the history of openly manifested (and some merely perceived) subregional threats projected by Japan in the 1940s, Malaya in the 1950s and 1960s, Vietnam from the 1960s to the 1980s, China from the 1950s to the 1980s, and Malaysia in the 1980s, Singaporean foreign policy has been geared toward meeting the "threat from the north."[13] In responding to the "northern threat," one goal of Singaporean diplomacy has been the consummation of treaties that secure access to Malaysian water resources, such as the waterworks at Kota Tinggi and Scudai in Johore, Malaysia. To secure this north-south line of communications, entrepôt Singapore compensates for its resource-poor vulnerabilities with an ardent advocacy of "free trade" in international fora. Singapore has even sought to further secure its northern approaches by assisting its former adversary, the People's Republic of Vietnam. In the early 1990s, Senior Minister Lee Kuan Yew became an economic and political adviser to Vietnam (and China).

To meet the threat from the north by co-opting potential adversaries, Singapore has forged informal and semiformal security arrangements with other nations. Singapore trains its military in Australia, Bangladesh, Brunei, Indonesia, New Zealand, Taiwan, and the United States; it also participates in bilateral and trilateral military exercises with Australia, Brunei, Malaysia, New Zealand, the Philippines, Thailand, and the United States. Formerly under the terms of the Anglo-Malaysian Defence Agreement (AMDA) and currently under the auspices of the Five Power Defence Arrangements (FPDA), Singapore also conducts joint military exercises with Australia, Malaysia, New Zealand, and the United Kingdom.

Numerous security confidence-building measures in the subregion have included information sharing on intelligence and defense policies, thus crafting enhanced transparency. Singapore also participates in a rapidly evolving network of security dialogs among the ASEAN countries and their trading partners. These communication networks, which constitute a security architecture for Singapore, consist of the following: the ASEAN Senior Officials Meetings (SOM); the ASEAN Foreign Ministers Meetings (AMM); the ASEAN Post-Ministerial Conferences (PMC); the ASEAN Regional Forum (ARF); the Asia-Pacific Roundtable series, organized by the Institute of Strategic and International Studies in Malaysia; the ASEAN security institutes (ASEAN-ISIS); the Council for Security Cooperation in the Asia-Pacific (CSCAP); the Asia-Pacific Economic Cooperation (APEC), with a Secretariat in Singapore; and the Pacific Economic Cooperation Council (PECC). Further reducing the threat from the north, ASEAN's Treaty of Amity and Cooperation has been signed by all Southeast Asian countries as well as a dozen or so outside the region, a confidence-building measure drafted on Singapore's terms.[14]

Nevertheless, subregional tensions with its neighbors re-manifested themselves in November 1986, when Israeli President Chaim Herzog visited Singapore. Upset, some Muslims led anti-Singapore demonstrations in Malaysia for over five weeks. Acts of political violence included burning effigies of Prime Minister Lee Kuan Yew and the national flag of Singapore, public demands for the severance of diplomatic relations with Singapore, threats to Singapore's water supply, and the random stoning of Singaporean automobiles after they entered Malaysia via the Causeway. Claiming that extending the invitation to the Israeli president was a legitimate prerogative of a sovereign nation-state, Singapore conducted numerous open mobilization exercises within its territory at the time. Moderates within both countries and the modest mediation of Indonesian President Suharto brought the mini-crisis to a close. Reflecting the new harmony, when several Singaporean soldiers strayed up a river in Johore Bahru in 1987, Malaysia was quickly appeased when the Singaporean government promised to discipline them.[15]

When New Zealand's FPDA battalion departed from Singapore in 1990, the island nation was bereft of foreign troops for the first time since Sir Stamford Raffles founded the British colony in 1819. The Ministry of Defence partially filled the vacuum with a base-access agreement, the U.S.-Singapore Memorandum of Understanding, in 1990. The agreement, modest when compared to American prerogatives at the former American bases in the Philippines, has the following provisions:[16]

- U.S. Navy ships can dock at the Sembawang and Jurong shipyards for repairs, general maintenance, supplies, and crew rest-and-recreation.
- U.S. Navy vessels may be permitted to "increase the duration and number" of their visits to Singapore.
- Four U.S. Air Force F-16 fighters may be based at Paya Lebar Air Base for a 6- to 7-month period annually.
- Additional U.S. Air Force aircraft may be deployed to the island nation several times annually for training exercises of several weeks duration.
- Some 160-170 U.S. military personnel may be bivouacked in the vacated barracks of the withdrawn New Zealand battalion.

A supplemental Protocol, signed in January 1992, relocated the U.S. Seventh Fleet's Logistic Headquarters for surface ships in the Pacific (i.e., CTF-73), also known as the Commander Logistics Group Command Pacific ("Comlog Westpac"), from Subic Bay in the Philippines to Sembawang in Singapore and transferred 150 naval personnel to Singapore's major naval ship repair yard.[17] Even before the base-access agreements were signed, Singapore Foreign Minister Suppiah Dhanabalan wistfully conceded in 1985 that his country "would like to be left alone, but we have to be realistic. . . . A U.S. presence is needed to keep the balance of power [in the region]."[18]

Meeting the "Threat from the West"

U.S. influence, however, has not always been welcomed. Through the application of the Total Defence Doctrine and other diplomatic mechanisms, the Singapore government seeks to protect its society against a host of perceived foreign cultural, economic, and political threats. The island nation's ideological opponent during the twilight years of the Cold War and deep into the "Cold Peace" of the 1990s was (and is) the West, with the liberal traditions of the United States singled out for special negative attention by the Singaporean government.

Trade disputes. The earliest notable dispute between Singapore and Washington was over copyright infringements, as Orchard Road was filled with vendors selling pirated copies of software produced by American companies. In January 1987, Washington threatened to rescind duty-free access of Singapore products into the American market unless the island republic, the "world's capital of piracy" according to an International Intellectual Property Alliance report,[19] changed the situation. One month later, Singapore passed a copyright law acceptable to the United States.

During the same year, policy makers in Washington contemplated "graduating" several erstwhile "developing countries" from the U.S. Generalized System of Preferences (GSP) in the spirit of the Trade Act of 1984, which specified that a country with per capita income of US$8,500 would no longer be eligible for the GSP. In July, when one of the countries to be removed from the GSP was identified as Singapore, despite the apparent promise that Singapore would retain GSP status in exchange for its new anti-piracy law, the PAP government went into political shock.[20] Accordingly, the government sought to protect its economic interests by successfully pressuring American multinational corporations with business operations in Singapore (e.g., AT&T, Apple Computers, Caterpillar, Kenner Parker Toys, Philip Morris, the Toy Manufacturers Association of America, and Westinghouse) to create a lobbying group, the "GSP Coalition of U.S. Businesses," in order to influence the U.S. Economic Policy Council. As a result, President Ronald Reagan adopted policies favorable to Singapore.[21] In addition, Singapore attempted to enlist ambassadors of ASEAN countries in Washington to follow the example of East Asian governments by lobbying the American public outside Washington.[22]

In February 1988, a protest note to the U.S. ambassador over Singapore's removal from GSP was delivered via a labor solidarity march of some 4,500 members of the National Trade Union Congress (NTUC), which rallied outside the U.S. Embassy. A former head of the Trade Development Board suggested an economic boycott in retaliation, and Singapore also filed a protest with the General Agreement on Tariffs and Trade (GATT) in Geneva, Switzerland.[23] Nevertheless, unlike the outcome in a GSP dispute with New Zealand in 1983, Washington finally announced that the island republic would forfeit its remaining GSP privileges because it had demonstrated "remarkable advancement in development" and "recent improvements in trade competitiveness," thus making it eligible for full "graduation."[24]

In October 1987, however, Lee Hsien Loong angrily complained that a trade bill introduced into the U.S. House of Representatives referred to Singapore as a "major trading competitor" of the United States.[25] Sinnathamby Rajaratnam, former foreign minister, commented that the relatively affluent country was being punished for its prosperity because economic success instilled envy in both allies and adversaries.[26] Enforcement of the copyright law, meanwhile, has been lax; legal action by the Association of American Publishers commenced in 1993 but to no avail.[27] Piracy, hard to control, continues today, though there are stiff fines.

"Interference in domestic politics." While the copyright/GSP dispute brewed, Singapore was also seeking to define the emerging Asia-Pacific political culture. The first arena of this contest of clashing values centered on the foreign press, as described in the chapter by Derek Davies, for allegedly interfering in the internal domestic politics of the island republic. When criticized by the Western media, the Singapore government claimed an unlimited "right of reply" in the attacking journal or newspaper regardless of the length of the response. The right of reply, still exercised today, was perceived by the PAP government as a necessary component of social, psychological, and (in some cases) economic defense. The authorities would not tolerate any "cultural pollution" or political information contrary to the government's positions filtering in from the outside world without the guarantee of an official "last word" by PAP Cabinet hardliners or their bureaucratic minions.

The Singapore government began this clash of political and cultural values with the United States in 1988, when it expelled a U.S. diplomat, Political Counselor E. Mason ("Hank") Hendrickson, for allegedly interfering in the parliamentary election campaign. Singapore claimed that a "conspiracy" to create a large pro-American liberal opposition had been organized by Hendrickson, using Law Society President Francis Seow as an agent of U.S. foreign policy to transform the island republic into a democracy. To further the alleged conspiracy, the government claimed, Hendrickson and Seow met with a "Mr. Y" (Deputy Assistant Secretary of State David F. Lambertson) in Singapore and with a "Mr. Z" (Lambertson's superior, Joseph Snyder) in Washington.[28] The sequence of events leading to the expulsion can be traced to the detention of twenty-two alleged "Marxist conspirators" in

1987 and the later release and re-arrest of several of these persons in 1988. One day after Seow sought to represent two of the re-detainees at a habeas corpus hearing in May 1988, Seow was himself detained, and the government demanded the recall of Hendrickson from Singapore.

In the month following Hendrickson's departure, parliament was suffused with anti-American rhetoric.[29] The original government statement fell short of accusing the United States of overt neocolonialism, but subsequent statements from the younger parliamentarians made harsher claims, such as an American attempt to sabotage Singapore. Lee Hsien Loong suggested that Hendrickson, Lambertson, and Snyder would have been arrested and detained without trial, with Internal Security Act authorization, if they had not been covered by diplomatic immunity. PAP propaganda organs announced that the American advocacy of democracy and human rights was a veiled economic sword piercing the prosperity of Singapore and the other Asian newly industrializing economies.[30] One fear expressed was that Americans were, in the name of democracy, encouraging trade-unions in poorer countries to strike for high pay in order to save American jobs. Publicly billed as a "Protest Rally Against Foreign Interference," the National Trade Unions Congress organized an enormous anti-U.S. rally in Singapore's central business district. Hand-lettered signs at this rally, which I attended, said, "Out CIA Agent, Out Hendrickson," "We Are Independent—CIA Stay Out," "Singapore is Not a US Colony, US Spys Out!," "America Don't Meddle and Break Our Rice Bowl," and "Foreign Interference Threatens Our Jobs and Security." There were numerous speeches hostile to the United States.

These belligerent statements, especially by Prime Minister Lee's son, surprised and angered the U.S. government, which was concerned about human rights abuses but hatched no "conspiracy" to undermine the government. Rumors swept Washington, D.C., that the speech of Lee Hsien Loong spurred the Pentagon into drafting rescue contingency plans for American nationals in Singapore.

Prime Minister Lee Kuan Yew's two-hour parliamentary speech, in contrast, was more pragmatic and conciliatory.[31] While claiming that the United States turned down an offer to mediate the "dispute," he expressed the fear that the Hendrickson affair would drive the United States into neo-isolationism, possibly costing Singapore the protective services of the U.S. Seventh Fleet. At the same time he articulated his certainty that American liberal democracy would destroy the cultural, economic, and political fabric of Singapore. According to Lee, a United States military role in the subregion was only acceptable if American activity was contained within unobtrusive and finely defined nonpolitical parameters.

During the election campaign later in 1988, PAP continued to harp on the theme of American subversion of Singapore, though I learned of differing opinions on the anti-American campaign within the top leadership. The government manipulated the Hendrickson affair to communicate a larger political lesson to the Singaporean people: An American-style democracy would destroy the island republic. One Singapore diplomat whom I interviewed in December 1988 indicated that the Hendrickson-Seow incident was motivated by a fear that the United States would bring about the downfall of Lee Kuan Yew in the same manner as Ferdinand Marcos in the Philippines. But he also asserted that the Singapore's success in foiling the so-called "black operation" was further significant evidence of a new post-Pax Americana, post-hegemonic Asia-Pacific order that had been evolving in the region even before the termination of the Cold War. According to a second foreign ministry official, the "second generation" PAP leadership had demonstrated "toughness" during the Hendrickson affair, setting the stage for an emerging "Asian Renaissance."

Seow was released after seventy-two days of detention in July 1988, but he was soon charged with tax evasion. In 1989, while in the United States to seek treatment for a heart condition and to attend a human rights conclave, two private detectives hired by the government of Singapore approached Seow in Manhattan, after weeks of surveillance. They offered to find him a more prestigious cardiologist, hoping to dupe him into a negative diagnosis that would compel his return to Singapore in order to face tax evasion charges, though his American physician had earlier informed him that he was too sick for air travel. Learning of the surveillance, the Deputy Director of Human Rights Watch sought the U.S. government's assistance, and the State Department asked the government of Singapore to "comment on allegations that it ordered the surveillance."[32] Under the U.S. Arms Export Control Act, sanctions could have been applied to Singapore for "intimidation or harassment" of an individual on American soil.

Opposition to human rights. From the ashes of the Hendrickson—Seow affair emerged a new political struggle over regional cultural values. A primary goal of Singaporean foreign policy then was to defeat Western liberal interpretations of human rights. Lee Kuan Yew, in retirement as Senior Minister, embarked on a second career as a global pundit, traveling from one capital to another, denouncing American-style democracy and allegedly perilous liberal interpretations of human rights in the belief that "Westerners have abandoned an ethical basis for society . . ."[33]

Kishore Mahbubani, Singapore's Permanent Secretary within the Ministry of Foreign Affairs, announced a diplomatic campaign to urge non-Western governments to oppose Western definitions of democracy and interpretations of human rights, which he claimed have been promoted in the "euphoria" over the triumph of the West over the Soviet bloc. He characterized this struggle as a Manichean competition for the future of the Asian-Pacific region, a contest between the norms of non-Western "communitarian" group conformity and Western individualism and diversity: "If the powerful Soviet bloc had to capitulate in the face of Western ideas on human rights and democracy, how could the rest of the world resist this tide?"[34] He opined that a "Moderate South" interpretation of human rights was the wisest strategy for Singapore and ASEAN, rather than totally rejecting the legitimacy of all human rights per se, in order to combat the Lockean liberal tidal wave from the West. He postulated the norm of cultural relativism, which assumes that each and every culture has its own standards for human rights. Mahbubani advocated the political philosophy of "communitarianism," not as a balance between the rights of the individual and the rights of society at large, as would Amitai Etzioni,[35] but rather as a form of neo-Confucian authoritarianism. He asserted that Singapore must meet basic human material needs as the first step in the pursuit of comprehensive security before attempting to achieve higher standards of human rights: "Therefore, the expectation of a society on human rights behavior should depend on the level of its development."[36] Singapore's cynical attitude toward human rights was further revealed by Bilahari Kausikan, Director of the East Asian and Pacific Bureau of the Ministry of Foreign Affairs, who saw American human rights rhetoric as an ideological smokescreen, an inexpensive and camouflaged weapon for international economic warfare by a declining hegemon.[37]

Singapore's resistance to the Clinton Doctrine of democratic enlargement and free-market democratization[38] was first challenged in a public forum at the World Conference on Human Rights at Vienna during July 1993. Singapore's Foreign Minister Wong Kan Seng was applauded by delegates from more than seventy Asian and African nations for his remark, in "defense of diversity," that "Only those who have forgotten the pangs of hunger will think of consoling the hungry by telling them they should be free before they can eat."[39] Projecting its Total Defense Doctrine onto the international stage, Singapore allied itself with such hardliners as China and Myanmar (Burma) against the West at the conference to gain control of the conference's secretariat. As a direct result, West-leaning nongovernmental organizations were expelled from the committee that drafted the conference's final declaration. Singapore also supported China's initiative to prevent the Dalai Lama from addressing a plenary session of the conference. The Vienna Declaration and Program of Action, the final conference document, reflected Singapore's position on "cultural relativism."

Michael Fay affair. The Singapore government's diplomatic offensive against the global dissemination of Western conceptions of democracy and human rights was brought home to Singapore in 1994, when a teenage American schoolchild was caned by prison authorities. Although the incident was designed to instruct citizens and resident foreigners in Singapore about the dangerous "decadence" of Western lifestyles and cultural influences, the island republic's real lesson was its arrogant disregard of basic principles of justice.

The caning was the outcome of a day in October 1993, when several automobiles in Singapore were spraypainted. Soon, police arrested three Americans, two Malaysians, a Thai (who had diplomatic immunity), a Hongkong teenager, and three other adolescents. Of the ten, five were charged with vandalism. One was Michael Fay, the son of a chief executive officer of an Ohio automotive supply company and the stepson of the managing director of Pacific regional office of Federal Express. For nine days, Fay was held virtually incommunicado (no conversation allowed with any lawyer, his family, or U.S. Embassy diplomats), seven days more than the legal norm in Singapore, while suffering physical and psychological torture (deprived of sleep, forced to stand naked, grabbed by the hair, threatened with a hosing down with ice-cold water in a freezing room, mocked, slapped, and called various names). When his resistance cracked, he confessed to a crime that he later denied committing; he did so in the belief that he would merely be fined and deported.[40]

Fay pleaded guilty to two counts of vandalism, two counts of criminal mischief, and one count of receiving stolen property (the latter for having a Singapore street sign in his room at school). Although the paint on the automobiles was easily removed, the American adolescent was sentenced to four months in prison, a fine equivalent to US $2,215, and six strokes of a rattan cane (to be administered by a martial arts expert). No individual in Singaporean history, either citizen or foreign resident, had ever received a caning sentence for removable spraypainting, though the indelible defacement of public property had been punished by flogging in the past. The sentence was an unprecedented extension of the 1966 national security law which banned, upon penalty of caning, the defacement of all public buildings with political slogans and symbols, at a time when the Malayan Communist Party was still an active presence in Singapore. The law's new application was not only an extension from public to private property; it was also an extension from political messages to apolitical non-messages.

Official outrage was swiftly communicated to the Singaporean government. During a period of nearly six months of behind-the-scenes diplomacy, U.S. foreign service officers attempted to reduce the vandalism charges to criminal mischief, the normal charge for an offense of this nature. The U.S. chargé d'affaires in Singapore condemned the court's judgment: "We see a large discrepancy between the offense and the punishment. . . . the accused is a teenager, and this is a first offense."[41] President Bill Clinton announced that his government had submitted a "strong protest" note to the Singaporean government; at a White House press conference, he declared that the "punishment is extreme," and he expressed a desire for a reconsideration.[42]

After Fay was sentenced, an appeal was filed. One basis for overturning the sentence was that the court failed to follow procedures set forth in the Probation of Offenders Act of 1993, which provided that a court in such cases should defer a sentence while ordering a report on Fay's suitability for probation.[43] However, Fay's appeal was rejected on March 31, 1994. After the appeal was rejected, President Clinton and twenty-five U.S. Senators communicated with President Ong Teng Cheong to request clemency.[44] I then wrote to President Clinton for clarification. A reply from Senior Advisor to the President for Policy and Strategy, George R. Stephanopoulos, expressed doubt that Fay was guilty or had confessed voluntarily. Clinton's reply expressed the belief that "the punishment of caning is excessive, and . . . his youth and status as a first-time offender justified clemency, especially when compared to other cases of this kind that have been tried in Singapore."

The hypersensitive Singapore government realized that a foreign policy crisis had emerged. Responding to a full Cabinet directive, the Ministry of Home Affairs conducted an internal investigation of police behavior in the case and concluded that there was no evidence of police brutality.[45] The headline of a *Straits Times* editorial, "Spare the Rod, Mr. Clinton?," reflected the government's perspective and general condescending tone.[46] The editorial derided the "interference" of the White House and mocked President Clinton for taking time from the "deepening personal crisis" of the Whitewater scandal and various alleged American foreign policy crises to deal with the Fay Affair. The editorial also patronizingly sneered at the American people: "Singaporeans who find his intervention objectionable need to understand that heroic gestures go down well with the American public."

Lee Kuan Yew claimed that Singapore's national sovereignty (and the political legitimacy of the ruling People's Action Party) was at stake in the Fay Affair:

> Can we govern if we let him off and not cane him? Can we then cane any other foreigner or our own people? We'll have to close shop. . . . I'm an old-fashioned Singaporean who believes that to govern you must have a certain moral authority. If we do not cane him because he is an American, I believe we'll lose our moral authority and our right to govern.[47]

At the National Press Club in Canberra, Australia, Lee ratcheted up the level of his rhetoric: "To adopt any lenient methods would make Singapore more dangerous, scare off investment and force Singaporeans to emigrate."[48]

American public opinion was divided on the issue, but elite opinion leaders were almost unanimously opposed to the caning of Michael Fay. In a poll of the general American population, conducted on April 7-8, 1994, 52 percent of the respondents were opposed to the Fay caning, while 38 percent approved of the punishment.[49] Right-wing opinion mobilization networks, using "burst fax" machines, targeted direct mail lists, telephone banks, and computer link-ups, encouraged a deluge of calls to radio and television talk shows and letters to local newspapers and politicians' offices, and the Singaporean Embassy in Washington. Indeed, whispers in the capitol indicated that the embassy was directly feeding the American right-wing networks with propaganda points, yet another overseas manifestation of the Total Defence Doctrine in action. Editorials from the most respectable organs of opinion from coast to coast totally opposed the caning sentence, including the *New York Times*, the *San*

Francisco Chronicle, the *Washington Post*, and many other newspapers.[50] Foreign Minister Shanmugan Jayakumar responded by attacking what he considered to be a "hysterical campaign" that demonstrated "unprecedented naïveté" in attempting to force Singapore to "cave in," which would have the effect of preventing the government from "govern[ing] effectively if its citizens see the government as having succumbed to U.S. press pressure."[51]

As the deadline for President Ong's clemency decision drew near, the pressure increased. Former President George H. W. Bush and former Secretary of State George Shultz visited Michael Fay's mother at her home in Singapore. Singapore's embassy in Washington was completely overwhelmed with telephone calls.

On the advice of the Cabinet, President Ong reduced the sentence on May 4, 1994, from six to four strokes of the cane. In a supercilious official statement, the government proclaimed:

> Even though the cabinet found no merit in Fay's petition, it sought a way to accommodate President Clinton's appeal without compromising the principle that persons convicted of vandalism must be caned. . . . To reject his appeal totally would show an unhelpful disregard for the president and the domestic pressures on him on this issue. . . . However, the government values Singapore's good relations with the United States and the constructive economic and security role of the United States in the region.[52]

President Ong's decision was interpreted by some as a direct insult to President Clinton, since in 1989 and 1990 Singapore relented under pressure from Thailand and India, respectively, to grant clemency to illegal guestworkers from the two countries who might otherwise have been caned for violating the recently revised Immigration Law.[53] Whereas Thailand even threatened to send warships for purposes other than retrieving some 10,000 nationals,[54] Clinton politely commented: "I think it was a mistake . . . not only because of the nature of the punishment related to the crime but because of the questions that were raised about whether the young man was in fact guilty and had involuntarily confessed."[55]

Many American opinion leaders were incensed that Fay was taken hostage so that he could be used and objectified as a symbol of alleged American libertinism. With Singapore plagued by more than thirty secret societies for adolescents who roam the streets, carry large knives, engage in shoplifting, and break out in fights in front of crowded shopping centers, the message to Singapore's youth was simple: "If we can thrash an American, we can certainly thrash you . . ."[56] In short, the caning of Michael Fay was manipulated by the government as a warning to Singapore's adolescents, an attempt to "educate" and intimidate—a form of internal deterrence, aimed at the enhancement of the nation's economic, psychological, and social defense.

Reprisals Against Singapore

Once the caning sentence had been administered by prison officials, the American media began to demand that Singapore itself should be punished.[57] George Fay, the boy's father, threatened that he would file a lawsuit against Singapore in U.S. courts and actively promote an economic boycott of Singapore.[58] His stepfather quickly moved the Pacific headquarters of Federal Express from Singapore to Subic Bay.

Singapore received at least six sanctions from the U.S. government in due course. The first sanction against Singapore occurred on the day following the caning, when Singapore's ambassador to the United States, S. R. Nathan, was summoned to the State Department by Winston Lord, Assistant Secretary of State for East Asia and the Pacific, who informed him sternly that President Clinton was very disappointed by this decision and that the U.S.-Singapore bilateral relationship would be permanently downgraded.[59] The Fay case destroyed Ambassador Nathan's diplomatic effectiveness in Washington, who was eventually replaced by Professor Chan Heng Chee. In response to the formal diplomatic reprimand by Assistant Secretary Lord, a spokesman at Singapore's foreign ministry meekly stated that it would be "regrettable" if the Fay Affair "were allowed to affect bilateral relations."[60] Two Singaporean writers then published books to justify the government's action. Asad Latif, in *The Flogging of Singapore*, argued that Singapore was the primary victim in the Fay Affair, which was a "symbol of American vulnerability in an age of change."[61] Dr. Gopal Baratham, in *The Caning of Michael Fay*, said,

> In the past it was the communists and their supporters who threatened our system. Now it was western values that was [sic] corrupting our perfect eastern system. . . . Michael Fay epitomized all that was rotten in the west, its decadence: the breakdown of the family, the under-achievement at school, the pointless destruction of property. They were all the things that were threatening to undermine our society and

destroy its efficient running. In some way this was connected to human values and the rights of the individual. . . . The entry of high-powered politicians, right up to the President of the United States, the blitz on television, the news stories that went beyond hype into gross inaccuracy, the insinuations of economic reprisals, all conspired to cause Fay to lose public sympathy in Singapore. We saw ourselves, a little David, standing up to mighty Goliath. . . . we were damned if we were going to let a meta-power, which had been bullying the world for the better part of the century, force us to do things other than in our own way.[62]

Thus, Singaporeans perceived themselves as victims in the Michael Fay incident, and demonstrated that they were still psychologically burdened with a grudge against Caucasians, which emanated from their occasionally painful colonial past.

The second punitive response involved the venue for the first ministerial meeting of the new World Trade Organization (WTO), a location that was understood to be Singapore as the site for its permanent headquarters. The island republic had already alienated the Clinton Administration by refusing to support the establishment of a permanent WTO committee charged with the drafting of an international labor rights policy, thus projecting Singapore's economic and social defense interests into the realm of international economic policy.[63] A few days after the Fay caning, U.S. Trade Representative Mickey Kantor stated that the first ministerial meeting "ought to be held somewhere else [beside Singapore]."[64] Kantor then lobbied the G-7 trade ministers to support the search for an alternative first meeting and headquarters site.

In response to such a noticeable defeat and humiliation in international politics, Singapore successfully "conducted a very extensive and frenetic campaign" to retrieve the hosting privileges for the first WTO ministerial meeting, a diplomatic offensive composed of "pleadings and threats of contract discrimination."[65] While Singapore "persuaded" some seventy-six countries to support its meeting venue before the WTO General Council on January 31, 1995, Kantor prepared a compromise, offering support for Singapore as the venue for the second ministerial meeting in 1998, but not the first meeting in 1996. Geneva was then confirmed as the choice for a permanent WTO headquarters.

The third American retaliation against Singapore emanated from Congress. In 1993, the Malaysian defense ministry successfully placed orders for eighteen MIG-29M "Fulcrums" and eight McDonnell-Douglas F/A-18D "Hornet" fighters along with the installation of a flight simulator and a maintenance training package, giving Kuala Lumpur a significant strategic advantage over its neighbors.[66] To deter potential threats from the north by purchasing the most sophisticated aerial combat technology available, Singapore requested permission from the United States in early April 1994 to buy eighteen "Hornets," too.[67] Incensed over the Fay affair, several House of Representatives staffers secured a briefing on the proposed sale three weeks later with representatives from the Defense Department and the State Department.[68] Following the meeting, a Resolution of Disapproval on Arms Sales to Singapore was drafted and discussed among members of Congress; however, it was not formally introduced by its authors for a vote by the entire legislative body. Instead, Congressman Benjamin Gilman met with Ambassador Nathan, vehemently denouncing Singapore's handling of the Fay affair, and Singapore ended up buying eighteen of the less sophisticated F-16s.

The fourth type of reprisal consisted of premeditated diplomatic snubs of the prestige-anxious mini-state. One day after Michael Fay was caned, President Clinton "laid out the red carpet" for an Oval Office meeting with Prime Minister Mahathir Mohamad of Malaysia, thereby serving notice that the United States no longer acknowledged Singapore's leaders as de facto international spokespersons for Southeast Asian countries.[69] In November 1994, before the annual APEC meeting, Clinton spoke before the U.S. War Cemetery at Corregidor, the site of the Philippine-U.S. last stand against the forces of Japanese fascism in 1942. During his speech, he extolled the virtues of democracy in Asia while branding neo-Confucianism and alleged "Asian Values" as undemocratic.[70]

At the APEC Trade and Investment Treaty signing ceremony, a triumphantly smiling Mahathir was awarded a diplomatically significant place of honor beside Clinton, with Indonesian President Suharto occupying a similar place of honor on Clinton's other side, while Prime Minister Goh was relegated to a spot seven leaders removed from the American chief executive, a humiliation that marked the end of the appeasement of Singapore.

The fifth punitive response was the publication of an official warning about Singapore's severe laws and harsh punishments in the U.S. State Department's travel advisory bulletin on May 9, 1994, four days after Michael Fay's caning:

> Visitors should be aware of Singapore's strict laws and penalties for a variety of offenses that might be considered minor in the United States, including jaywalking, littering, spitting, as well as the importa-

tion and sale of chewing gum. Singapore imposes a mandatory caning sentence on males for vandalism offenses. Caning may also be imposed for immigration violations and other offenses. . . . This replaces the Consular Information Sheet dated July 9, 1993, to include information on strict laws and severe punishments in Singapore.[71]

This travel advisory was designed to discourage not only American tourists but also U.S. businesses from entering Singapore.

The final sanction involved Singapore's request to join the North American Free Trade Association (NAFTA). Prior to the Fay incident, Singapore was placed second on an informal NAFTA accession list generated by the U.S. government. Afterward, Argentina replaced Singapore in the list's second position, thereby soiling the island republic of its vaunted image as "free traders."

Two other sanctions were considered. One was to imposes trade sanctions, under Section 301 of the Trade Act of 1988, because Singapore then did not allow American banks operating in Singapore to accept local deposits. Clinton also could have eliminated all U.S.-government guarantees for American investment in Singapore under the rationale that taxpayers should not underwrite U.S. capital and technology transfer to a city-state that abuses American citizens.

Singapore paid for the caning incident in other ways. Rather than pursuing the vandalism and mischief charges against Stephen Freehill, Fay's seventeen-year-old classmate, the government accepted a plea bargain; in exchange for a guilty plea for one count of possessing stolen property, Freehill was fined the equivalent of US$516, and was released to his family's custody.[72] Singapore also relented on charges that would have carried caning sentences for the third American adolescent. Vandalism and mischief charges were dropped against a fifteen-year-old Malay youth who had been arrested (and partially deafened during police interrogation) in exchange for a guilty plea for possession of stolen property (four Mercedes-Benz automobile emblems).[73] The Hongkong student, arrested along with Fay, was caned six times not long afterward.

The Fay Affair also widened the political schism between PAP's hardline and moderate wings. Prime Minister Goh Chok Tong sided with the moderates when the decision was made to reduce the caning sentence by two strokes, whereas Senior Minister Lee Kuan Yew supported hardliners who opposed any reduction of sentence, fearing that any appearance of submission to foreign powers would reduce PAP's capacity to govern.[74]

The Government appeared to realize that it had reached the outer frontier of its capacity to project its Total Defense Doctrine into foreign polities. Singapore succeeded in alienating many in the American business community, which had earlier aided the republic's campaign to retain GSP status, because Fay was one of their own, the son of an expatriate American business executive. Singapore also forfeited any likelihood that the United States would come to the aid of the island republic in the event of a military threat from Indonesia or Malaysia.[75] Due to concerns over the safety of Americans in Singapore, American expatriates in the city-state felt targeted for harassment "as part of a government crusade against American values," perceiving them as a living contagion, a source of the Western liberal white peril within the Singaporean body politic.[76] Rumors in Washington gave assurances that U.S. commanders would transfer an errant American sailor or airman out of the island republic long before the Singaporeans had a chance to prosecute, much less cane or hang, any hapless service personnel.

Within the United States, rumors circulated in both Washington, D.C., and in California that bomb threats had been lodged against the Singaporean embassy and the Singapore Airlines head office. The incident also brought harm to the Chinese-American community in San Francisco, where vandals spraypainted hostile graffiti slogans over many buildings in the Chinatown district during the 1994 Fourth of July weekend.

Conclusion

Singapore's leaders did not become more cautious in their foreign policy dealings throughout the rest of 1994. The Total Defense Doctrine was apparently operational once again in October, when Christopher Lingle, an American economist serving as a Senior Fellow at the National University of Singapore, wrote an article for the *International Herald Tribune* entitled "Smoke Over Asia Obscures Some Profound Concerns,"[77] which was critical of unnamed authoritarian regimes in Asia. As noted in Chapter 5 by Derek Davies, Lingle was interrogated and searched. With heavy fines, incommunicado detention, and imprisonment likely, Lingle hurriedly left Singapore because the police had "intimidated the hell" out of him.[78] The State Department declared that it "was disappointed at this apparent attempt by Singaporean authorities to intimidate Professor Lingle," and press comments were was full of reproach and condemnation.[79] The republic's official response, as always, was vigorous, reiterating themes about the government's "integrity."[80] Lingle's riposte was that Singapore "is a republic of fear" that "politicizes crime and criminalizes politics."[81] He then launched an offensive against one element of Singapore's Total Defense strategy—the future candidacy of PAP loyalist Tommy Koh for the position of Secretary-General of the United Nations.[82] Singapore's former ambassador to the United Nations and the United States, Koh had distinguished himself by his work on the Third UN Conference on the Law of the Sea and the preparatory work on the 1992 UN-sponsored Rio Earth Summit on the Environment and Development, but his consolation prize in due course was to be named the head of an unimportant multilateral research institute (the Asia-Europe Foundation in 1997).

Singapore's pursuit of the Total Defense Doctrine in the Lingle affair further alienated important power centers within the United States. Such alienation in an important export market and source of investment did not enhance economic security.

In short, Singapore's leaders badly tarnished the country's public relations image. It can certainly be argued that the Total Defense Doctrine has been applied in such a way as to reduce security for the island republic.[83] Meanwhile, according to the leader of the opposition Singapore Democratic Party, "If and when the economy takes a turn for the worse, Singapore will come apart at the seams."[84]

Comment in 2014 (by Richard A. Deck)

Singapore's relations with the United States have improved since the deep freeze in relations during the 1994-1998 period. Lee Kuan Yew has stated that he wants the United States to maintain a presence in the Asia-Pacific region as an external balancer.

PAP is somewhat fearful of the growing ambitions of China, which is perceived as being more aggressive in territorial disputes. Alarm bells were raised when a Chinese naval vessel made an incursion into Malaysian territorial waters. Singapore supports the Philippines' proposal for a multinational Code of Conduct for the South China Sea, rather than a more restrictive China-ASEAN Treaty of Peace and Friendship (as proposed by China). In the pursuit of this balancing mechanism, I believe that Singapore has permitted the home porting of four U.S. Navy vessels in the island republic.

The United States is pursuing free trade with Singapore through the Trans-Pacific Partnership negotiations. The parley involves more than a dozen nations, including Malaysia, Brunei, Vietnam, Chile and Canada.

It seems that Singapore has more or less dropped its Asian Values campaign. The chief ideologue of this campaign, Kishore Mahbubani (the author of *Can Asians Think?*), has been sent packing from the foreign ministry to the academy. (He is now Dean of the Lee Kuan Yew School of Public Policy at the National University of Singapore.) I think that Lee Kuan Yew said that everyone should forget what he opined about Asian Values. Singapore failed to cane an American national for overstaying his visa a year or two ago. U.S. State Department diplomacy was more effective than it was during the bad days of the Michael Fay affair.

Epilog (by Michael Haas)

During the twenty-first century, there has been much more cooperation in recent years between Singapore and the United States. The main transformation of the self-perceived vulnerable city-state occurred after the terrorist attack on September 11, 2001.

Back in 1989, when the Cold War was winding down, protection of the island state's military vulnerability was not an urgent element of its foreign policy agenda. When the Philippines decided that year not to renew the American presence on military bases, Singapore agreed to let the U.S. Navy use its naval base at Changi Naval Base as a port stop; agreements were signed in 1990 and 1992.

However, Washington's post-Cold War emphasis on human rights was viewed as meddling in Singapore's internal affairs. The "Asian Values" concept was a strange development that was at odds with Washington, which had hitherto been seen as a protector of Singapore sovereignty, nestled as it is between more powerful neighbors.

But the "Asian Values" concept was quietly dropped after the 1997 financial crisis that hit Indonesia, South Korea, and Thailand. Indeed, observance of some of those very values may have contributed to the crisis in the affected countries.

Meanwhile, the Cooperation and Readiness Afloat (CARAT), initiative started in 1995 as bilateral naval exercises between the United States and Thailand. Brunei, Indonesia, Malaysia, the Philippines, and Singapore joined in 1996. Today, CARAT bilateral training also extends to the navies of Bangladesh, Cambodia, and Timor Leste.[85]

When the foreign policy agenda of the United States changed after terrorist attacks on September 11, 2001, Singapore responded by arresting members of an Islamic organization, as noted in Chapter 6 above. Singapore was in support of the Afghan and Iraq wars, serving as a transshipment port for weapons not manufactured in the island republic. During 2001 a U.S. Navy carrier battle group docked at Changi Naval Base for the first time.[86]

Following free trade agreements with New Zealand in 2001 and Japan in 2002, Singapore and Washington adopted a free trade agreement in 2003. One benefit to the United States was the potential to stop piracy of intellectual property.

In 2005, the Singapore and the United States signed the bilateral Strategic Framework Agreement for a Closer Cooperation Partnership in Defense and Security, which absorbed the U.S.-Singapore Memorandum of Understanding of 1990 and the Protocol to the agreement in 1992. Defense officials from both countries have consulted annually since the agreement went into effect.

But in looking for a model to deal with terrorism, memory of the public's reaction to the Michael Fay affair seemed subliminally revived. In the eyes of the Singapore government, after all, Fay was committing the crime of terrorism. Just as many Americans supported the torture of the teenager regardless of his guilt or innocence, there were few objections to the torture and indefinite detention without trial of those incarcerated in Abu Ghraib, secret prisons abroad, and at Guantánamo. In short, American foreign policy became Singaporeanized.

Piracy at sea, a form of international terrorism, had been a concern in the Straits of Malacca and Singapore for many decades, but 9/11 gave the issue more salience. For many years, Japan had hoped to establish a regional organization to combat piracy. Its patience bore fruit in 2001 with the establishment of the Regional Cooperation Agreement on Combating Piracy and Armed Robbery Against Ships in Asia, an organization with fourteen regional members, extending from South Korea and China to India and Sri Lanka, including even landlocked Laos.[87] Although Singapore joined, becoming the headquarters for the organization's Information Sharing Center, Indonesia and Malaysia have attended meetings, but they did not join, preferring to rely on the Piracy Reporting Center of the International

Maritine Bureau.

In 2002, Singapore joined another initiative coming out of Washington:[88] The Southeast Asian Cooperation Against Terrorism (SEACAT) was set up in 2002 to share information on regional terrorism and conduct training exercises; Singapore hosts its Multinational Operations and Training Center. The name changed to Southeast Asian Cooperation and Training in 2012. CARAT exercises are now integrated into SEACAT. In 2005, as noted above, a Strategic Framework Agreement was signed between Singapore and the United States to increase diplomatic contact, military exercises, and research cooperation,[89] but three months later outgoing American ambassador Frank Levin criticized Singapore for "limited political expression."[90]

In recent years, Singapore has tried to improve relations with ASEAN countries,[91] though the island republic has preferred bilateral trade agreements while awaiting an ASEAN free trade agreement to come to fruition. Nevertheless, Singapore has blocked admission of Papua New Guinea and Timor Leste from membership in ASEAN, thereby occasioning criticism from Jakarta.[92] Whereas ASEAN was united during the Cold War, consensus building has become more difficult since international terrorism arose, with divergent approaches among the members.[93]

Canberra, with strong ties to Indonesia and Timor Leste, has sought to be recognized as an important partner with ASEAN. However, in 2003 Prime Minister Goh Chok Tong infuriated Prime Minister John Howard when he said that Australia would only be welcomed in the region when the country became majority nonwhite.[94]

When Singapore planned to add a landfill that might intrude into Malaysian waters, the parties in 2003 agreed to submit the case to the International Tribunal for the Law of the Sea, which ruled that Singapore should abandon its plan because of potential damage to the marine environment. The issue was resolved by 2006. Four years later, Malaysia agreed to vacate its railway station inside Singapore and to relocate the facility at the border.

Over the years, haze from slash-and-burn fires from Sumatra, Indonesia, darkened Singapore skies. In 1997, the haze was so bad that air travel was affected, and Singaporeans stayed indoors for days. A treaty on the subject was proposed, as losses were con-siderable. An ASEAN Agreement on Transboundary Haze Pollution was adopted in 2002, providing for a haze monitoring system to stop burning from developing into toxic haze. Singapore signed in 2003, but Indonesia held up ratification. When Lee Kuan Yew criticized Jakarta for harboring leaders of the allegedly terrorist Jemaah Islamiyan in 2002, a protest was held around Singapore's embassy in Jakarta, and the Indonesian interior minister responded that the conflict was "based on democratic pluralism . . . [versus] . . . authoritarianism," but made the arrests anyway in 2003.[95]

Lee Kuan Yew has proved that he was still lost in past quarrels.[96] As Minister Mentor, he publicly complained in 2006 about the mistreatment of Chinese in Indonesia and Singapore. In 2007, he again opined that Singapore might join the Federation of Malaysia again if Kuala Lumpur would abolish special treatment for Malays. Denunciations from Malaysia followed. Jakarta responded in a different way by refusing to sign the anti-haze treaty until Singapore extradicted Indonesians living in Singapore who were wanted on charges of corruption.

Although Singaporean and Malaysian patrol boats had clashed in 1992 near the disputed island of Pedra Branca, in 2007 the International Court of Justice awarded the island to Singapore and neighboring islands to Malaysia. In 2009, Kuala Lumpur assisted in the capture of the head of Jemaah Islamiyan, who had escaped from Singapore prison one month earlier; as a terrorist; he remains in custody on an indefinite basis.[97]

In 2007, Indonesia held up a shipment of sand to Singapore for land reclamation until Singapore signed an extradition treaty with Indonesia so that Jakarta could arrest corrupt officials who had fled to the island republic for sanctuary. That same year negotiations broke down between the two countries on another matter: Indonesia shelved an agreement proposed by Singapore that would allow the military to use Indonesian airspace, sealanes, and train in Area Brava. In 2009, however, the maritime border between the two countries was settled.

When Cyclone Nargis devastated Myanmar in 2008, some ASEAN countries sought to provide aid. When acceptance of the aid was delayed, Singapore spoke up to criticize Yangon, something that ASEAN countries in the past were reluctant to do. In 2009, Senior Minister Goh Chok Tong indicated that investment in Myanmar would increase as the country became more democratic.

Singapore's relations with China improved during the twenty-first century. In 2001, Singapore provided financing for the Suzhou Industrial Park, and in 2002 Beijing offered the use of Hainan Island as a venue for Singapore military training. A highlight was the signing of a free trade agreement, effective 2009. However, when Prime Minister Lee Hsieng Loong visited Taiwan in 2004, Beijing so strongly objected that he made a speech strongly opposing the independence of the Republic of China.[98] Continuing to provide project assistance, an agreement was reached in 2008 on the Sino-Singapore Tianjin Eco-City Project, which would build housing to accommodate some 85,000 persons.[99]

In 2010, after a liquidity crisis had arisen in Europe and the United States, Singapore's offer was accepted to provide a secretariat for the proposed Asian Monetary Fund (AMF), as an alternative to the International Monetary Fund. AMF is capitalized at $120 billion. The following year Singapore agreed to host the ASEAN+3 Macroeconomic Research Office.

In sum, Singapore has been successful in military cooperation. Singapore's role in regional economic cooperation is now second to no other country in Asia.

Notes

1. R. S. Milne and Diane K. Mauzy, *Malaysia: Tradition, Modernity, and Islam* (Boulder, CO: Westview, 1986), 24.
2. Dennis Bloodworth, *The Tiger and the Trojan Horse* (Singapore: Times Books International, 1986), 116-121.
3. Milne and Mauzy, *Malaysia*, 49.
4. Bloodworth, *The Tiger and the Trojan Horse*, 268.
5. Ibid., 274.
6. Charles E. Morrison and Astri Suhrke, *Strategies of Survival: The Foreign Policy Dilemmas of Smaller Asian States* (St. Lucia, Australia: University of Queensland Press, 1978), 190.
7. *Straits Times*, 7 October 1978.
8. Timothy John Huxley, *Indochina as a Security Concern of the ASEAN States, 1975-81* (Canberra: Ph.D. thesis, Australian National University, 1986), 164. See also Lee Kuan Yew, BBC interview, repeated on the Singapore radio home service, 8 February 1979 (SWB FE/6040/A3/15, 12 February 1979); Goh Keng Swee, "Vietnam and Big-Power Rivalry" in *Asian Security in the 1980s: Problems and Policies for a Time of Transition*, ed. Richard H. Solomon (Cambridge, MA: Oelgeschlager, Gunn and Hain, 1980), 163.
9. Singapore Ministry of Foreign Affairs, *From Phnom Penh to Kabul* (Singapore: Ministry of Foreign Affairs, 1980); S. Rajaratnam. 19 January 1979 (SWB FE/6022/A3/16, 22 January 1979).
10. According to a journalist "close to the Singapore leadership" quoted in Huxley, *Indochina as a Security Concern of the ASEAN States*, 166.
11. Sydney Schanberg, "Bush Backing Asia's Nazis," *Honolulu Advertiser*, 21 May 1990, A6.

12. Michael Haas, *Cambodia, Pol Pot, and the United States: The Faustian Pact* (New York: Praeger, 1991), 19.

13. Richard A. Deck, "Singapore: Realpolitik in Comprehensive Security," in *Conflict, and Strategic Culture in the Asia-Pacific Region*, ed. Russell Trood and Kenneth Booth (London: Macmillan, 1997); Shuhud Saaid, "The Singapore Armed Forces, Pt. I: Girding Up for `Total Attack' Through Total Defence," *Asian Defence Journal*, February 1987, 7.

14. Richard A Deck, "Singaporean Security Culture." Paper presented at the workshop on Peace, Conflict, and Strategic Culture, Griffith University, St. Lucia, Australia, 15-17 August 1994. The nonregional countries signing the treaty are Australia, Bangladesh, China, France, India, Japan, Mongolia, New Zealand, North and South Korea, Pakistan, Russia, Sri Lanka, the United States, and the European Union.

15. Suhaini Aznam, "Room to Manoeuvre: Singapore-Malaysian Exercises Signal Improved Ties," *Far Eastern Economic Review*, 23 February 1989, 27.

16. *Fact Sheet: U.S.-Singapore Memorandum of Understanding* (Washington, DC: Department of State, 1990); *Joint U.S.-Singapore Statement: United States and Singapore Announce Agreement On Increased U.S. Use of Singapore's Military Facilities* (Washington, DC: Department of State, 1990); Mike Fonte, "A Shot Across the Bow," *Far Eastern Economic Review*, 19 July 1990, 10-11; Patrick E. Tyler, "U.S. Close to Singapore Deal on Access for Pacific Forces," *International Herald Tribune*, 7-8 July 1990, 1, 5; William T. Tow, *Encountering the Dominant Player: U.S. Extended Deterrence Strategy in the Asia-Pacific* (New York: Columbia University Press, 1991), 321-322.

17. Zara Dian, "Viewpoint: The Bush Visit," *Asian Defence Journal*, February 1992, 3-4.

18. Quoted in Robert O. Tilman, *Southeast Asia and the Enemy Beyond: ASEAN Perceptions of External Threats* (Boulder, CO: Westview, 1987), 48.

19. International Intellectual Property Alliance, *Trade Losses due to Piracy and Other Market Access Restrictions Affecting the U.S. Copyright Industries: A Report to the United States Special Trade Representative on 12 `Problem' Countries* (Washington, DC: IIPA, 1989), 80.

20. Patrick Daniel, "US May Strip S'pore of Duty-Free Status," *Straits Times* (Institute of Southeast Asian Studies Clippings File), 1.

21. "S'pore Awaits US Decision as Chile Becomes No. 6 to Lose GSP Status," *Straits Times*, 29 December 1987, 9; "Privileged Fewer: The Four Dragons GSP Benefits Are Threatened," *Far Eastern Economic Review*, 19 November 1987, 70.

22. Tommy Koh, "A Lilliputian in the Land of the Giants: The Work of the Singapore Embassy in Washington," Occasional Seminar, Institute of Southeast Asian Studies, Singapore, 2 July 1987.

23. Anne Koh and Loong Swee Yin, "NTUC Leaders Hand Letter to US Embassy: 4,500 Protest Against GSP Move," *Straits Times*, 6 February 1988, 1; "Act Not in Anger," *Straits Times*, 5 February 1988 (editorial).

24. Nayan Chanda, "Concessional Bending: The U.S. Cuts Trade Benefits for Four Asian Exporters," *Far Eastern Economic Review*, 11 February 1988, 68.

25. Ong Ming Seing, "US Will Benefit From Understanding the Asia-Pacific: BG Lee," *Straits Times*, 9 October

1987.

26. "The Resentment That Prosperity Brings—Raja," *Straits Times*, 22 November 22.

27. "Caveat Vendor," *The Economist*, 1 May 1993, 33; Association of American Publishers, Inc., *Status Report on Copyright Reform and Anti-Piracy Activities in 62 Countries* (Washington, DC: AAP, September 1993), 22; Tuan Vu, "Piracy in Singapore," *slideshare.net*, 30 March 2010, accessed 20 February 2014.

28. "A Tale of Two Plots: Foreign Interference," *Petir* (publication of People's Action Party) May 1988, 5; "Beware Foreign Influences," *Straits Times*, 7 May 1988; Lau Teik Soon, "The Hendrickson Affair and the Anti-Singapore Lobby: A Comment," *Petir*, May 1988, 3; Government of Singapore statement, 7 May 1988, quoted in *Recent Developments in Malaysia and Singapore* (New York: Asia Watch, 1988), 8.

29. "Parliament Debates Hendrickson Affair: Foreign Interference," *Petir*, May 1988, 10; Chandra Das, "Economic Motives May Be Behind US Bid to Destabilise Three NICs," *Straits Times*, 2 June 1988, 25; "Kan Seng Warns Against Imposing US Model on S'pore," *Straits Times*, 2 June 1988, 25.

30. Seah Chiang Nee, "What the Americans Are Up To," *Petir*, May 1988, 8-9; Election Night Broadcast, SBC-TV, 3 September 1988.

31. "Full Text of PM's Speeching Rounding Up Debate on the Hendrickson Affair," *Straits Times*, 2 June 1988, 24.

32. Lee Lescaze, "Singapore Dissident Finds Surveillance Follows Him Even to the United States," *Wall Street Journal*, 15 December 1989; N. Balakrishnan, "Eyes on the Job: Dissident Under Watch in New York," *Far Eastern Economic Review*, 26 January 1989, 12; Marcus Gee, "Surviving Singapore's Dark Side," *Toronto Globe and Mail*, 5 April 1994, A12-A13, C1-C2; "Outside Looking in: An Exile Talks About Himself—and Lee Kuan Yew," *Asiaweek*, 9 February 1994, 30. For more details, see Francis Seow, *To Catch a Tartar: A Dissident in Lee Kuan Yew's Prison* (New Haven, CT: Yale University Council on Southeast Asia Studies, 1994).

33. Fareed Zakaria, "Culture Is Destiny: A Conversation with Lee Kuan Yew," *Foreign Affairs*, March/April 1994, 109-126.

34. Kishore Mahbubani, "New Areas of Asean Reaction: Environment, Human Rights and Democracy," *ASEAN-ISIS Monitor*, V (Oct.-Dec. 1992): 13-14.

35. Amitai Etzioni, *The Spirit of Community: Rights, Responsibilities, and the Communitarian Agenda* (New York: Crown Publishers, 1993).

36. Mahbubani, "New Areas of Asean Reaction: Environment, Human Rights and Democracy. See also Kishore Mahbubani, "The West and the Rest," *The National Interest*, Summer 1992, 3-13.

37. Bilahari Kausikan, "Asia's Different Standard," *Foreign Policy*, Fall 1993, 26-27.

38. Winston Lord, "A New Pacific Community: Ten Goals for American Policy," Opening Statement at Confirmation Hearings before the Foreign Relations Committee, U.S. Senate (Washington, DC: Department of State, 31 March 1993; Susumu Awanohara, "Containing Enlargement: New Clinton Foreign Policy Doctrine Gets Cool Response," *Far Eastern Economic Review*, 21 October 1993, 13.

39. Wong Kan Seng, "Debate Over Rights: Rejecting Western Pressure, Asia Tables Its Own Definition,"

Asiaweek, 30 June 1993, 25.

40. William Branigin, "Jail Tactics in Singapore Assailed: American's Caning Case Puts Focus on Charges of Prisoner Abuse," *Washington Post*, 20 April 1994, A14; David Grogan, Karen Emmons, Luchina Fisher, and Tom Nugent, "Whipping Boy: U.S. Teenager Michael Fay Pleads With Singapore to Spare the Rod," *Weekly People*, 18 April 1994, 42-43.

41. Charles P. Wallace, "Ohio Youth To Be Flogged in Singapore," *Los Angeles Times*, 4 March 1994, A12.

42. Grogan et al., "Whipping Boy," 41.

43. Francis T. Seow, "S'pore's Brutal Charade: The Pain and the Punishment," *Bangkok Post*, 26 May 1994.

44. Senate (Legislative Day of 2 May 1994), *Congressional Record: Proceedings and Debates of the 103d Congress, Second Session*, CXL (5 May 1994); telephone interview with David Rubin, legislative aide to U.S. Senator Howard M. Metzenbaum, 5 May 1994.

45. See Francis T. Seow, "Singapore and Caning," *Wall Street Journal*, 27 June 1994.

46. "Spare the Rod, Mr. Clinton?," *Straits Times* (editorial); summarized in Philip Shenon, "A Flogging Sentence Brings a Cry of Pain in U.S.: Singapore Journal," *New York Times*, 16 March 1994, A4.

47. James R. Gaines, Joelle Attinger, William Dowell, and Sandra Burton, "A Rigorous Case for Morality: Singapore's Lee Kuan Yew Speaks Out on Caning," *Time*, 9 May 1994, 47 (interview).

48. Quoted in Seow, "S'pore's Brutal Charade."

49. Michael Elliot et al., "Crime & Punishment," *Newsweek*, 12 April 1994, 18-19. Cf. "Americans Deeply Split Over Caning Sentence," *San Francisco Chronicle*, 21 April 1994, A11.

50. "Condemn Singapore's Brutality," *New York Times*, 10 April 1994 (editorial); William Safire, "Torture in Singapore: As Old as Civilization," *San Francisco Chronicle*, 8 April 1994, A21 (reprinted from the *New York Times*); "Torture in Singapore," *San Francisco Chronicle*, 5 April 1994, A18 (editorial); James Hoagland, "The Writing on the Wall," *Washington Post* article quoted in Susumu Awanohara, "Whipping-Boy: Americans Get Worked-Up About Michael Fay's Caning," *Far Eastern Economic Review*, 28 April 1994, 25; Mike Royko, "If You Want Blood, Why Stop at Flogging?," *San Francisco Chronicle*, 11 April 1994, A19; Mike Royko, "Cut By the Lash of Guilt," *San Francisco Chronicle*, 12 April 1994, A21 (reprinted from the *Chicago Tribune*); Robert Benjamin, "Singapore's Brave New Totalitarianism: Efficient, Clean and Almost Crime-Free, City-State Also Is a Bit Chilling," *San Francisco Chronicle*, 18 April 1994, A10 (reprinted from the *Baltimore Sun*); Stan Stesser, "Singapore, the Orwellian Isle," *New York Times*, 30 April 1994, 15; Karen Nakamura, "A View From the Left," *San Francisco Examiner*, 10 May 1994, A15; Stephanie Salter, "It's a Grand Old Flog," San *Francisco Examiner*, 10 April 1994, A19; Richard Cohen, "This Caning in Singapore Won't Make America Safer," *International Herald Tribune*, 6 April 1994, 7 (reprinted from the *Washington Post*); Ellen Goodman, "Six Lashes And You're Out," *San Francisco Chronicle*, 14 April 1994, A23 (reprinted from the *Boston Globe*).

51. "Singapore Bends a Little on Caning," *San Francisco Chronicle*, 4 May 1994, A9.

52. William Branigin, "Singapore Reduces American's Sentence: Teen's Parents Still Angry at 4-Lash Edict," *Washington Post*, 5 May 1994, A33, A37.

53. Ibid., A33.
54. N. Balakrishnan, "A Touch of the Stick: Clampdown on Foreign Workers Annoys Thailand," *Far Eastern Economic Review*, 30 March 1989, 13.
55. William Branigan, "Singapore Canes American Teenager: U.S. Said to Voice 'Disappointment'," *Washington Post*, 6 May 1994, A27.
56. "Young and Restless: Rising Violence Among Youth Gangs Worries the Government," *Asiaweek*, 14 July 1993, 24-26; Elliott et al., "Crime and Punishment," 22.
57. Ibidem; James Walsh, "The Whipping Boy," *Time*, 2 May 1994, 80; "Shame on Singapore," *International Herald Tribune*, 9 May 1994, 8 (editorial); "Singapore Justice On Trial," *New York Times*, 5 May 1994, A20 (editorial); "Four Unfortunate Lashes," *San Francisco Chronicle*, 6 May 1994, A24 (editorial); Jon Carroll, "Raising Cane and Other Issues," *San Francisco Chronicle*, 5 May 1994, E10; "Citizen Caned: Singapore Can't Be Proud of 'Reducing' Fay's Torture to 4 Lashes," *San Francisco Examiner*, 5 May 1994, A18 (editorial); "Condemn Caning, Flogging; Torture Merits No Applause—Singapore's Harsh Ways Are Too High a Price to Pay for Safer Streets, Here or Abroad," *USA Today*, 6 May 1994 (editorial). Both the American Medical Association and the American Bar Association condemned the caning.
58. Carol J. Castaneda, "Caning Over But Outrage Still Burns," *USA Today*, 6 May 1994, 1.
59. Statement by Christine Shelly/Acting Spokesman, "Lord Meeting With Singapore Ambassador," Press Release, Office of the Spokesman, U.S. Department of State, 5 May 1994.
60. Quoted in William Branigin, "Mother Denounces Caning as Torture: Teenager Shows His Wounds to a U.S. Consular Official," *International Herald Tribune*, 7-8 May 1994, 5.
61. Asad Latif, *The Flogging of Singapore: The Michael Fay Affair* (Singapore: Times Books International, 1994).
62. Dr. Gopal Baratham, *The Caning of Michael Fay* (Singapore: KRP Publications, 1994), 93-94.
63. Peter Behr, "New Trade Group Sets Talks on Labor Rights," *Washington Post*, 8 April 1994, D1-D2.
64. U.S. Trade Representative official, telephone interview. See also "Tit-for-Tat," *Asiaweek*, 18 May 1994 (newsmap section); "Singapore Opposed as Trade Summit Site," *San Francisco Examiner*, 10 May 1994, A13; Philip Shenon, "Caned U.S. Youth, Freed, Is Saying Farewell to Singapore," *New York Times*, 22 June 1994, A5.
65. Telephone Interview with Joseph Damond, Director, Southeast Asian Affairs, United States Trade Representative's Office, 30 March 1995.
66. Aidah Husin, "Offset Deal Signed with McDonnell Douglas," *Asian Defence Journal*, November 1993, 51; Zara Dian, "Of Fulcrums and Hornets in the Malaysian Skies," *Asian Defence Journal*, August 1993, 3-4.
67. "Singapore: Lockheed Deal," *Far Eastern Economic Review*, 21 July 1994, 13; "U.S. May Sell F-18 Fighters to Singapore," *Washington Post*, 22 May 1994, A29; "Big Sting," *Asiaweek*, 1 June 1994 (Newsmap section). The deal was also to have included twenty-four AIM-9 "Sidewinder" missiles, fifty AIM-7M "Sparrow" missiles, ammunition for air canon, and spare parts.
68. Telephone interview with a Republican staffer on the Committee on Foreign Affairs, 20 September 1994.

69. "Back on the Rails: As the U.S. Image Improves, Clinton Is Learning the Asian Way," *Asiaweek*, 22 June 1994, 24-25.

70. "An American in Manila," *Asiaweek*, 23 November 1994, 33 and U.S. television news broadcasts.

71. *Singapore—Consular Information Sheet* (Washington, DC: Bureau of Consular Affairs, Department of State, 9 May 1994).

72. Associated Press, "Singapore Drops U.S. Teen's Vandalism Charge," *Washington Post*, 18 May 1994, A18.

73. Associated Press, "Malay Youth, 15, Escapes Caning in Singapore," *Los Angeles Times*, 27 May 1994, A7.

74. "The Michael Fay Caning," *Asiaweek*, 1 June 1994, 1.

75. Cf. Nayan Chanda, "U.S. Legislators Are Concerned About Secrecy in Singapore Pact," *Asian Wall Street Journal*, 26 November 1990, 20.

76. Philip Shenon, "American Protests 'Intimidation' by Singapore," *New York Times*, 7 November 1994, A7.

77. Christopher Lingle, "Smoke Over Asia Obscures Some Profound Concerns," *International Herald Tribune*, 7 October 1994.

78. Shenon, "American Protests 'Intimidation' by Singapore."

79. Ms. Christine Shelly, *EAP Press Guidance: Final Version* (Washington, DC: Bureau of East Asian and Pacific Affairs, Department of State, 18 January 1995; Jim Hoagland, "Singapore's Great Helmsman," *Washington Post Weekly Edition*, 31 October 31—6 November 1994, 29.

80. See Chak Mun, "Singapore Responds," *Far Eastern Economic Review*, 29 December 1994—5 January 1995 (letter); Kieran Cooke, "Goh Battles to Bolster His Standing: For Most in Singapore, Ex-Premier Lee Is Still a Force," *Financial Times* (London), 10 January 1995, 4; Shenon, "American Protests 'Intimidation' by Singapore."

81. Quoted in Philip Shenon, "Singapore Court Finds a U.S. Scholar and Newspaper Guilty of Contempt," *New York Times*, 18 January 1995, A5.

82. Ibidem.

83. Christopher Lingle, "Singapore Repression Reveals Regime's Insecurity," *Yomiuri Shimbun*, 2 December 1994. Unlike some other analysts, Lingle believes that the linchpin of the Total Defense Doctrine is psychological defense (not economic defense). He argues that the government's application of psychological defense is schizophrenic, first exhibiting phobia of the West and then later extolling the inevitable fusion of all Pacific Rim cultures, the theme that "East Meets West."

84. Cooke, "Goh Battles to Bolster His Standing," 161.

85. "SEACAT 2013 Exercise Builds Multilateral Cooperation in Maritime Southeast Asia," *Naval News Service*, September 2; "Cooperation Afloat Readiness and Training (CARAT)," *globalsecurity.org*, c. 2003.

86. Tim Huxley, "Singapore in 2001: Political Continuity Despite Deepening Recession," *Asian Survey*, XLII (2002): 163.

87. John F. Bradford, "Shifting the Tides Against Piracy in Southeast Asian Waters," *Asian Survey*, XLVIII (2008): 473-491.

88. Ibidem.

89. Garry Rodan, "'Vibrant and Cosmopolitan' Without Political Pluralism," *Asian Survey*, XLVI (2006): 185.
90. Ibidem.
91. Andrew Tan, *Intra-ASEAN Tensions* (London: Royal Institute of International Affairs, 2000).
92. Tim Huxley, "Singapore in 2000: Continuing Stability and Renewed Prosperity amid Regional Diversity," *Asian Survey*, XLI (2001): 207.
93. Kim Hyung Jong and Lee Poh Ping, "The Changing Role of Dialogue in the International Relations of Southeast Asia," *Asian Survey*, LI (2011): 953-970.
94. William Case, "Singapore in 2003: Another Tough Year," *Asian Survey*, XLIV (2004): 120.
95. Jonathan T. Cow, "ASEAN Counterterrorism Cooperation Since 9/11," *Asian Survey*, XLV (2004): 309.
96. Chua, "Singapore in 2006: An Irritating and Irritated ASEAN Neighbor," 211; Chua Beng Huat, "Singapore in 2007: High Wage Minisers and the Management of Gays and the Elderly," *Asian Survey*, XLVIII (2008): 58.
97. Narayan Gasesan, "Singapore in 2009: Structuring Politics, Priming the Economy, and Working the Neighborhood," *Asian Survey*, L (2010): 253-259.
98. Garry Rodan, "Long-Awaited Leadership Transition," *Asian Survey*, XLV (2004): 144.
99. Narayan Gasesan, "Singapore in 2008: A Few Highs and Lows While Bracing for the Future," *Asian Survey*, XLIX (2009): 213-219.

8

Mass Society
Michael Haas

The task of this chapter is to explain the twenty or so puzzles about Singapore that have been identified schematically in Chapter 1 and presented more graphically in later chapters. Implicitly, several explanations have been advanced thus far in the volume. The government, as noted particularly in the chapter on Singapore's history (Chapter 2), prefers to justify its peculiar behavior in terms of a strategic action-reaction theory; that is, when crises have emerged, the government has responded preemptively, hoping to solve problems quickly. Clark Neher's case for Singapore (Chapter 3) argues subliminally for another theory, to which the government also subscribes; this is a trade-off theory, namely, that the exigencies of economic progress require political repression. Christopher Lingle and Kurt Wickman (Chapter 4), however, attempt to refute trade-off theory by showing that that the economic progress of Singapore depended entirely upon modeling the island republic on Hongkong's economic policies. Derek Davies and Francis Seow (Chapters 5-6) appear to favor a "great man" theory, namely, that Singapore's oddities can be traced primarily to the personality of Lee Kuan Yew and to the structure of governance that he established, which will doubtless persist even when Lee is out of the picture. Richard Deck (Chapter 7) explains the blunders of Singaporean foreign policy in similar terms—as an extension of individual narcissism to the state level. In contrast, I offer mass society theory.

The concept of Singapore as a "mass society" is not new. Indeed, the first presentation of this thesis was by Lee Kuan Yew himself. During his National Day address in midsummer 1987, I was in front of the television set at my Singapore residence, listening and watching intently as he applied mass society theory to his country, though he did not carry the analysis far enough, as will be seen below. In any case, I agree with Lee Kuan Yew that Singapore has a mass society.

Mass Society Theory

A "mass society" exists when there is a vast gulf between rulers and ruled. The gulf is the absence of independent organizations that can mediate between the governed and those who govern. The sum of these independent organizations is known as "civil society." When a mass society exists, there is alienation or rootlessness among the governed. When the masses are alienated, various manifestations of discontent appear, from self-destructive behavior to anger against others, including defiance of the rulers.

There are two major ways to bring about a mass society. Classically, mass society emerges unplanned from the social change associated with rapid industrialization and urbanization. Those living in rural areas move to cities in search of newly created jobs, but in so doing they leave behind family and other social ties and find difficulty in establishing social connections in the burgeoning cities, which then seethe with social problems (alcoholism, homicide, rape, suicide) and political problems (racial unrest, riots, and strikes). Newcomers, in short, find difficulty in locating institutions of civil society that will provide assistance in adjusting to the new urban environment. No society has undergone the socioeconomic transformation from traditional society to modernity without experiencing manifestations of mass society.

The second way to bring about a mass society is through planning. Feigning endless "crises," a government can construct a totalitarian mass society. Through the power of the state, independent institutions of civil society can be made illegal, and the government can seek to monopolize the public discourse. Rulers can then effect rapid change without consulting the masses—or by setting up pseudoconsultative institutions that enlarge the ability of the regime to control the thoughts of the people. Because the masses are buffeted around without a voice, they become alienated from the regime and fearful of linking up with one another. The results are futile efforts to reconstitute civil society, apathy and passive submission, a breakdown of primary friendships and institutions, a desire to migrate elsewhere, and even efforts to undermine the regime.

Classical mass society theory comes from sociologist Émile Durkheim, who sought to explain why deviant social behavior skyrocketed during the industrial revolution of the late nineteenth century.[1] The second variant of mass society theory, as developed by sociologist William Kornhauser, seeks to explain how totalitarian regimes arise and hold power by such strategies as demanding absolute loyalty to the ideology of a single political party, criminalizing an independent civil society, allowing only government-controlled associational groups, maintaining a communications monopoly, unleashing a terroristic police force, and ruling the economy.[2]

Lee Kuan Yew is clearly familiar with classical mass society theory. As he once commented,

> The speed of change has caused disruptions. About 80% of Singaporeans have been resettled into new homes in new towns. Their new homes are better. But they are living in the midst of strangers and in totally unfamiliar new surroundings. They miss their relatives and old neighbors and friends. They are disorientated. Some feel stress, many feel a sense of loss, a rootlessness, a void in their lives.[3]

However, Lee has not demonstrated much familiarity with the totalitarian variant of mass society theory. His informant on mass society theory appears to be a book by Michael Hill and Lian Kwen Fee, who explicated classical mass society theory, citing Durkheim, in *The Politics of Nation Building and Citizenship in Singapore* (1995), which she coauthored with Michael Hill.[4] Interestingly, although the book also quotes Kornhauser, there is no mention of totalitarian mass society theory in her book. Nevertheless, Lee Kuan Yew's Singapore systematically has destroyed civil society in the manner suggested by Kornhauser, with predictable consequences.

Consistent with mass society theory, social change due to rapid economic growth in Singapore has atomized individuals in society, resulting in deviant behavior. The government of Lee Kuan Yew and the second generation of leaders are very much aware of various types of asocial behavior among the masses, but their remedy has been to use the power of government to embark on various sudden, repressive, and unexpected crackdowns against what they perceive to be undesirable behavior. As Lee Kuan Yew puts it,

> I am often accused of interfering in the private lives of citizens. Yes, if I did not, had I not done that, we wouldn't be here today. And I say without the slightest remorse, that we . . .would not have made economic progress, if we had not intervened on very personal matters—who your neighbor is, how you live, the noise you make, how you spit, or what language you use. We decided what's right. Never mind what the people think.[5]

The manner in which the crackdown campaigns emerge, entirely without warning, suggests that the rulers of Singapore, too, are alienated from the rapidly changing reality. Seeking to control a reality that appears intractable, they have set up the second type of mass society, and Singapore has been totalitarianized, though they do not completely control the economy.

According to David Brown, the watershed year was 1981. Before the election of Benjamin Jeyaretnam to parliament, the ruling People's Action Party (PAP) and the government were "exclusionary," maintaining a certain distance from the masses, but afterward there has been an "inclusionary" effort to control associational groups so that PAP and the government could pretend to consult the masses.

The rulers of Singapore believe that government has been the friend of the masses in bringing prosperity and stability. Rapid economic growth and ultrastability have taken a severe toll on the masses, however. The ruled of Singapore are fearful of a government that behaves erratically. There appears to be no way to stop further alienation and further totalitarianization. Mass society theory, I believe, explains most of the anomalies about Singapore today. Evidence for my thesis now follows.

Singapore's Mass Society

Mass society theory focuses on the behavior of both ordinary people (Durkheim) and those who govern (Kornhauser). The evidence of Singapore's mass society will therefore begin with mass behavior and then turn to elite behavior.

Clearly, the ingredients of mass society are present in Singapore, which has rapidly changed from a humble port stopover into one of the top three richest countries in per capita income, so traditional forms of employment have been eclipsed by newer occupations requiring higher levels of skill. Since independence, many Chinese from neighboring countries have arrived in Singapore, which has the largest percentage of immigrants within Asia (43 percent) except for Brunei and Macao.[6] In addition, most Singaporeans have experienced an urban development that has entailed movement from single-story houses into high-rise apartments. No country in Asia has been so uprooted in so short a period of time.

Some deviant behavior has resulted.[7] Although Singapore is often perceived as the safest country in Asia, in 1993, Singapore had a murder rate of 59.4 per 100,000 population annually, but by 2013 the island republic had only .3 homicides per 100,000, safer than any Asian country but Hongkong. When rates of juvenile delinquency were increasing, the government in 1997 decided to ban "tea dancing" among persons under age 16. A study in 1998 revealed that the explanation was that delinquents were from homes with many siblings and high-income fathers, but by 2012, the problem was greatly reduced. The suicide rate (10.3 cases per 100,000) ranks 48th in the world, higher than other Southeast Asian countries but lower that East Asia. Suicide is most common in housing projects; attempted teenage suicide has also risen in recent years. Drug rehabilitation cases went up 50 percent from 1990 to 1995, but arrests slowed to a 5 percent increase in recent years. Draconian laws on drug possession have forced those needing treatment to go outside the country and are not counted in government statistics.

Divorce rates, 1.5 per 1,000 population in recent years, with a divorce/marriage rate of 28, higher than other Southeast Asian countries but below East Asia. Although divorces increased in the 1990s, they have leveled off in recent years.

At a more personal level, Singaporeans are "crass, selfish and egoistic," according to former Prime Minister Goh Chok Tong. There are few avenues for Singaporeans to assert their discontent, as the conventional approach of supporting an opposition party is risky. One mass society way of displaying displeasure with overregulation is to deliberately place chewing gum on the doors of mass transit cars in order to prevent them from closing, a practice that led to the banning of chewing gun, yet another example of what Korea's President Kim Dae-Jung has called Singapore's "Orwellian extreme in social engineering." One estimate is that 20 percent of all Singaporeans want to migrate from the island republic, and many in fact do so. The net out-migration rate (16 per 1,000 population) is the fourth highest in the world, below only Qatar, United Arab Emirates, and Zimbabwe.[8]

The pressures of Singapore's highly materialistic society are often cited as responsible for some of the various forms of deviant behavior. The increasing economic gap between rich and poor has been acknowledged by Prime Minister Lee Hsien Loong,[9] with top management increasing salaries over the years while the masses have improved their lot at percentages less than the annual growth rate. Compared to other countries, Singapore's inequality is exceeded only by African and Latin American countries. While there is a long queue to buy a Mercedes, most in Singapore cannot own a car. The moderate-wage policy, however, is said to be necessary because of competition from other countries with even lower wages. As Lee Kuan Yew has admitted, economic growth has proceeded "unequally, often unjustly."[10] Housing costs have increased dramatically while an absence of true collective bargaining has prevented wages from rising to keep up. Because living costs are sailing beyond wages, both parents tend to work, leaving children unsupervised when they come home from school. As a result, some join youth gangs that engage in fights in front of shopping malls. In addition, job hopping, to increase salaries, is endemic.

The educated elite are not immune from the alienation.[11] Many are afflicted with kiasu, namely, competitive selfish anxiety. Tens of thousands, according to a tearful Lee Kuan Yew, leave the country each year for residence elsewhere. Even at the Institute of Southeast Asian Studies and the National University of Singapore, I found that faculty and students are in mortal fear of expressing politically incorrect opinions. As Chris Lingle and Richard Deck report, spies in university classes take notes on those who express politically incorrect views.

The connection between the economic squeeze and rude behavior has been acknowledged by the government. In early 1997, Prime Minister Goh Chok Tong said, "Singaporeans cannot just be materialistic, self-centered and impatient to get rich quick."[12] He then urged a more "gracious" society, a theme that Lee Kuan Yew first sounded in the 1960s.

To say that Singaporeans need to be gracious is an accusation that they are not gracious today. Such rhetoric is part of a general tendency of the government to find scapegoats. According to the official line, domestic dissidents and foreign meddlers should pay heavily for making trouble, and many citizens agree. At the same time, government officials do not hesitate to carp at ordinary citizens, who are told to "conform" because their opinions are unimportant.[13] Chinese who speak English are told that they are too Westernized. Non-English-speaking Chinese are chided for being out of touch with current realities. All Chinese are told to stop using dialects and instead to speak to one another in Mandarin. Indians, meanwhile, are berated for being too outspoken, and Malays are instructed that they are not in the mainstream. All Singaporeans are told that they lack "cultural ballast" and are uncreative. In this apparent insultocracy, everyone is at fault for all the problems but the government, which acts boldly, unapologetically, and without graciousness.

As documented by the previous chapters, the government seeks to stamp out all organizations autonomous of the state until the masses are co-opted. Newspapers and religious organizations with contrary perspectives are punished. News leaks, even of correct facts, result in retribution. Government-appointed judges make the "right" decisions in politicized trials. Autonomous interest groups, such as the Law Society, are muzzled or co-opted. Opposition party candidates are vilified and bankrupted. Americans, whether diplomats or teenagers, are deliberately humiliated. To effect greater control over the masses, the Societies Act requires all organizations with more than ten members to register; no reason need be given for denying registration, as in the case of People Like Us, which in 1997 was denied registration and thus became an "unlawful society." Any member of an unlawful society or person attending a meeting of an unlawful society is subject to a three-year jail sentence and a S$5,000 fine. Police must approve any public assembly as well as the speakers at the rally. The government has sponsored community-based and ethnic organizations as well as debates on proposed policies in letters to the editor, thereby increasing supervision over how ordinary citizens think.[14] Private clubs are no longer acceptable, and many Singaporeans believe that their phones are tapped.[15] To further limit privacy, cameras are installed in public toilets to ensure that urinals are flushed.

The government also attempts to establish a dominant public discourse. In the search for a national ideology, citizens have been told to eschew Western Values for shared "Asian Values," although all Singaporeans left their homelands to escape traditional societies, and produced a prosperous country by applying Western Values. The local press disseminates the party line and answers foreign critics with specious arguments, presenting the image of a be-leaguered Singapore. Decisions to lock up those who try to exercise freedom of speech and assembly are made on the basis of such catchphrases as the need to "nip in the bud" any pos-sible unrest because the country might face some supposed impending disaster that needs to be averted. With the masses fed nonsense in this manner, they are assumed all the more to be nincompoops, whose views can be ignored. Meanwhile, the possibility of a "kinder, gentler Singapore" or an eventual democracy has been dangled like a lollipop before masses who are urged to be patient. Many party officials and bureaucrats even believe the propaganda, as noted in the previous chapters.

The word "total" in the Total Defense Doctrine gives a further clue of the totalitarian reach of the government. Anything viewed as unfavorable, however minor, is depicted as a major threat, requiring the mobilization of all possible diplomatic, economic, psychological, and social resources, in order to advance Singapore's interests in the world. Thus, Singapo-reans lobby for special privileges in Washington, attack mere statements of American offi-cials as interference in internal affairs, and mobilize non-Western nations to oppose universal human rights standards.

I believe that I have now established the case that Singapore has a mass society. The mass society that flows from rapid social change was inevitable, and the government should not judge itself or its citizens too harshly for the results. However, the regime has invoked governmental repression in order to cope with the social effects of mass society, resulting in totalitarianization. In the rest of the chapter, I will address the various puzzles identified in previous chapters in order to explain some of the dynamics at work in Singapore in light of mass society theory.

The Economy

There are three major puzzles about Singapore's economy. One is why Singapore has been so successful economically, while other Third World countries have failed to achieve pros-perity. Second, how can we classify the economy? Is the economy truly a "free market" economy, and is Singapore a "developed" or a "developing" economy? In addition, the occa-sional lack of confidentiality of business transactions requires an explanation.

The Singapore government assumes credit for the economic progress of the country and stakes its reputation on continued prosperity. Most observers assume that the government is responsible for the country's economic success. In Chapter 4, however, Christopher Lingle and Kurt Wickman argue that Singapore's status as a small island in a geographically fortunate location presented limited options. Singapore had no alternative but to trade. Lacking domestic capital, the country had to invite foreign investment. They argue that the logic of economics for a city-state meant that the path taken by Lee Kuan Yew's government would have been taken by any other sane Singaporean government. In other words, Singapore should thank Adam Smith, David Ricardo, and the other giants of economic thinking much more than Mr. Lee, who merely followed in their footsteps.

Nevertheless, Singapore might have taken the wrong path. For the Singapore government to argue that its policies spurred economic growth, specific policies need to be identified. Lingle and Wickman, however, find no such innovative policies. They point out that Singapore simply copied noninterventionist policies already adopted in Hongkong. They also note that the most important managers of the economy have not been government officials; instead, management of government corporations has been assigned to corporate executives drawn from the private sector. Moreover, when Singapore tried an original policy, failure resulted: The import substitution policy of the early years resulted in stagnation,[16] and the high-wage policy in the early 1980s caused recession.

Lingle and Wickman also note that there is a dual economy in Singapore, wherein the larger corporations are free from government regulations, but small businesses are overregulated.[17] Thus, they assert that the economic success of Singapore has been artificial—due to foreign corporations in free trade zones that tapped into the booming international economy rather than into any domestic dynamism. In *Singapore's Authoritarian Capitalism*, Lingle further argues that public investment in Singapore (in which the government has dipped into the Central Provident Fund to assist favored businesses) has "one of the lowest returns on capital investment in the world," and he cites data to show that only 1.75 percent of total real growth of domestic income from 1960 to 1991 was due to increased productivity.[18] Lee Hsien Loong evidently conceded this latter point, urging Singaporeans to be more creative.[19]

To answer the second question, how to classify the Singapore economy, an authoritative definition is needed. Lingle and Wickman describe a "dual economy" because the rules that apply to the domestic economy are waived for foreign corporations, which employ most of the workers.[20] Within the domestic economy, the government started many corporations or took over the regulation of existing corporations, so the term "socialist" may be partly applicable. However, in the late 1980s, Singapore began to privatize many government corporations. Lingle has elsewhere referred to Singapore's domestic economy as "crony capitalism."[21] The most blatant example occurred when Lee's brother, head of Hotel Properties Ltd., sold luxury apartments at a discount to Lee and his son in 1996. Kurt Wickman provides other examples: Lee's youngest son was the chief executive officer of Singapore Telecom, his wife was a majority owner in a bus and taxi firm that receives government contracts, and Lee & Lee (a law firm in which Lee Kuan Yew's brother and spouse are partners) handled all housing contracts for government flats. Lingle also challenges the belief that Singapore strictly enforces anti-corruption legislation by noting that penalties are not severe for PAP officials and that several Singapore firms are fronts for smuggling operations.[22] Accordingly, Lingle choose the term "authoritarian capitalism" because Singapore combines political centralization with economic decentralization.

Singapore's quality-of-life index ranks 11, the highest in Asia.[23] The Organization for Economic Development and Cooperation (OECD) classifies Singapore, as a "developed" country, and the International Monetary Fund (IMF) classifies Singapore as an "advanced" economy. In 1992, only 10 percent of the labor force had had any postsecondary education, but that figure rose to 41 percent in 2002 and 50 percent in 2012, when 29 percent were degree holders. Singapore workers are productive, ranking 17th in the world and the highest in Asia, but nearly two-thirds as much as Americans. Although there is 92.5 percent literacy, about 20 percent are literate only in their vernacular languages. Some 10 percent of the population lived below the poverty line in 1990, but one estimate is that there was a significant increase to 26 percent by 2011, a statistics that the government refuses to release. Nearly all the advanced technology is brought into the country by foreign corporations; two indigenous Singapore companies are in the Fortune 500 list of the world's largest corporations, Flextronics and Wilmar. In addition, some 28 percent of the labor is imported, including Filipina housemaids and Thai construction workers. Without the incomes of the managers of expatriate firms and their employees, leaders of the island republic concede, Singapore would be classified as a Third World country.

In short, the Singapore government has done much less to deserve credit for statistical indicators of success than is generally thought, yet has developed the myth that the People's Action Party (PAP) is the goose that has been laying golden eggs. In the domestic sector, government control is dominated by a few large firms and a declining percent of local entrepreneurs.[24] In the foreign sector, the government defers to the multinational corporations unless they appear to meddle in domestic politics; in the latter case, the confidentiality of banking and business transactions is breached by political considerations.

"Asian Values"

For a time in the 1990s, Singapore leaders championed the concept of "Asian Values" in a country that is highly Westernized. Moreover, the concept of "Asia" itself was a Western invention developed once upon a time as a myth to contrast the hardworking, thrifty European with the lazy, profligate Asian who needed the help of the imperialist white man in order to advance. Why would Singapore, a former colony, seek to dredge up this colonial racist rhetoric?

Clearly, the prosperity of Singapore required a large part of the population to have work habits acceptable to foreign corporations. The younger generation had to reject the traditional values of their families in order to adopt the more competitive orientations of the world economy. However, as the Westernized younger generation has increased in size, challenges to the ruling party have emerged.

In the early years of the republic, PAP encouraged Singaporeans to adopt pragmatic Westernized attitudes in order to advance economically; the stress on meritocracy cultivated individual competition. Those who overasserted the interests of separate ethnoreligious groups were called "chauvinists," but the major ethnoreligious groups were still allowed to have their own educational track. When voters began to reject PAP rule, the Western idea of democracy was declared a threat. As conversions to Christianity increased rapidly, Lee Kuan Yew attributed this development to the alienation associated with rapid social change, fearing that PAP rule would be undermined by the liberation theology movement that toppled Philippine President Ferdinand Marcos.

Accordingly, a new national ideology was needed so that an antidemocratic discourse would receive popular support, and this meant relying on the root cultures of the diverse Singapore population. The first attempt to develop an antidemocratic ruling philosophy focused on Confucianism, but this failed because it appealed only to a part of the population—to Chinese whose families had left China some time ago because they rejected Confucianism, which relegates merchants to a low position in society. The next antidemocratic concept was "Asian Values," but this was later changed into the "shared values" movement, which seeks to combine the best elements of Asian and Western cultures.[25]

Nevertheless, the "Asian Values" theme was asserted by government officials outside Singapore as a way of building solidarity with a region that is increasingly dominated by China. An essay on the subject by one editorial writer for the *International Herald Tribune* prompted PAP leader Kishore Mahbubani to respond, whereupon Christopher Lingle penned a rejoinder in the same publication. As a result, libel lawsuits were filed against both Lingle and the *Tribune* in Singapore.[26]

What, then, are "Asian Values"? In Chapter 4, Lingle and Wickman formulate one version. The official definition is similar: (1) community before self, (2) the family as the basic unit of society, (3) consensus rather than contention to resolve conflicts, (4) racial and religious tolerance and harmony, and (5) community support for the individual. Interestingly, the fifth point was added in 1991, and a sixth proposed item—honest government—was rejected.[27] Of course, many Westerners accept all these points and admire Asians for many more reasons,[28] but the subtext is that Western civilization (1) puts the individual before the community, (2) does not support family values, (3) is too contentious, (4) is intolerant of diversity, and (5) forces individuals to rely on government rather than their own communities. In addition, this Occidentalphobic construction posits that Western civilization (6) has peaked and is on the decline, (7) is parochial and thus its concept of human rights is not universal, (8) does not encourage its people to make sacrifices for their beliefs or their continued prosperity, and (9) is the source of much evil in the world—or at least in Singapore.

The idea that Eastern organic collectivist values have a competitive advantage over Western atomistic individualism is certainly not new. Perhaps the first to state the thesis was Ezra Vogel, who tried to explain the success of Japan in *Japan as Number One* (1979) and then broadened his thesis in *Ideology and National Competitiveness* (1987).[29] Samuel Huntington's thesis that Western Values are parochial added support to the "Asian Values" movement.[30]

Critics of the "Asian Values" thesis are not confined to Westerners. Goh Keng Swee, principal architect of Singapore's economic policies, argued that the so-called "Asian Values" are in reality "Victorian values." Opposition leader Tang Liang Hong characterized the government's "Asian Values" as a dangerous pretext for paternalism that will "bury" true Asian Values. President Kim Dae-Jung of Korea, who argues that "Asian Values" are a cover for antidemocratic practices, quotes Chinese philosopher Meng-Tzu (372–289 BCE) as an advocate of democracy.[31] Asians have come forward to criticize the myth of a homogeneous Asia. Asian Americans, similarly, resent Singaporeans who broadcast the stereotype of the "invulnerable Asian overachiever," which, as Richard Deck notes, has produced a backlash against Asian Americans within the United States. Rather than engaging the debate about the content or validity of the "Asian Values" thesis, with which I have much sympathy,[32] the point to be stressed here is that the attempt to forge a new identity for Singaporeans is crafted in response to the perception that alienated citizens are loyal only to themselves, with the objective of branding those who favor democracy as "un-Singaporean." The "core values" approach, according to Lingle and Wickman, is used to persuade the public that any deviation from PAP rule would bring economic disaster to Singapore. PAP's response to the mass society caused by rapid social change, in short, is to intensify the mass society imposed by the government by telling the people what to think.

Media Censorship

In Chapter 5, Derek Davies notes that Lee Kuan Yew expressed a strong commitment to freedom of the press before becoming prime minister, but then jettisoned his commitment afterward. Once in power, Lee quickly took over government-controlled radio; television followed in 1963. In regard to newspapers, he turned the once-vibrant domestic press into lap dogs. Instead of having PAP members start a newspaper of their own, to compete with independent news dailies by presenting the official "truth," the power of government was used to silence alternative visions of reality.

The most repeated rationale for limiting press freedom takes the form of the argument that "when reporting has been left to the marketplace of ideas, it has from time to time led to civil commotion, riots and mayhem."[33] But only three cases of alleged newspaper incitement to riot have been cited to justify media repression, the only one after independence being the arrest of executives of *Nanyang Siang Pau* in 1971, when no such riot occurred. Later, foreign control of the local press was a pretext to shut down voices alternative to PAP, whereas in fact the editorial writers questioned policies that Lee could not adequately defend. As soon as the government took over the main daily, the *Straits Times*, the range of criticism of government narrowed considerably. More recently, according to Lingle and Wickman, the justification for strict control of the media is that any deviation from the PAP party line risks economic collapse. For Derek Davies, the real explanation is somewhere inside the psyche of Lee Kuan Yew, whom he suggests has a "garrison mentality," is enamored of power, and manifests paranoia.

When the domestic press was tamed, articles appearing in the foreign press were increasingly perceived as major challenges to the legitimacy of the ruling elite. Rather than running rebuttals in the domestic press or banning foreign publications, which would have displeased human rights watchdogs around the world, the government decided to limit the number of copies that offending publications could distribute, but the effect has been the same— censorship for making politically incorrect statements.[34]

Presumably, criticism is fair if it is stated humbly; the same words are perceived as unfair criticism if they are stated in an aggressive, disrespectful, or vituperative manner. Singaporean law is similar to British law in allowing officeholders to sue for libel. Nevertheless, libel lawsuits have been carried very far because of a belief that any negative coverage, however minute, exposes officeholders to ridicule, such that they will "lose control," and the consequence "will not be more freedom, but confusion, conflict, and decline."[35] Ironically, in the Lingle case, Lee Kuan Yew and others were offended and sued because of a vague reference to unnamed governments that bankrupt opposition politicians, but in court the government documented eleven such cases, admitting that the statement applied to Singapore, and thus that Lingle was correct. Of course, the outcome of a libel suit filed by the Singapore government is never in doubt. The practice of collecting damages for stating the truth clearly restricts the possibility of fair criticism.

From the mid-1980s to the 1990s, when the *Straits Times* urged readers to comment on proposed policies in letters to the editor, objections to some of the proposals were indeed

printed, some pseudonymously. However, the government rarely modified its planned legislation or regulations, the *Straits Times* insisted that letter writers must disclose their names,
and the public was left with the impression that a negative letter would be placed into an individual's file at the Internal Security Department. As Prime Minister Goh reminded Singaporeans, "the Western idea of the press . . . as an adversarial watchdog of government goes
against our goal of consensus politics . . ."[36] More bluntly, Lee Kuan Yew called glasnost a
mistake that led to the toppling of the Soviet Union, and he preferred to have foreign reporters to stay short assignments so that they would not, in his words, "get to the truth."[37]

Most newspapers extend the courtesy of a reply when a person or an organization objects
to inaccuracies in a news story. In Singapore, the government has elevated this practice to a
"right," a longstanding English term that has its origin in a belief that there are areas where
governments may not restrict personal liberty. Singapore's "right of reply," however, does
not apply to individual citizens, as alleged misdeeds of Singaporeans are often played up in
the press, and their voices are never heard. The "right of reply," instead, applies to what the
foreign press says about the Singapore government. Whenever news or opinion has an "incorrect" slant, government agencies have demanded that overlong, nitpicking rejoinders must
be printed.[38] Even though the *Far Eastern Economic Review* decided to print all governmental replies in 1987, the government decided to cut its circulation in 1988 without demanding
the right of reply when a particular news report differed from the Singapore government's official version.

However, if the foreign press makes a misstatement, the Singapore government can easily reply in the domestic press. The *Straits Times* reprinted the *New York Times* columns of
William Safire along with snide rebuttals in order to prompt Singaporeans to rally around the
government, since their country has allegedly become the West's whipping boy by observers
with a lot of "chutzpah." The government, thus, denies the "right of reply" to all but itself,
sues even when the right of reply is still available, and cuts circulation whether or not the
right of reply is denied. The foreign press, as Lingle and Wickman note, cannot fight back
because they are so logistically dependent upon Changi airport.

Once again, the danger of social mass society (civil chaos) is used as a rationale for imposing governmental mass society (restrictions on media). However, the likelihood of civil
chaos due to incidents of "press misconduct" in independent Singapore has been nonexistent.

The government informs the public that a tight control over the press is expected to last until the country reaches a point of greater national stability and unity, but the stifling of fair criticisms and alternative news only delays national stability and unity. The public in Singapore, meanwhile, gives the *Straits Times* as much credibility as Soviet citizens used to give to *Pravda*.[39]

Rule of Men, Not Laws

The criminal justice system in Singapore, according to Francis Seow in Chapter 6, was more fair under the British than under PAP today. A major puzzle is that Lee Kuan Yew once championed the rule of law, pointing to excesses under British rule, yet while in office has brushed aside trial by jury and the independence of the judiciary. Related puzzles are why Singapore authorities use torture, employ preventive detention, and pick on certain inconsequential victims so blissfully.

According to Singaporean sociologist Chua Beng Huat, there is no rule of law or constitution in the Anglo-American sense in Singapore:

> [T]he legal system . . . is an instrument of social control and of rectification of social behavior, tailored to the needs of the issues at hand by the legislative Parliament, the sole authority in law-making. Instances abound in which laws are changed and invoked retroactively to punish violators; statutes are changed to better suit enforcement immediately after they were successfully contested by litigants, such as the removal of the Internal Security Act from judicial review after one of the government's indictments was reversed in the Supreme Court; and finally, constitutional changes are undertaken with speed because of the absolute majority of the PAP.[40]

Singapore's parliament does not view law as an effort to translate moral principles into various limitations on government. According to Chua, law is seen as a pragmatic tool to be shaped and reshaped in order for Singapore (and PAP rule) to survive and prosper.

Francis Seow reports that the abolition of jury trials can be traced to two trials.[41] In 1963, Lee kept in frequent touch with Seow, who was the prosecutor in the trial of Jamit Singh. Lee's nervousness over the outcome was relieved when Singh was found guilty of embezzling union funds, thereby removing a political opponent from the landscape. Shortly thereafter, jury trials were abolished for all but capital offenses. Four years later, Lee displayed anxiety in a murder trial of Freddy Tan in which the defense had called Dr. Wong Yip Chong, who repeatedly obtained vacationing psychiatrists to testify that accused persons were psychopaths and not fully responsible for their actions. After the jury brought in a verdict of manslaughter rather than first or second degree murder, and a life sentence rather than hanging was imposed, Lee had parliament abolish jury trials in all cases. With independent juries out of the way, Lee then chipped away at the independence of judges, a story that occupies much of Francis Seow's narrative in Chapter 6.

Clearly, Lee's political agenda prevailed over concerns for justice. While keeping the forms of an independent judicial system, the decisions rendered by courts in political trials have been entirely predictable. If the Singh case is an example of neutralizing someone who provoked a riot, and the Freddy Tan case was viewed as symptomatic of allowing murderers to cop insanity pleas to obtain lesser sentences, we can understand that Lee had in mind preventing the chaos of a mass society by controlling the otherwise uncertain proceedings of courts, wherein opponents might "confuse" the public with facts at variance with the PAP party line. Thus, in seeking to avoid a classical Durkeimian mass society, Lee established a governmentally based totalitarian mass society.

Singapore leaders inexplicably seem proud that police authorities use torture, knowing that most of those arrested will crack under pressure, resulting inevitably in false confessions. The use of torture by police and internal security officials, who claim to be professionals at their business, can be traced to two sources. One is the introduction of such methods to the security department by Japanese during World War II,[42] when Lee Kuan Yew's political consciousness emerged. The second source is Joseph Stalin's Soviet Union, which developed methods that are practiced around the world by regimes with totalitarian agendas.[43] Pride in the use of torture, thus, is an eloquent way in which to tell citizens of the awesome power of the state, which must not be questioned. Singapore is known worldwide as "Torture City."

Caning was introduced into Singapore by British colonial authorities. British schools, not courts, used caning, so the inference is that the colonials used the cane on the colonized because they believed the latter to be immature. The same belief that ordinary people are immature persists within the Singapore government, which carries on endless campaigns about hair length, flushing toilets, and the like, thereby telling citizens that they lack discipline and must be treated like children; even lawyers are told what shade of tie to wear in court.[44] Thus, the criminal justice system in Singapore tends to be less interested in whether an individual is guilty or innocent of a crime than in deterrence. As noted above, statistics show that criminals in Singapore are not deterred. Rather than being interested in the root causes of crime or of opposition to the regime, the penalties have increased to theatrical levels, provoking counterreactions from concerned observers around the world that Singapore's brand of justice, to quote opposition leader Chee Soon Juan, is "barbaric."[45]

British colonial authorities used preventive detention while there was an active Communist underground. Singapore's detention of Chia Thye Poh in 1966 was premised on this threat, but Chia has never confessed to being a Marxist, which contradictorily would have been a condition of his release. The events of 1987 best explain why Singapore retains the Internal Security Department tool of preventive detention in the absence of any real threat to internal security: A so-called threat to internal security is used as a cover for some other political motive. In 1987, when twenty-two young professionals were detained under the terms of the Internal Security Act, some form of subversive conduct had to be identified. Accordingly, they were portrayed as "Marxists" under the alleged control of Tan Wah Piow, who in turn was supposedly in league with Malcolm Caldwell, a deceased professor in England whom Singapore authorities believed to be a "Euro-Communist." Caldwell, however, was merely an academic exponent of the theory of dependency, which had been attacked by academic Marxists for being un-Marxian, a fact that was suppressed by Singaporean authorities.[46]

In 1988, Francis Seow was detained for seventy-one days on the bizarre accusation that he was plotting with and receiving financing from the American government to defeat PAP by running candidates for office in forthcoming elections. In all the cases cited above, there was not a shred of truth to the accusation that led to preventive detention, and even torture failed to extract hard evidence of anything incriminating. In short, preventive detention is used not only to "nip in the bud" actual or even potential threats to security but also to deal with imagined threats. Meanwhile, the objective of neutralizing the victim is accomplished by vilification of supposed enemies in the controlled press so that "stability" will be maintained, the "moral integrity" of the government will be unblemished, and the public will know that PAP does not trust its citizens.[47]

Those abused by the criminal justice system have generally been scapegoats, that is, individuals whose alleged misconduct is characterized by a scripted catchphrase and then broadcast to the public as a warning. Alleged Communists (Chia Thye Poh, 1966), ethnic chauvinists (editors of *Nanyang Siang Pau* in 1971, Tang Lian Hong in 1996), Marxists (Tan Wah Piow in 1975, Vincent Cheng in 1987), those causing "public disquiet" (J. B. Jeyaretnam in 1986), American collaborators (Francis Seow in 1988), and even Americans themselves (E. Mason Hendrickson in 1988, Michael Fay in 1994, Christopher Lingle in 1995) have been crucified by the Singaporean news media so that the public will fear that there is a line of misconduct that they must not cross—but the public never knows when that line will be redrawn, when the goalposts will be moved forward. That the evidence against these recent "enemies" is thin or nonexistent[48] is important, too, so that the public will fear the totalitarian aims and powers of the state.

According to the New York City Bar Association, the

> campaign against the rule of law is part of a broader effort by the current Singapore government to secure its hold on power. It parallels a similarly motivated effort to strangle the independent institutions of civil society and thus prevent the emergence of an effective and organized opposition.[49]

The leaders of Singapore want the public to believe that chaos is likely to emerge if "dangerous" ideas gain currency. What better way to preempt every conceivable "disaster" than by totalitarianizing the institutions of law and order?[50] The Singaporean rule of men, not laws, is the very disaster that has produced a mass society.

Foreign Policy

How Singaporean leaders could possibly believe that they can defend their country militarily is yet another puzzle. The tendency to antagonize neighboring countries and pull at the coattails of Uncle Sam is also in need of an explanation.

One reason why Britain wanted to incorporate Singapore into Malaysia in 1963 was the fear that an independent state might go Communist, as leftists in coalition with Communists controlled the government by 1959. Singapore's expulsion from Malaysia, Lee Kuan Yew's biggest political disappointment, occurred when the government in Kuala Lumpur could no longer tolerate Lee's contentiousness. In Chapter 7, Richard Deck carefully notes the many real threats, internal more than external, which faced the survival of newly independent Singapore. Riots broke out when the government prior to PAP rule did not take preventive measures, and in the early years of PAP hegemony there was an inability to perceive early warning indicators of impending unrest.

Accordingly, as Deck describes, Lee Kuan Yew's government adopted a "Total Defense Strategy," only one element of which involved military defense. Lee established the framework for responding to potential internal turmoil, as follows: When early warning indicators of trouble emerge, the situation is labeled a "crisis" that threatens the survival of the state; those viewed as troublemakers, especially the "mastermind," must then be arrested by the Internal Security Department so that the conspiracy "cancer" will be "nipped in the bud." This procedure, originally retail in scope, became wholesale when press freedom and judicial independence ended. Opportunities for threats of the state were reduced to a minimum because, in the cliché-prone parlance of PAP, a small state has "a low margin for error."

The military component of the Total Defense Doctrine was designed after consultation with the government of Israel, a small state that has managed to survive despite being surrounded for many years by hostile neighbors. The Israeli strategy was copied in at least two respects. One is the development of a modern air force, which is advertised in Singapore as an invulnerable protector of the state because it is more advanced technologically than that of its neighbors. The second element in the defense strategy is compulsory military service for all Singaporean males from age eighteen to twenty and one half, with all trainees kept on reserve after national service and subject to immediate recall for military exercises until age forty. However, national service is not conceived in narrow military terms. In the 1960s, it was already represented as an experience that would make "the community conscious that they must be fit and disciplined to protect the prosperity they were creating."[51] In 1987, when Lee Hsien Loong indicated that Malays would only be deployed in the rear of battle, the primary objective of national service was conceded to be maintaining a subservient population— that is, psychological defense.[52]

Why, then, annoy other countries? Since an overargumentative Lee Kuan Yew prompted the expulsion of Singapore from Malaysia, abrasiveness became an emblem of an independent-minded country that sought to survive. Barking is one way to deter intruders and to justify enormous military expenditures.[53] Lee's persuasive vituperation paid off in the form of concessions from Britain, Malaysia, and the United States over the years.[54] However, the subtext of negative remarks about Malaysia is an arrogant sense of superiority. PAP leaders believe that their country is "annoyingly prosperous" and need not be concerned about how other countries perceive Singapore.[55] Repeated undiplomatic moves encourage the public to believe that the city-state is winning victories against regional dinosaurs. During 1997, the escalating war of words across the Causeway was entirely unprecedented: Kuala Lumpur believed itself to be defamed by the tactlessness of Lee Kuan Yew and the *Straits Times*. Singapore then had to scramble to find alternative sources of water.

Tugging at Uncle Sam's beard only occurred within the 1990s. Lee Kuan Yew's effort to cultivate friends in the United States, so as to attract economic investment and military ties, was largely successful until the mid-1980s. His candid wisdom antagonized the rest of Southeast Asia but impressed Americans, who saw him as the most Westernized leader in Asia. At the same time, Lee was apprehensive about the United States in several respects. First, the United States has exercised the power to topple unfriendly regimes, so he was apprehensive of Washington's tendency to retaliate against those who cross American interests. Second, American culture lionizes adolescence, thus producing a cultural generation gap that is very un-Confucian. Third, the first idealist nation, as Woodrow Wilson once characterized the United States, has a missionary zeal to promote democracy and human rights, though some of the zeal is supplied by labor leaders and progressive interests who are incensed that Americans are losing jobs to plants which are set up in dictatorships that suppress trade-unions and pay low wages.

During the Cold War, Lee's anti-Communism made him popular in Washington, which ignored matters of human rights. When the Cold War ended, Lee's anti-Communism became anachronistic. With the expulsion of E. Mason Hendrickson and the caning of Michael Fay, Singapore dramatically ended the honeymoon with Washington. The Hendrickson/Seow episode proved that Singapore's leaders do not respect Americans.[56] The Fay affair showed that leaders of the city-state are willing to harass and even torture an American resident, whether guilty of a crime or not, rather than deal with the root causes of mass society that cultivate Singaporeans to engage in juvenile delinquency. In addition, many in academic communities and news organizations within the United States are enraged at Singapore for restricting the flow of information, using courts as political instruments, financing heroin smuggling, and loudly proclaiming that Western civilization is on the decline.[57]

The divorce between Singapore and the United States appeared irreparable so long as leaders of the island republic preferred to depict themselves as victims of a Western plot to impose destabilizing foreign values on Singapore.[58] Yet the English-speaking island republic has Westernized itself without any prodding in order to become internationally competitive. Once again, the fear of chaos (socially-based mass society imported from the West) is justified as grounds for maintaining firmness (governmentally-based mass society in Singapore).

Classifying and Rationalizing Singapore's Polity

Singapore's leaders claim to have a "democracy," and indeed Lee Kuan Yew once said that the best method for preventing the success of the Communist movement in Singapore and elsewhere was to uphold the "free choice of a people, by secret ballot, at periodic intervals."[59] But terms other than democracy have been proposed to describe the island republic. Since any classification depends upon the initial definition, I begin with a statement that was intended to convey the meaning of "democracy" to Lee Kuan Yew in the 1960s:

> some measure of popular will, of popular support; that from time to time, as accurately as is possible with trying to find out what human beings in a large group want or feel or think, one tries to act in accordance with the wishes of the majority. . . . but also [to] respect the need to accommodate a large dissenting minority.[60]

Singaporean political scientist Bilveer Singh, with the apparent approval of the ruling party, has defined a "competitive election," which is central to democracy, as follows:

> All law-abiding adult citizens are entitled to vote; elections are held regularly; political organizations are free to put up candidates, debate their merits freely, and criticize opponents; political organizations campaign with the objective of winning; each voter casts one vote in secret and is not hindered in expressing a choice; votes are honestly counted and the results faithfully reported; the candidate, party, or coalition with the most votes wins; the losing individual or party does not try to use force to alter the outcome or prevent the winner from taking office; and the party in power does not restrict political participation and competition which are within the parameters of existing rules.[61]

Perhaps the most authoritative definition of "democracy" in the social sciences is that of political scientist Robert Dahl, who indicates that "populist democracy" stresses the requirement that voters have equal weight in selecting among alternatives, whereas "Madisonian democracy" requires checks and balances, that is, a separation of the powers of branches of government, to ensure that no minorities will be deprived of "natural rights."[62] Dahl, thus, presents the well-known distinction between majority rule (substantive democracy) and minority rights (procedural democracy), which he tries to reconcile by combining the two elements into a unified definition of "polyarchic democracy."

In the Singapore case, there is no doubt that substantive, majoritarian democracy exists at the polls. Voter turnout is high. Candidates with the most votes are declared the winners and are subsequently seated in parliament. However, the majority of voters are not involved when the ruling party decides to expel individual parliamentarians. Moreover, when parliamentary seats are vacated, they are not always filled promptly, as in the case of the seat once occupied by J. B. Jeyaretnam, which was left vacant for several years after his expulsion. Lee Kuan Yew's antidemocratic idea of giving two votes for those aged twenty to forty has not been adopted, but the proposal does show contempt for the concept of democracy. Some Singaporeans even believe that there is no such thing as a secret ballot in Singapore.[63]

The main problem with Singapore's political system is that basic procedural rights are violated, such that minority interests, including those represented by opposition parties, are not given an equal chance to be represented in parliament. In Singh's words, the opposition party is not "free to put up candidates, debate their merits freely, and criticize opponents."

Opposition parties are discouraged in several ways. First of all, it is difficult to attract candidates to run for any party. As opposition politician Jeyaretnam has put it, "People whom we would like to have enrolled as candidates were saying, 'No way, after seeing what happened to you. You must think we are fools.'"[64] In other words, prospective opposition candidates do not expect a free and open debate because of a high probability that they will be sued and bankrupted after elections for libel or expelled from parliament for a slip of the tongue.[65] Any candidate of an opposition party needs funds to run a campaign, but government officials hound financial backers of minority parties in order to deter them from making monetary contributions.[66] For candidates who have the courage to run on opposition party slates, the Group Representation Constituency (GRC) device requires parties to put up slates of candidates, thus mathematically diluting the voting strength of minority ethnic groups within formerly single-member districts. No opposition candidate has ever been elected from one of these GRCs, which are reportedly gerrymandered (geographically distorted) on the basis of past support for opposition parties.[67] The ethnic minority candidates selected by PAP to run on these slates are, thus, Uncle Toms (members of a minority who parrot PAP's party line) who are not allowed to have their own constituencies. Similarly, the Nominated Members of Parliament and Non-Constituency Members of Parliament are co-opted by PAP; the latter inevitably serve as Uncle Toms.

Not all democratic politics, however, is confined to political parties and elections. In a democracy, the people have a right to petition for the redress of their grievances between elections. In order to petition, the people must be free to form groups that will lobby a government. Competing political parties in a democracy generally vid for the support of these groups, which are variously called "interest groups" or "pressure groups." In Singapore, however, such groups are branded today as "political sanctuaries" that supposedly are run in a manner similar to the Communist front organizations that operated in Singapore from the 1940s to the 1970s.[68] PAP's opposition to the idea of autonomous interest groups was most clearly stated in 1987, when the government stripped the Law Society's power to comment on proposed legislation, forced the shutdown of several religious organizations, and told those involved in activities of the interest groups that they could only become involved in politics by joining political parties. Later, PAP tried to feign consultation with or otherwise to control various independent organizations, thereby robbing the groups of their autonomy.

Nonetheless, PAP sincerely believes that allowing a very few ethnic, environmental, and other interest groups to exist without allowing them to be assertive is a democratic breakthrough. When one group acts to save treecutting, for example, PAP pats itself on the back for opening up the political process.[69] In 1994, however, when an article in the *Straits Times* reported some public discontent over a decision to peg salaries of high-ranking government officials at a percentage of the top private-sector employees, the writer was also told that if she wanted to express opinions of that sort, she should go into politics.[70] In short, in the politics of Singapore today, the people are repeatedly told that politics should be left to politicians.[70] Some consultation is doubtless genuine, but much is pseudoconsultation.[71] One obvious result is a depoliticized citizenry.

The current generation of PAP leaders is quite candid in rejecting democracy.[72] According to former Prime Minister Goh, a two-party system is "not realistic" for Singapore. For Lee Hsien Loong, "If we follow the examples of South Korea, Taiwan or the Philippines, in the name of democracy and human values, we shall come to grief." Instead, as National Development Minister Lim Hong Kiang has said, Singaporeans are supposed "to trust your leaders to represent your interests," even though the leaders give every sign of not trusting the voters. PAP leaders sometimes claim that democracy is alien to Asia, but this cultural premise is contradicted by the above quote from Lee Hsien Loong as well as the flurry of anonymous letters from Singaporeans to the *Far Eastern Economic Review* during 1987 and to the *Straits Times* during periods when PAP allows the public to express opinions on proposed policies. The reported reason for opposition to democracy, according to Lingle and Wickman, is a fear of economic decline if special interests in the public demand changes in the law that would render Singapore less competitive in the international economy.

Since Singapore leaders reject democracy, and have driven their most prominent opponents into exile, what type of government does the island republic have? Various observers differ.[73] Although Singaporean scholars prefer such terms as "restrictive democracy," "controlled democracy," "communitarian democracy," or "consociational democracy," most Westerners agree that the rule is "authoritarian." One Western scholar has characterized Singapore as "corporatist" because all political loyalty must be to the state. A book coauthored by an Australian and a Singaporean uses the term "civic republic" instead of choosing between the democratic versus authoritarian options. The term "near-authoritarian" is also used.

In the beginning of this chapter, I presented a definition of a "totalitarian" regime. Clearly, Singapore meets all but one of the criteria; the exception is that foreign firms are able to operate freely in the economy, though of course their executives are now well aware that their sons might be caned any day in a show trial after a coerced confession for something that they might not have done. But let us use the definition of "totalitarian" from Lee Kuan Yew:

If it is not totalitarian to arrest a man and detain him when you cannot charge him with any offense against any written law—and if that is not what we have always cried out against in Fascist states—then what is it?[74]

As President Kim Dae-Jung of Korea has said,

the biggest obstacle [to democracy in Asia] is not its cultural heritage but the resistance of authoritarian rulers and their apologists. . . . The fact that Lee's Singapore, a small city state, needs a near-totalitarian police state to assert control over its citizens contradicts his assertion that everything would be all right if governments would refrain from interfering the private affairs of the family.[75]

In short, Kim believes that Singapore's "near-totalitarianism" creates a mass society in which there are no independent institutions to intervene between the people and the state. Not even the family is sacrosanct, contrary to "Asian Values" and "shared values" pronouncements.

Nevertheless, the voters of Singapore baffle many observers by supporting PAP at each election with huge majorities. PAP has the advantage of setting the groundrules for all political activity in Singapore, so the public is socialized to respect the ruling party, and opposition candidates are subjected to the sanctions mentioned above. Moreover, opposition parties have not always contested enough seats to pose a challenge; PAP has already won enough seats to command a majority in parliament before the votes are counted. Although the opposition cannot find enough candidates to run and has not demonstrated competence to run the government if it won a majority, the real reason for limiting the number of contested seats is so that voters will be assured that a vote against PAP will send a message of protest but not unleash a repressive hurricane.

Why are voters generally satisfied with PAP rule? One of the reasons cited is that there is widespread home ownership. According to Chua Beng Huat, Singapore is a "home-owning democracy" in which 80 percent of the population lives in public housing, where 90 percent are owner occupants.[76]

PAP has the advantage in any election campaign, which may be called on short notice. The election campaign is only a ten-day affair. The repeated PAP tactic of threatening to give second-class treatment to constituencies that elect opposition candidates may also play a role in continuing to command a majority.

Voters have surprised everyone by voting increasingly for opposition candidates in recent years. Singapore's leaders were shocked to learn that some voters did not consider PAP parliamentarians to be honorable men who were governing in the best interests of the country as a whole. PAP's public analysis of the 1984 election, in which the ruling party's support declined 13 percent, was Confucian—that the masses were immature and ungrateful for the decades of progress and thus that a new consensus had to be forged. PAP quietly conceded that middle-class voters were alienated by the authoritarian management style, so various concessions were made.[77] To provide more consultation, the Ministry of Community Development established a Feedback Unit, and organizations at community centers and residences were allowed to air grievances. In addition, GRCs, Nominated Members of Parliament, and Non-Constituency Members of Parliament were instituted to dilute and co-opt the opposition.

But the most spectacular event was the arrest of the twenty-two young professionals in 1987, a summertime docudrama that was calculated to frighten voters into believing that all economic progress would evaporate if PAP rule were to end. However, PAP evidently forgot that political repression delegitimated the Lim Yew Hock government. When opposition candidates posted a 1 percent gain in the 1988 election, PAP realized that the public was unimpressed with the "Marxist cancer cell" charade of 1987, and polling data expressed even deeper discontent than the anti-PAP vote indicated.[78] Indeed, efforts to appease the middle class after the 1984 election resulted in increased working class defections. Lee Kuan Yew then expressed the fear that the opposition might be voted into power in a "freak" election in which a majority of voters decided to cast protest votes, still believing that PAP would win.[79] The 1991 election, in which there was yet another 1 percent decline in support for PAP, showed that working-class voters supported opposition candidates who protested rising medical and transport costs while Prime Minister Goh babbled about his so-called "kinder, gentler" style.[80] During the campaign of 1997, PAP repeated the threat to place opposition constituencies last on the queue for community upgrading, which in turn provoked a negative State Department comment on the threat. PAP was then able to rally voters by sending a message that Washington should mind its own business. Although PAP support rebounded by 4 percent in 1997, the popularity of the ruling party still remained 11 percent below the level attained in the election of 1980. Then came the startling results of the 2011 election, when PAP was repudiated by 40 percent of the voters. Evidently, PAP has been generally supported for economic reasons, but the working class is disaffected by rising costs, and the middle class is impatient for democracy.

Accordingly, it is possible to explain the paradox that democratic forms and values have declined while the prosperity of the country has skyrocketed. Whenever the public exercises the independence of thought that better education brings, "a danger to be nipped in the bud" or some similar cliché is articulated as the basis for repression. For example, Lee Kuan Yew, in his National Day Address of 1987, justified the detention of the twenty-two professionals as an effort to avoid the turmoil then occurring in Seoul, where the mass public demanded democracy. He predicted that South Korea would suffer economically as a result of the unrest. But when the year ended, statistics showed that the growth rate in increasingly democratic South Korea was twice that of increasingly totalitarian Singapore.[81] Later, Prime Minister Goh Chok Tong mused that the island republic could not "have done even half of what was achieved in the last thirty years if we had a multiparty system and a revolving-door government."[82]

The conundrum is that lack of democracy was supposedly a precondition to economic prosperity, yet prosperous Singapore presumably cannot afford democracy lest prosperity will be in jeopardy. No such correlation or precondition, however, has empirical support in the social science research.[83] According to Goh, "As our society becomes better educated and more mature, limits for expression will widen."[84] But the opposite is true. For example, according to the party line, the imagined "Marxist conspiracy" of 1987 showed "how little things have changed since the 50s and 60s."[85] In the early years of the republic, social turmoil came primarily from the working class, but the so-called crises of the 1980s and 1990s have involved the not so silent middle class, which is better educated and acts in a more mature manner than the prime minister, who once admitted to being "furious, flabbergasted and floored" when criticized.[86] In short, the mass society designed by the government to meet the delusionary crises of the early years has been rejected by the better educated and more mature citizenry. A vicious cycle, therefore, has been created: With support for PAP uncertain, new crises are concocted as if times have not changed, and the mass society worsens.

Social Problems

Three puzzles refer to Singaporean society. One is the policy regarding marriages among the most intelligent to "enhance the gene pool" despite scientific evidence that no such policy is feasible. The second is the policy toward ethnic groups, which appears to be muddled, alternating between communalism and anticommunalism. The third puzzle is why there is a problem of social alienation despite the economic achievements of the country.

The concept of having the more intelligent Singaporeans intermarry in order to produce "superpersons" is the harebrained scheme of Lee Kuan Yew, whose ignorance of biology and fascination with the goal of human perfection reveal peculiar elements of his personality. Based on the unsurprising fact that working-class families have more children than middle-class families, Lee leaped to the conclusion that Singapore, where the only resource is human intelligence, was doomed to decline if something were not done to reverse a supposed trend toward mediocrity. Accordingly, monetary incentives were offered if working class families would "stop at two" and if female college graduates married and had children. Although a matchmaker unit was established in a government agency in 1984, marriage rates continued to drop.[87] The policy clearly told the less well educated that they were expendable, lectured the better educated on how to live their personal lives, and informed all that Big Brother's mass society was now in the bedroom.

The marriage policy touched a nerve in the ethnic communities of Singapore. The public deconstructed the marriage policy to mean that Chinese college graduates should have more children, whereas Malays should be sterilized.[88] The long litany of events and statements in which Chinese PAP leaders have deprecated other ethnic groups need not be repeated here.[89] What remains odd is why government leaders continue to be so culturally insensitive. The obvious explanation is Chinese ethnocentrism, which feeds on the belief that Chinese are the superior race, as evidenced by the apparent fact that Chinese have built a prosperous Singapore in a region of less affluent Malay peoples. Even the policy of residential integration, which limits the minority percentage in units of public housing, is viewed by the government as necessary to forestall the possibility of "ethnic confrontations."[90] The rulers of Singapore, thus, operate a racist society in which one ethnic group is designated as the norm, while others are portrayed as deviant.

Social alienation, finally, is acknowledged by the leaders of Singapore. Explanations, however, differ. As Lee Kuan Yew has noted, Singapore grew too fast to have a smooth transition from a lowly position in the world to become among the top ten countries in per capita income: "We concentrated on wealth creation, not redistribution. We rewarded excellence more than mediocrity."[91] In this respect, Singapore does not differ from any other industrializing society, as described in the writings of Durkheim and other mass society theorists. For example, rising living costs in Singapore have forced both parents to work, so they are unable to manage their families at home, and their children are free to roam the streets for excitement, such as fistfights and shoplifting.[92] Increasing conversions to Christianity were cited by Lee in the National Day Address of 1987 as a visible sign that he felt that alienation is a problem in Singapore.

However, alienation in industrial societies has led to political protests and strikes to ameliorate conditions, and the eventual result has been democratization. Within Singapore, the opposite has occurred: Protests and strikes have been suppressed, and democracy has receded. Lee Kuan Yew's strange understanding of history, moreover, is that democracies would have prevented the Industrial Revolution in England.[93] Accordingly, he has responded to the alienation caused by economic growth by constructing a mass society through the institutions of government, which in turn has driven many among the best educated to greener pastures in other countries.

Lee Kuan Yew

At the center of Singapore's mass society is unquestionably its architect, Lee Kuan Yew. To understand Singapore requires some insight into the personality of this brilliant intellect, who achieved honors at Cambridge and has impressed audiences and political leaders around the world for decades, yet who is so insecure about his reputation that he sues for defamation even when he is not personally defamed.

Minibiographies of Lee Kuan Yew are found tucked within almost all writings on Singapore. There are official biographies by Alex Josey and Anthony Oei.[94] However, the unauthorized biographies of T. J. S. George, James Minchin, and T. S. Selvan are the most penetrating.[95] Although very few persons can write about him without expressing extremely favorable or unfavorable judgments, my task here is not to pin such labels as "alienated," "elitist," "Darwinist," "ethnocentric," "megalomaniac," "messianic," "narcissistic," "paranoid," "schizophrenic"—or even to accept his self-conception as a "thug."[96] Instead, I seek to explain some of the puzzles of Singapore by understanding him somewhat better. My only personal experience is as a member of the television audience while he spoke in an eloquent, humble, learned, yet forceful manner, reminiscent of the fireside chats of Franklin Delano Roosevelt. Besides, no one could ever engage in an in-depth interview with Lee Kuan Yew, a man who shies away from psychological self-analysis.[97]

Born in 1923, he had two heart operations in 1996 for narrowing of the arteries. His life expectancy is such that one of the chapter writers has expressed chagrin that Lee might not live to read what has been written in the pages of this book.

Lee Kuan Yew's parents came together in a traditional arranged marriage and were later separated. He, thus, probably never experienced a love relationship at home, and his later statement that "falling in love" is a Western fantasy[98] doubtless explains his inability to understand objections to his marriage policy. His anticommunalism may perhaps be explained by the fact that his parents were Straits Chinese—that is, Chinese who acculturated to Malay society before Britain established colonies in the region. His mother was one-sixteenth Malay. His parents were both hardworking entrepreneurs: His father worked for a foreign oil company, and then retired to work in a jewelry store; his mother gave cooking lessons.

His early life provided many opportunities to develop strategies for coping with conflict. During the Great Depression, his family accepted borders, some of whom doubtless used course language and had undisciplined, libertinistic personalities, thus perhaps accounting for Lee's prudery, contempt for hedonists, propensity to use sexual metaphors, and male chauvinism. As the first-born child, his biographers claim that he was spoiled. Nevertheless, especially when his parents separated, he assumed responsibility for producing a semblance of order for his younger siblings out of the daily chaos at home. As prime minister, he continued to play this role for all Singaporeans without first asking whether they wanted to be treated as children.

The turbulence of the conditions in which he grew up precluded learning how to exercise finesse in dealing with fellow humans, and the reins of power emboldened him to heights of abrasiveness totally at variance with Confucian and diplomatic norms. As a schoolboy, he established his identity as a bright student who could rise above others, not only in the classroom but also in aggressively dominating others outside of class, for which he was caned. He evidently used knowledge and morals disseminated by Christian educators not only to critique the turmoil at home but also to formulate anticolonial ambitions.

Although he grew up under British paternalistic rule, the dawn of his political consciousness evidently came when Japan took control of Singapore away from Britain in 1942. Nearly carted away to death, he learned how to stay alive by appearing to collaborate with black marketeers and Japanese colonial administrators. In the process, he learned how an Asian country could exercise totalitarian control, and much of contemporary Singapore has reproduced conditions not unlike Japanese occupation. He also learned how to reinvent himself, a feat that came in handy many times thereafter. Similarly, he has tried to reinvent Singapore from a relaxed backwater to a modern metropolis.

After World War II, Lee studied economics at the London School of Economics and law at Cambridge University. Through his university experience, he developed Anglophilia, a zeal for advanced learning, economistic ways of perceiving reality, clever debating skills, Fabian socialism, and knowledge of how to use the law as an instrument of control in a British colony. He also must have found intellectual reinforcement for Darwinistic predilections from his university experience, in which success accrues to those who have superior intelligence and determination. He set progressive goals for Singapore, relying on rationality rather than emotion, motivated by the desire to achieve ambitious goals for his country rather than to sit back and enjoy the good life.

At the same time, Lee is sentimental. When he returned home from his studies abroad in 1950, he married. He loves his wife and family very much, and he has provided his children with what he lacked in childhood—the stability of a considerate parent. Tears have fallen from his eyes on a few occasions—not for himself personally, but instead when his dreams for Singapore have not been fully realized.

He has orated in the manner of a parent, telling his children to be very careful to do the right thing or risk disaster or punishment. As the father of his country, he has expected filial piety in the Confucian tradition, believing that loss of face is intolerable. His need for approval, sometimes manifest as intolerance of open dissent, gives some evidence that he has a personality typical of a mass society—isolated and neurotic. He has few friends outside his immediate family, and he does not mind terminating friendships over policy differences by causing others to lose face.

After his marriage in 1950, he devoted himself to bringing Singapore into the modern world. As an anticolonialist, he put his legal skills to work by defending many clients, from Communists to Malays accused of killing British, although many of his clients disgusted him. He was particularly contemptuous of juries, who often acquitted defendants on the basis of sentiment rather than evidence, so his later abolition of the jury system must have appealed to his preference for rationality over emotion. In 1952, he achieved fame as an attorney for the union of postal workers, which achieved a major victory after a strike.

He then entered politics, where he had to bargain with the British while outmaneuvering chauvinists and Communists, both of whom could mobilize the masses demagogically. He did so by befriending a wide range of persons, including journalists and Internal Security officers, and then picking and destroying enemies one at a time. Whereas the island republic has been fully assured of stability, he has continued to believe that Singapore's very existence is fragile, and his early experience with Britain's timidity in dealing with Communists told him that it is better to stop an imagined dangerous trend early than to mop up too late.

Lee rose to power with the aid of a close group of likeminded, multiethnic patriots of Singapore. Early in his political career, he established his preeminence in oratory, and he met and discussed matters with ordinary people. Once in office, he became impatient with the undisciplined public, and he did not hesitate to stop those whom he thought to be misguided. After his first libel lawsuit, Internal Security detainee, and newspaper shutdown, the second time was much easier.

Quite often, political allies form cabals. To run the country, he installed a braintrust of Singaporeans dedicated to modernizing the country. He operated as a godfather, on the lookout to reward talent by elevating extremely able civil servants and politicians to positions of responsibility on the condition that they would owe absolute loyalty to him and his policies. When those whom he appointed proved "incompetent," that is, dilatory in implementing sweeping changes to achieve almost impossible goals, he discharged them summarily. When his favors were not returned, as when he elevated Francis Seow to Solicitor General who soon resigned to enter a private legal practice, he doubtless felt betrayed and suspected ulterior motives. But he bided his time so that he could pick the occasion to clobber what he has perceived as his opponents, whom he has then portrayed as part of some grand conspiracy to destroy all that he tried to do in building up his native land. As a result, few of Lee's early compatriots have retained his support.

Abroad, Lee has achieved fame on the international lecture circuit with eloquent epi-grams for nearly every occasion. His seemingly profound analyses of complex problems have been applauded by many politicians around the world. His disdain for all the social sciences but economics is probably due to the fact that human behavior is less controllable than he would wish and more creative in ways that he does not appreciate. He prefers impatiently to accept mere hypotheses about human behavior as substitutes for evidence. He has tried to create and package reality for the masses rather than recognize that humans, imperfect as we are, need to extract meaning from life by making up own minds. Lee is clearly a perfectionist who is not amused by dilettantes or fools, and his brashness has alienated many. Although he wants to portray an image of an all-knowing fatherly watchdog for his beloved Singapore, he has advanced a few foolish policies, and has later reversed course (notably in regard to eth-noreligious issues). Concerned with "face," he was not human enough to admit a single mis-take while in power. As mentioned in Chapter 2, he admitted that he was mistaken to have denigrated Malays during the 2011 election.

In his prime, Lee overstressed himself. The result has showed up in failing health. In 1965, when his dream of incorporating Singapore into Malaysia was destroyed, he nearly collapsed, and he took drugs to calm him down and pick him up. Thereafter, he stopped meeting ordinary persons at the grassroots. He smoked to the point of developing an allergy to tobacco, and indeed he became allergic to many foods. He has been known to overreact to events, flying into a rage, resulting in the nickname "Thunderclap."

After 1980, when his mother died and Singaporeans began to reject his overpaternalistic rule, his daily regimen slowed considerably, with many quiet hours of reading and golfing. Withdrawn and isolated, surrounded by handpicked appointees, he has increasingly appeared out of sync with the reality of the post-Cold War world, conjuring images of disaster on the basis of little evidence. His ability to outdebate everyone has waned; he suffered ridicule by attempting to outthink Francis Seow in 1987 and by whining in court during the trial of *Lee Kuan Yew v Derek* Davies (1989). His resignation as prime minister in 1990 permitted him the luxury of kibitzing when the next generation of leaders tried to carry on in his footsteps, appearing out of the loop while in fact having decisive influence on important matters.

When the Cold War ended, Lee's anti-Communism became an anachronism. His efforts to control the foreign press and to condone the arrest of "Marxists" lost far more face than the minor issues that prompted repression. His desire to alienate neighboring countries and the United States demonstrate an abandonment of a career built on pragmatism that appears to be culminating in a death wish. He is his own man.

The Future of Singapore

Since the next generation is indeed in power, the final puzzle is where Singapore is headed. Alternative scenarios vary considerably. In Chapter 4, Lingle and Wickman suggest that Singapore has reached its apogee and will decline as the First World relies more on robotics and Third World countries develop a sophisticated workforce that accepts lower wages than Singapore. They also argue that the increasing size of the middle class points toward eventual democratization, as there may be more wisdom outside PAP on how to respond to problems of increased international competitiveness. In Chapter 5, Davies suggests that things may indeed improve after Lee Kuan Yew dies. In Chapter 6, Seow hints that increasingly intelligent Singaporeans will force democratization. In Chapter 7, Deck outlined how Singapore was being downgraded strategically by the United States. All five authors, thus, believe that Singapore will either democratize or decline economically, whereas Lee and company are convinced that democratization would produce a catastrophe for Singapore.

PAP leaders appear confused. In 1987, the arrest of twenty-two professionals on trumped-up charges of being "Marxists" was greeted with the comment that the so-called conspiracy "shows how little things have changed since the 50s and 60s.[99] On the other hand, the results of the 1991 and 2011 elections showed that Singaporeans cannot be expected to reelect PAP on the rhetoric of the 1950s and 1960s. Prime Minister Goh Chok Tong adopted a "kinder, gentler" philosophy in 1990, suggesting that democracy might prevail in the long run, but in 1991 he responded to disappointing election results by dropping the "nice guy" posture, and state-funded nurseries were, for example, closed in errant constituencies.[100] Nevertheless, the *Straits Times* pats the government on the back whenever the government make concessions to suggestions from nongovernmental quarters, thereby giving credence to sociologist Liak Teng Kiat's prediction that the long-term prospect is for quiet democratization from the top down but repression if citizens demand democracy on their own terms.[101]

In addition to the dichotomous democratization-totalitarian and rise-or-fall scenarios, another possibility is a "Third China" scenario. Currently, Singapore is very much involved economically with China, one of the world's largest violators of human rights. Trade missions have been dispatched, Singaporeans manage the Suzhou industrial enclave.[102] Similarly, Lee Kuan Yew has cozied up to Myanmar and Vietnam and once had pretensions of being on the winning side in a struggle with Western countries, which will no longer be able to "impose their will and their values on us."[103] Evidence of this possible scenario cost Singapore the support of the United States in the 1990s.

The scenario that this chapter offers for the future is a continuation of Singapore's mass society. So long as the ruling elites fail to allow greater voice to the educated professionals and diligent members of the working class, thereby permitting a change in repressive policies, more deviant behavior and unsuccessful government crackdowns appear inevitable. Singapore may become a nastier place to live and work, with increasing class conflict. Out-migration will be maintained as a safety valve for the discontented, and thus few policy changes will be demanded.

Since a small state without an autonomous middle class provides few opportunities for alternative leaders to establish themselves, I expect that the People's Action Party, one of the causes of the mass society, will not give up power for some time, but may become more overtly factionalized. If factions do not lead into alternative political parties and democratization, then the third generation of voters may become fed up, either because the economy and society will falter or, more likely, because the public will become bored with PAP and its Kafkaesque melodramas. Only democracy can cure the ills of mass society.

Alternatively, mass society may have run its course. New leaders may instead recognize that democratization can heal the wounds and advance the country on a more self-assured path toward political maturity. A government that decides increasingly to trust its citizens can happily shed the oblivion of so many puzzles.

Epilog (by Michael Haas)

The 2006 film *Happy Feet* depicts a penguin named Mumble who cannot sing, as required of all penguins. Instead, he can tap dance. When some penguins try out and enjoy tap dancing as a fun activity, leaders of the penguins see the new activity as a threat to their authority. They then crack down on the practice, and Mumble is ejected from his community. Before the film's ending, *Happy Feet* is a paradigm that could be applied to Singapore, where thousands voluntarily leave a highly regimented society each year because their creativity and desire for real democracy is systematically suppressed.

Singapore leaders patted themselves on the back for having greater state control of the economy and society, thereby supposedly avoiding the financial crisis elsewhere in Asia during 1997-1998, but contradictorily adopted reforms for greater transparency in disclosure of accounts and in economic information, which previously had been carefully censored.[103] The liquidity crisis of 2008-2009, however, did not affect Singapore very much.

In an effort to have the government appear less centralized, Singapore was divided into five districts in 2001. Each district has a mayor and is managed by a Community Development Council. The mayors, who are members of parliament, are assigned Cabinet-level ranks. Government closer to the people should bridge the gap, but the aim was administrative, not political.

Top-down government continues. The bureaucracy is highly politicized rather than neutral to political winds, and the public essentially has not been able effectively to complain either to the bureaucracy, including the Feedback Unit, which was renamed in 2006 as REACH (for Reaching Everyone for Active Citizenry @ Home) and did e-polling.[104] In 2008, the government decided to allow anyone to speak at the Speaker's Corner in Hong Lim Park without first obtaining a police permit,[105] but such a gesture was as diminuitive as the Remaking Singapore movement set up in 2004 and Our SG Conversation instituted after the 2011 election.[106]

On the other hand, some new interest groups, intervening between government and the people, have made a dent in public policy.[107] The Association for Women in Research and Education (AWARE) has successfully pressed the government to allow more women in parliament, but they had to wait until 2009 before the first one rose to Cabinet rank, Lim Hwee Hua. The Singapore Nature Society has protested projects to cement in undeveloped land; in 2002, the Society successfully had the government set up a bird sanctuary. The arts community has also been innovative. On the other hand, the Association of Muslim Professionals has been unable to protest discrimination in the island republic.

The real purpose of public consultation is to sell policies that have already been made. Everyone in Singapore knows that true democracy will not arrive at the pace of such incremental openings but instead when PAP is out of power.

As the twenty-first century has unfolded, the government seems increasingly out of touch with the Singapore public. Lee Kuan Yew, who once characterized Singaporeans after the Cold War as the "overconfident generation,"[108] has stumbled as he has attempted to tell citizens in recent years that they should kiss his posterior because once upon a time he saved the country from disaster. But times have changed. Memories of that struggle to bring prosperity to Singapore are now elipsed in the high fashion shopping malls of the country.[109] Lee, who boasts of pragmatic decisions that boosted his country's role in the world, was exposed as elitist and racist during the 2011 election and no longer resonates with the younger population.[110]

Although the National Integration Council was established in 2008 to bridge the gap between the races as well as between old and newer members of the island, the election of 2011 proved that the gap is primarily a perception of Chinese leaders who view other communities as of lesser value within "Singapore, Inc." Remarks about Malays being too religious or reluctant to fight against neighboring countries continue to rankle.

From the government's standpoint,[111] the Chinese, Indian, and Malay groups must be harmonious for the state to prosper. But each racial group has subgroups, which could complicate governance. Accordingly, one tactic has been to encourage all to speak English and the native language of each group, and the educational system only allows Mandarin Chinese in order to wean the Chinese away from the very dialects that originally populated the country. In 2004, however, the bilingual campaign was abandoned as a failure.

The census, similarly, only counts the three groups, not the various subgroups. The establishment of Racial Harmony Day, July 21, is another way for the government paternalistically to give respect to different groups culturally. The counterpart politically is the selection of non-Chinese to stand for election in group constitencies. Socially, quotas ensure that no race can dominate public housing. The subtext of all these efforts is that the corporatist state is seen as indispensible for the management of multicultural harmony, rather than a democracy in which interest groups representing the various communities would mediate between the government and the people. As a result, minority communities feel that their influence is minimal, though they are propagandized into believing otherwise by government-established organizations, namely, the Chinese Development Assistance Council, the Council for the

Education of Muslim Children, and the Singapore Indian Development Association. After 9/11, the government set up Inter-Racial Confidence Circles in each constituency to counter any racial suspicions.

Any attempt to assert communal identity outside what the government prescribes is viewed as a threat to the state. Poverty among the Malays is never discussed in terms of race but instead as a matter of class.

Similarly, the effort to encourage more marriages among the affluent has also been a failure: The fertility rate of the brightest citizens is below replacement level, as is common in industrial societies.[112]

But the age of the Internet and social media has broken through the government's effort to manufacture consent and restrict ties in the civil society of Singapore. Although theatrical productions are subjected to strict censorship and a mandate to project an image of a "new Asia," theater workers have used clever means to evade government restrictions.[113]

Although there are no signs of the "awakening" that visited Arabic-speaking countries in 2010, the election results of 2011 brought PAP to such a low point in percentage of vote support that a united opposition might win in the next general election. PAP's efforts to appeal to the voters may contain the ferment, but time will tell. Mass society tends to regenerate itself until extraordinary events occur. The defeat of PAP would do so.

Current cracks in the totalitarian control of the population may result in an avalanche of reform if the opposition wins. Meanwhile, crackdowns and scapegoats have been noticeably absent from PAP's political discourse. The future appears to be for the development of democracy in Singapore soon rather than later.

Notes

1. Émile Durkheim, *The Division of Labor in Society* (New York: Free Press, 1949); *Suicide: A Study in Sociology* (New York: Free Press, 1951). Originally published in 1893 and 1897, respectively.
2. William Kornhauser, *The Politics of Mass Society* (Glencoe, IL: Free Press, 1959); Carl J. Friedrich and Zbigniew Brzezinski, *Totalitarian Dictatorship and Autocracy* (2nd edn., Cambridge, MA: Harvard University Press, 1965), 21. When a government adopts only the first three of these characteristics, it is sometimes called "corporatist." See David Brown, "The Corporatist Management of Ethnicity in Contemporary Singapore," in *Singapore Changes Guard: Social, Political and Economic Directions in the 1990s*, ed. Garry

Rodan (New York: St. Martin's Press, 1993), 22.

3. "Out of the Recession—Thanks to Younger Leaders, Workers," *Straits Times*, 9 August 1987, 13.

4. Michael Hill and Lian Kwen Fee, *The Politics of Nation Building and Citizenship in Singapore* (London: Routledge, 1995).

5. *Straits Times*, 20 April 1987; Steve Vines, "The Deepening Tendency to Control," *Honolulu Star-Bulletin & Advertiser*, 1 September 1987, E1.

6. Brown, "The Corporatist Management of Ethnicity in Contemporary Singapore," 18.

7. The data in this paragraph come respectively from the *World Competitiveness Report* (1993); Jacqueline Wong, "Violent Youth Rebel in Singapore," *Reuters*, 7 May 1997; Ramthan Hussaid, "Singapore MP Frets Teen Violence May Turn Racial," *Reuters*, 24 July 1997; T. J. S. George, *Lee Kuan Yew's Singapore* (London: André Deutsch, 1973), 212; "Singapore Teenage Suicide Attempts on the Rise—Report," *Reuters*, 3 April 1996; Matthew Lewis, "S'pore PM Wants Decent Press But Not 'Bootlickers'," *Reuters*, 15 July 1995; Christopher Lingle, *Singapore's Authoritarian Capitalism: Asian Values, Free Market Illusions, and Political Dependency* (Fairfax, VA: Locke Institute, 1996), 100; Chua Beng Huat, *Communitarian Ideology and Democracy in Singapore* (London: Routledge, 1995), 34-35, 117; "Singapore Divorce Rate up 14.6 Percent to 4,100," *Reuters*, 23 October 1996; Devin Nair, "Foreword" to Francis T. Seow, *To Catch a Tartar: A Dissident in Lee Kuan Yew's Prison* (New Haven, CT: Yale University Southeast Asia Studies, 1994), xiv; Mastercard International survey of 1997 reported by the news survey of Australia's Ministry of Foreign Affairs and Trade; Philip Bowring, "Traveller's Tales," *Far Eastern Economic Review*, 8 September 1988, 47; Chiew See Kong, "National Identity, Ethnicity and National Issues," in *In Search of Singapore's National Values*, ed. Jon S. T. Quah (Singapore: Times Academic Press, 1990), 66-79; Kim Dae Jung, "Is Culture Destiny?," *Foreign Affairs*, LXXIII (November-December 1994), 190; *The Economist*, 10 March 1990; Jason Kai Ming Lum, "Singapore—Where Caning Is a Way of Life," *Honolulu Star-Bulletin*, 15 September 1995, A15 (op-ed column); V.V. Bhanoji Rao, "Income Distribution in Singapore: Trends and Issues," *Singapore Economic Review*, XXXV (1990): 143-160; C. M. Turnbull, *A History of Singapore, 1819-1988* (2nd edn., Singapore: Oxford University Press, 1989), 313; *Straits Times*, 30 July 1991; Bilveer Singh, *Whither PAP's Dominance: An Analysis of Singapore's 1991 General Elections* (Petaling Jaya, Malaysia: Pelanduk, 1992), 118-121, 137-138; Liak Teng Kiat, "Life of the Party," *Far Eastern Economic Review*, 29 December 1994—5 January 1995, 20 (op-ed column); *Straits Times*, 6 February 1996; Amitav Acharya and M. Ramesh, "Economic Foundations of Singapore's Security: From Globalism to Regionalism?," in *Singapore Changes Guard: Social, Political and Economic Directions in the 1990s*, ed. Garry Rodan (New York: St. Martin's Press, 1993), 145; Christ Leggett, "Singapore's Industrial Relations in the 1990s," in ibid., 131; Goh Keng Swee, *The Practice of Economic Growth* (Singapore: Federal Publications, 1977), 159; Chua, *Communitarian Ideology and Democracy in Singapore*, 157; Wu Yuan, Chia Lee Lee, Lee Shin Yng and Lee Yueh Wun. *Factors Affecting Adolescent Delinquency in Singapore.* *Working Paper* 7-98, Nanyang Technological University *(http://www3.ntu.edu.sg/nbs/sabre)*; Singapore Police Force, *Annual Crime Brief 2012*; World Health Organization, "Suicide Rates per 100,000 by Country, Year and Sex (2012); James Goyder, "Drug Addiction

and Rehabilitation in Draconian Singapore," *blogs.independent.co.uk*, 23 May 2011; Singapore Central Narcotics Bureau, *Drug Situation Report 2012: CBN's Intensified Enforcement Efforts in 2012 See Increase in Drug Abuses Arrested and Drugs Seized*; "Divorce Demography," *wikipedia.com*; Singapore Department of Statistics, *Marriage and Divorces* (*singstat.gov.sg*); United Nations, *Trends in International Migrant Stock* (2013; UN Office on Drugs and Crime, *Global Study on Homicide* (2012).

8. U.S. Central Intelligence Agency, *Factbook 2012*.
9. Roger Mitton, "For Richer or Poorer: Who Will Care for the City-State's Deprived?," *Asiaweek*, 10 November 2000, 32, 34, 36; ibid.; Manu Bhaskaran, Ho Seng Chee, Donald Low, Tan Kim Song, Sudhir Vadaketh, and Yeoh Lam Keong, "Inequality and the Need for a New Social Compact." Background Paper, Lee Kuan Yew School of Public Policy, National University of Singapore. (*lkyspp.nus.edu.sg/wp-content/uploads/2013/04/SP2012_Bkgd-Pa).
10. Lee Kuan Yew, "The Socialist Dilemma," *Straits Times*, 14 November 1970, 8.
11. Ho Wing Meng, Value Premises Underlying the Transformation of Singapore," in *The Management of Success: The Moulding of Modern Singapore*, eds. Kernial S. Sandhu and Paul Wheatly (Singapore: Institute of Southeast Asian Studies, 1989), 670-691; "Phantom of the Opera," *The Economist*, 11 November 1989, 41; *The Economist*, 10 March 1990; Henry Kamm, "In Prosperous Singapore, Even the Elite Are Nervous About Speaking," *New York Times*, 13 August 1995.
12. Raj Rajenddran, "Ugly Singaporean Strikes Again," *Reuters*, 9 February 1997; James Minchin, *No Man Is and Island: A Study of Lee Kuan Yew's Singapore* (Sydney: Allen & Unwin, 1986), 252. See also "Lee Says Singapore Still Adjusting to New Wealth," *Reuters*, 8 January 1996.
13. *Straits Times*, 20 April 1987; Steve Vines, "The Deepening Tendency to Control," *Honolulu Star-Bulletin & Advertiser*, 1 September 1987, E1. Ethnic slurs are reported in *Straits Times*, 11 August 1987; Seow, *To Catch a Tartar*, 139; David Brown, "The Corporatist Management of Ethnicity in Contemporary Singapore," in *Singapore Changes Guard*, 24; "Singaporeans Told to Be More Creative," *Reuters*, 28 May 1996; John Clammer, "Deconstructing Values: The Establishment of a National Ideology and Its Implications for Singapore's Political Future," 47.
14. *Straits Times*, 24 January 24, 1990; Hill and Lian, *The Politics of Nation Building and Citizenship*, chap. 7; Chua, *Communitarian Ideology and Democracy in Singapore*, 23-25.
15. Francis T. Seow, *To Catch a Tartar*, 141-142; Lingle, *Singapore's Authoritarian Capitalism*, 159.
16. Jean-Louis Margolin, "Foreign Models in Singapore's Development and the Idea of a Singaporean Model," in Garry Rodan, ed., *Singapore Changes Guard*, chap. 6.
17. Ibid., 96.
18. *Ibid.*, 72, 81-82. Iain Buchanan, *Singapore in Southeast Asia: An Economic and Political Appraisal* (London: Bell & Sons, 1972), has questioned the accuracy of all government statistics in Singapore.
19. "Singaporeans Told to Be More Creative."
20. "Classless Society? You'd Have to Eliminate 650,000 HDB Flat Owners First," *Straits Times*, 6 July 1987, 12; "Singapore," *Asia Yearbook 1988* (Hongkong: Far Eastern Economic Review, 1989), 226; Nayan Chan-

da, "Concessional Bending," *Far Eastern Economic Review*, 11 February 1988, 69.

21. Lingle, *Singapore's Authoritarian Capitalism*, 72, 95. In 1986, National Development Minister Teh Cheang Wan committed suicide; he was under suspicion of being on the payroll of one or more foreign corporations. See also T. J. S. George, *Lee Kuan Yew's Singapore* (London: Deutsch, 1973), 201, 213, for a description of how friendship with the mighty in Singapore results in government favoritism.

22. Dennis Bernstein and Leslie Kean, "Singapore's Blood Money," *The Nation*, 20 October 1997, 11ff.

23. "Singapore Says It Still Not a Developed Economy," *Reuters*, 23 May 1997; Jerry Norton, "Singapore Still Has Some Catching up to Do—PM," *Reuters*, 20 August 1995; "Lee Says Singapore Still Adjusting to New Wealth"; Chua, *Communitarian Ideology and Democracy in Singapore*, 206; *Asia Yearbook 1992* (Hongkong: Far Eastern Economic Review, 1992), 189; Economist Intelligence Unit; Ministry of Manpower, *Singapore Workforce 2012*; U.S. Bureau of Labor Statistics, *International Comparison of GDP Per Capita and Per Hour, 1960-2011*; U.S. Central Intelligence Agency, *Factbook 2012*; Singapore Census 2000, "Literacy and Language" (*singstat.gov.sg*); Roy Ngerng, "26 Percent of Singaporeans Live Below the Poverty Line in Singapore," *the hearttruths*.com; Singapore, *Population Trends*, and other references cited in "Immigration to Singapore," *wikipedia.com*, accessed 17 January 2014.

24. Catherine Paix, "The Domestic Bourgeoisie: How Entrepreneurial? How International?," in *Singapore Changes Guard*, 193.

25. The search for a new discourse, from Confucianism to "shared values," is described in several chapters of Rodan, ed., *Singapore Changes Guard*, as well as in Chua, *Communitarian Ideology and Democracy in Singapore* and in Hill and Liat, *The Politics of Nation Building and Citizenship in Singapore*. See also Quah, ed., *In Search of Singapore's National Values*.

26. Philip Bowring, "The Claims About 'Asian Values' Don't Usually Bear Scrutiny," *International Herald Tribune*, 2 August 1994; Kishore Mahbubani, "You May Not Like It, Europe, But This Asian Medicine Could Help," *International Herald Tribune*, 1 October 1994; Christopher Lingle, "The Smoke over Parts of Asia Obscures Some Profound Concerns," *International Herald Tribune*, 7 October 1994.

27. Quah, ed., *In Search of Singapore's National Values*.

28. David Hitchcock, *Asian Values and the U.S.: How Much Conflict?* (Washington, DC: Center for Strategic and International Studies, 1994).

29. Ezra Vogel, *Japan as Number One: Lessons for America* (Cambridge, MA: Harvard University Press, 1979); George Lodge and Ezra Vogel, *Ideology and National Competitiveness: An Analysis of Nine Countries* (Cambridge, MA: Harvard University Business School Press, 1987).

30. Samuel P. Huntington, *The Clash of Civilizations and the Remaking of World Order* (New York: Simon & Schuster, 1996). See "American Don Now Praises Singapore Government," *Straits Times*, 31 December 1996, 15.

31. *Reuters*, 29 November 1997; *Straits Times*, 25 August 1984; Kim, "Is Culture Destiny?" See also David Brunnstrom, "Forum Hammers Asia's Authoritarian Rulers," *Reuters*, 1 December 1994; Ian Buruma, "The Singapore Way," *New York Review of Books*, 19 October 1995, 70; Barbara Crossette, "Ugly Americans with

Asian Faces: Westernization of Asia Is Being Accomplished by Asians Themselves," *Honolulu Star-Bulletin*, 17 May 1997, B1, B4.

32. In my *The Asian Way to Peace: A Story of Regional Cooperation* (New York: Praeger, 1989), I identified a sixfold operational code, the "Asian Way," which operates among diplomats in the region. My aim was to account for successful regional cooperation in such organizations as the Association of South East Asian Nations (ASEAN), though I cautioned readers that the "Asia Way" may have been derived from root cultures throughout the region but operated solely within the diplomatic arena.

33. The quote, from Foreign Minister Suppiah Dhanablan, appears in Francis T. Seow, *The Media Enthralled: Singapore Revisited* (Boulder, CO: Rienner, 1997), 151. See also *When the Press Misinforms* (Singapore: Information Division, Ministry of Communications and Information, 1987), 13, where Lee Hsieng Loong says that "unrestrained Babel leads to mayhem and riots."

34. Possession of *Playboy* is a crime in Singapore, though government-inspected prostitutes are easily available, as described by Gerry Cardinale, "Good Clean Fun," *The New Republic*, 26 May 1997, 10-11. *Cosmopolitan* was banned because of "advocating or celebrating fringe lifestyles," according to George Yong-Boon Yeo, Minister for Information and the Arts, quoted in Richard Hubbard, "S'pore Set to Marry Hi-Tech Media and Asian Values," *Reuters*, 2 November 1995.

35. *Straits Times*, 29 December 1994. See also Jawed Naqvi, "Lee Kuan Yew Says Falling in Love Western Fantasy," *Reuters*, 5 January 1996.

36. Matthew Lewis, "S'pore PM Wants Decent Press But Not 'Bootlickers'," *Reuters*, 15 July 1995.

37. "Lee Kuan Yew Calls Glasnost Mistake," *International Herald Tribune*, 21-22 September 1991, 2; "Cut and Thrust," *Far Eastern Economic Review*, 12 October 1989, 17.

38. Interestingly, Florida passed a law in 1913 guaranteeing the "right of reply" to candidates for office who believe that newspapers have unfairly maligned them. In *Miami Herald v Tormillo* (418US241), the U.S. Supreme Court in 1974 found the law to be unconstitutional, stating that it is censorship for a government to tell newspapers both what to print and what not to print.

39. Chua, *Communitarian Ideology and Democracy in Singapore*, 208. See also Singapore, *When the Press Misinforms*, 4.

40. Ibid., 193.

41. Seow, *To Catch a Tartar*, 28-31, 45-46.

42. One clue is that the face towel issued to Internal Security detainees is a face towel that was "a standard issue of the Japanese conquerors to Allied prisoners of war during their occupation of Singapore and Malaya." Ibid., 153.

43. See "Letter from an Iranian Prisoner," *New York Review of Books*, 10 April 1997), 52. "Russian confessions," as noted by Derek Davies in Chapter 3, were used as early as 1973.

44. Brendan Pereira, "Subordinate Court Rules Set Out in Book," *Straits Times* (weekly edition), 31 December 1994, 5. See also Clammer, "Deconstructing Values," 36-37.

45. "Singapore to Humiliate Sex Molester on Television," *Reuters*, 31 March 1995.

46. Liak Teng Kiat, "The Worries and Concerns Before the ISA Decision," *Straits Times*, 30 July 1987, 13; James H. Weaver and Marguerite Berger, "The Marxist Critique of Dependency Theory: An Introduction," in *The Political Economy of Development and Underdevelopment*, ed. Charles K. Wilber (3rd edn., New York: Random House, 1984, chap. 3. See also my letter in the *Far Eastern Economic Review*, 5 May 1988, 4-5.

47. "S'pre's Stability Result of Nipping Troubles in the Bud," *Straits Times*, 30 July 1987, 1; "More Important 'to Win Local Ground'," *Straits Times*, 25 March 1997; Chua, *Communitarian Ideology and Democracy in Singapore*, 181.

48. For example, Lee Kuan Yew referred to Tan Wah Piow as a "simpleton" and Vincent Cheng and his group as "stupid novices," as quoted by Friar Joachim Kang in "The Review's Defence," *Far Eastern Economic Review*, 19 October 1989, 12. When the term "Marxist" did not fit, the government referred to Cheng and the other twenty-one detainees as "leftists," whom the regime hoped would abandon their efforts to help Filipina guestworkers: Tommy Koh, "Article Contains Serious Errors and Omissions," *Straits Times*, 4 July 1987, 22; "The Answered Questions," *Straits Times*, 6 July 1987, 12; "Detention in Country's Best Interests: Zulfifli," *Straits Times*, 30 July 1987, 12. In regard to Francis Seow's detention, as reported in his *To Catch a Tartar*, even the Internal Security Department was convinced that there was not a shred of evidence that he was collaborating with the United States.

49. "The Decline of the Rule of Law in Malaysia and Singapore: Part II—Singapore," *The Record of the Association of the Bar of the City of New York*, LXVI (January/February 1991), 17.

50. The quoted words are from Lee Hsien Loong, commenting on the danger of the twenty-two so-called "Marxists," as reported in "Marxist Plot Show How Vulnerable S'pore Is," *Straits Times*, 15 June 1987, 1.

51. Alex Josey, *Democracy in Singapore: the 1970 By-Elections* (Singapore: Asia Pacific Press, 1970), 12.

52. "Four Tell Why It's Hard to Brainwash Men Who've Done NS," *Straits Times*, 22 June 1987, 15; George, *Lee Kuan Yew's Singapore*, 192-193.

53. George, *Lee Kuan Yew's Singapore*, 168.

54. Minchin, *No Man Is an Island*, chap. 8.

55. Rene Pastor, "Singapore Seeks to Hold onto Its Troops," *Reuters*, 8 December 1996, quoting Dr. Tony Tan. See also Rene Pastor, "Singapore 'Arrogance' Haunts Ties with Neighbors," *Reuters*, 22 March 1997; "More Important 'to Win Local Ground'."

56. On the one hand, Lee sees Americans as "cultural boors and political dilettantes." On the other hand, he is "paranoid about American and Americans." Seow, *The Media Enthralled*, 97; Seow, *To Catch a Tartar*, 234.

57. *Straits Times*, 6 February 1996; Kishore Mahbubani, "You May Not Like It, Europe, But This Asian Medicine Could Help"; Leslie Kean and Dennis Berstein, "The Burma-Singapore Axis: Globalizing the Heroin Trade," *Covert Action Quarterly*, LXIV (Spring 1998), 45-52.

58. "Singapore Under Attack in Larry King Show," *Straits Times*, 1 May 1994, 18; Shanmugam Jayakumar, "Shouldn't Other Countries Let S'pore Enforce Its Own Laws?," *Straits Times*, 5 May 1994, 26; "Goh 'Flabbergasted' at US Flak on Election Tactics," *Hongkong Standard*, 26 December 1996.

59. Josey, *Democracy in Singapore*, 12.

60. Ibid., 8, 16.
61. Singh, *Whither PAP's Dominance?*, 1-2, citing Richard Rose and Harve Mossawir, "Voting and Elections: A Functional Analysis" in *Empirical Democratic Theory*, eds. Charles F. Cnudde and Deane E. Neubauer (Chicago: Markham, 1969), 69-72; *Elections in Independent Africa* (Boulder, CO: Westview, 1987), 1-4; Austin Ranney, *Governing: An Introduction to Political Science* (5th edn., Englewood Cliffs, NJ: Prentice-Hall, 1990), 175-177.
62. Robert A. Dahl, A *Preface to Democratic Theory* (Chicago: University of Chicago Press, 1956).
63. George, *Lee Kuan Yew's Singapore*, 65; Chua, *Communitarian Ideology and Democracy in Singapore*, 154.
64. Raj Rajendran, "Singapore Polls Left Scars, Opposition Leader Says," *Reuters*, 27 January 1997.
65. In 1996, opposition leader Chee Soon Juan was sued for misplacing a decimal place in quoting figures in parliament, whereas in 1989 Lee Kuan Yew defended himself from the accusation that he was attacking the Catholic Church in parliament by saying that he was only speaking "loosely" in the debate: "Lee States His Case," *Far Eastern Economic Review*, 12 October 1989, 15.
66. Buruma, "The Singapore Way," 71.
67. Murray Hiebert, "Ring in the Old: Voters Extend the PAP's Lease on Power Yet Again," *Far Eastern Economic Review*, 16 January 1997, 17; Narayanan Ganesan, "Singapore in 2009: Structing Politics, Priming the Economy, and Working the Neighborhood," *Asian Survey*, L (2010): 254-249.
68. Chan Heng Wing, "There Are Limits to Openness," *Straits Times* (weekly edition), 31 December 1994, 23. According to Lee Kuan Yew, however, the twenty-two professionals detained in 1987 constituted a "new phenomenon—do-gooders who wanted to help the poor and dispossessed, getting perverted along the way to Marxism.," as reported in "Lee States His Case," 16.
69. Heng Chee Chan, "The PAP and the Structuring of the Political System," in *The Management of Success Success: The Moulding of Modern Singapore*, eds., Kernial S. Sandu and Paul Wheatley (Singapore: Institute of Southeast Asian Studies, 1989); Chua, *Communitarian Ideology and Democracy in Singapore*, 195-196; M. Shamsul Haque, "The State of Decentralization in Singapore: A Country Report," paper presented at the "Serving the Public Interest Through Decentralization" Conference, Manila, 29-31 January 1996; Tan Sai Siong, "Hang on, the Government Does Listen to Feedback," *Straits Times* (weekly edition), 24 December 1994, 13.
70. Chua Mui Hoong, "PM: No Erosion of My Authority Is Allowed; Respect for Office Must be Upheld," *Straits Times* (weekly edition), 10 December 1994, 1. This was a response to Catherine Lim, "One Government, Two Styles," *Straits Times*, 20 November 1994.
71. Seow, *The Media Enthralled*, 27, 94, contains quotes from Lee Kuan Yew and Goh Chok Tong to this effect. See also Chua, *Communitarian Ideology and Democracy in Singapore*, 179-181; Garry Rodan, "The Growth of Singapore's Middle Class and Its Political Significance," in *Singapore Changes Guard*, 58; Clammer, "Deconstructing Values," 38, 64-66. Interestingly, officials of the Internal Security Department regard politicians variously as "ignoramuses" and "political jokers and clowns," as reported in Seow, *To Catch a Tartar*, 206.

72. M. G. G. Pillai, "Singapore Not Yet Ready for Two-Party System," *SEASIA-L*, 18 July 1996; *Straits Times*, 12 August 1995, 4; "Upgrading Democracy at Work, Singapore Style," *Straits Times*, 5 August 1992, 2. See also Josey, *Whither PAP Dominance?*, 10; George, *Lee Kuan Yew's Singapore*, 182-185.

73. Chan Heng Chee, "Singapore: Coping with Vulnerability," in *Driven by Growth: Political Change in the Asia-Pacific Region*, ed. James W. Morley (New York: Sharpe, 1993), 219-241; *The Politics of Survival, 1965-1967* (Kuala Lumpur: Oxford University Press, 1971); Chua, *Communitarian Ideology and Democracy in Singapore*; Jon S. T. Quah, "Controlled Democracy, Political Stability and PAP Predominance: Government in Singapore" in *The Changing Shape of Government in the Asia-Pacific Region*, eds. John W. Langford and K. Lorne Brownsey (Halifax, Nova Scotia: Institute for Research on Public Policy, 1988), 125-169; N. Ganesan, "Democracy in Singapore," paper presented at the annual convention of the Association for Asian Studies, Honolulu, 11-14 April 1996; Garry Rodan, "Preserving the One-Party State in Contemporary Singapore," in *Southeast Asia in the 1990s: Authoritarianism, Democracy and Capitalism*, eds. Kevin Hewison, Richard Robison, and Garry Rodan (Sydney: Allen and Unwin, 1993), 108; Harold Crouch and James Morley, "The Dynamics of Political Change," in *Driven by Growth: Political Change in the Asia-Pacific Region*, ed. James W. Morley (New York: Sharpe, 1993), 277-309; James Cotton, "Political Innovation in Singapore: The Presidency, the Leadership and the Party," in *Singapore Changes Guard*, chap. 1; Brown, "The Corporatist Management of Ethnicity in Contemporary Singapore"; Hill and Lian, *The Politics of Nation Building and Citizenship in Singapore*; Lingle, *Singapore's Authoritarian Capitalism*, 159; Kim, "Is Culture Destiny?" Some of the terms have been misapplied. For example, according to Amitai Etzioni, *The Spirit of Community: Rights, Responsibilities, and the Communitarian Agenda* (New York: Crown Publishers, 1993), "communitarianism" refers to a movement in which there is a balance between the individual and society, with individuals encouraged to band together in communities without relying on the state. The meaning of "communitarianism" in Singapore has been distorted to mean that the society comes before the individual. Similarly, according to Arend Lijphart, *Democracies: Patterns of Majoritarian and Consensus Government in Twenty-One Countries* (New Haven, CT: Yale University Press, 1984), minority ethnic groups in "consociational democracies" can veto legislation proposed by the majority; in Singapore, the concept has been misapplied to refer to PAP cooptation of the Uncle Toms of ethnic minorities.

74. *Straits Times*, 14 July 1971.

75. Kim, "Is Culture Destiny?," 191. Kim's essay was written in rebuttal to the ideas expressed by Lee Kuan Yew, as reported from an interview by Fareed Zakaria, "A Conversation with Lee Kuan Yew," *Foreign Affairs*, LXXIII (1994): 109-126; "Public Housing in Singapore," *wikipedia*.com.

76. Chua, *Communitarian Ideology and Democracy in Singapore*, 129, 137.

77. *Straits Times*, 10 April 1985; Chua, *Communitarian Ideology and Democracy*, 21-24; Jon S. T. Quah and Stella Quah, "The Limits of Governmental Intervention," in *The Management of Success: The Moulding of Modern Singapore*, eds. Kernial S. Sandhu and Paul Wheatley (Singapore: Institute of Southeast Asian Studies, 1989); Singh, *Whither PAP Dominance?*, 10-15, 20; Rodan, "The Growth of Singapore's Middle Class and Its Political Significance," 57-58.

78. Poll results are reported in ibid., 58-62. See also Cheng Tun-Jen, "Is the Dog Barking? The Middle Class and Democratic Movements in East Asian NIC's," *International Studies Notes*, XV (1990): 10-16, 40; Chiew, "National Identity, Ethnicity and National Issues."

79. Chua, *Communitarian Ideology and Democracy in Singapore*, 22.

80. Ibid., 60-62; Singh, *Whither PAP Dominance?*, 91.

81. "Government Acted in the Interest of the Majority of the People," *Straits Times*, 30 July 1987, 12; "Regional Performance Figure," *Asia Yearbook 1988*, 6-7.

82. *Asiaweek*, 13 January 1997.

83. The source of this hypothesis is the undocumented thesis in Samuel P. Huntington, *Political Order in Changing Societies* (New Haven, CT: Yale University Press). Contrary evidence is available in a variety of sources: Milton Friedman and Rose Friedman, *Free to Choose: A Personal Statement* (New York: Harcourt, Brace, Jovanovich, 1990), 57; Michael Haas, *Improving Human Rights* (Westport, CT: Praeger, 1984); Hugh Patrick, "The Future of the Japanese Economy: Output and Labor Productivity," *Journal of Japanese Studies*, III (1977): 239.

84. Chan Heng Wing, "There Are Limits to Openness." See also Kishore Mahbubani, "The West and the Rest," *The National Interest*, Summer 1992, 3-13.

85. "Marxist Plot Shows How Vulnerable S'pore Is."

86. "Goh 'Flabbergasted' at US Flak on Election Tactics."

87. See Janadas Devan and Geraldine Heng, "State Fatherhood: The Politics of Nationalism, Sexuality, and Race in Singapore," in *Nationalisms and Sexualities*, eds. Andrew Parker, Mary Russo, Doris Sommer, and Patricia Yeager (New York: Routledge, 1992); Azlin Ahmad, "Singapore Government Matchmaking Thrives," *Reuters*, 2 January 1998.

88. Clammer, "Deconstructing Values," 39; Ministry of Social and Family Development, "State of Families in Singapore" (*app.msf.gov.sg/portals/0/Summary/-publication/SF2-MarriageAnnex*).

89. See Brown, "The Corporatist Management of Ethnicity in Singapore."

90. Hill and Lian, *The Politics of Nation Building and Citizenship in Singapore*, 112.

91. *Straits Times*, 6 February 1966. See also "Lee Says Singapore Still Adjusting to New Wealth."

92. Hussaid, "Singapore MP Frets Teen Violence May Turn Racial"; Wong, "Violent Youth Rebel in Singapore."

93. Josey, *Democracy in Singapore*, 10.

94. Alex Josey, *Lee Kuan Yew* (Singapore: Times Books International, 1968, 1980), 2 vols.; Anthony Oei, *What If There Had Been No Lee Kuan Yew?* (Singapore: Mandarin, 1992).

95 George, *Lee Kuan Yew's Singapore*; Minchin, *No Man Is an Island*; T. S. Selvan, *Singapore the Ultimate Island: Lee Kuan Yew's Untold Story* (Melbourne: Freeway Books, 1990).

96. See George, *Lee Kuan Yew's Singapore*, 180; Minchin, *No Man Is an Island*, 156, 254-255, 301-302, 316.

97 Ibid., 326. According to T. W. Adorno, Daniel J. Levinson, Max Horkheimer, and Else Frenkel-Brunswik, *The Authoritarian Personality* (New York: Harper, 1950), persons who resist psychological self-examination

tend to be authoritarian.

98   Jawed Naqvi, "Lee Kuan Yew Says Falling in Love Western Fantasy," *Reuters*, 5 January 1996.

99.   "Marxist Plot Shows How Vulnerable S'pore Is."

100. Jonah M. David, "Don't Count on Me, Singapore," *National Review*, 16 May 1994, 60.

101. Liak Ten Kiat, "Life of the Party," *Far Eastern Economic Review*, 29 December 1994—5 January 1995, 20.

102. David, "Don't Count on Me, Singapore," 61.

103. Gary Rodan, *Transparency and Authoritarian Rule in Southeast Asia: Singaore and Malaysia* (New York, Routledge, 2004).

104. Ho Khai Loong, *The Politics of Policy Making in Singa*pore (Singapore: Singapore University Press, 2000). See also Garry Rodan, "'Vibrant and Cosmopolitan" Without Political Pluralism," *Asian Survey*, XLVI (2006): 181; Rodan, "Consultative Authoritarianism and Regime Change Analysis." In *Handbook of Southeast Asian Politics*, ed Richard Robison (New York: Routledge, 2006), chap. 8

105. Narayan Ganesan, "Singapore in 2008: A Few Highs and Lows While Bracing for the Future," *Asian Survey*, XLIX (2009): 213-219.

106. Tim Huxley, "Singapore in 2000: Continuing Stability and Renewed Propsperity amid Regional Diversity," *Asian Survey*, XLI (2001): 204; Ho Khai Leong, *Shared Responsibilities, Unshared Power: The Politics of Policy-Making in Singapore* (Singapore: Eastern Universities Press, 2003); Boon Siong Neo and Geraldine Chen, *Dynamic Governance: Embedding Culture, Capabilities and Change in Singapore* (Singapore: World Scientific Publishing, 2007), 449; Ying-Kit Chun, "Kapitans in Singapore: Consuming Politics," *Asian Survey*, LIII (2013): 979-1004.

107. Chua Beng Huat, Liberalization Without Democratization: Singapore in the Next Decade." In *Southeast Asian Responses to Globalization: Restructuring Governance and Deepening Democracy*, eds. Francis Loh Kok Wah and Joakim Öjendal (Copenhagen: Nordic Institute of Asian Studies), 61-72.

108. The term is used in Lee Kuan Yew, *The Singapore Story: Memoirs of Lee Kuan Yew* (Singapore: Times Editions, Singapore Press Holdings, 1998).

109. Chua Beng Huat, *Life Is Not Complete Without Shopping in Singapore*. (Singapore: Singapore University Press, 2003).

110. Michael D. Barr, *Lee Kuan Yew: The Beliefs Behind the Man* (Richmond, Surrey: Curzon, 2000), 249.

111. This paragraph is based in part on Norman Vasu, "Governance Through Difference," *Asian Survey*, LII (2012): 734-753; Hussin Mutalib, "The Singapore Minority Dilemma," *Asian Survey*, LI (2011): 1156-1171. See also Narayan Gasesan, "Singapore in 2009: Structuring Politics, Priming the Economy, and Working the Neighborhood," *Asian Survey*, L (2010): 253-259.

112. Ho, *The Politics of Policy Making in Singapore*.

113. William Peterson, *Theater and the Politics of Culture in Contemporary Singapore*. Middletown, CT: Wesleyan University Press, 2001.

For Further Reading

Acharya, Amitav. *Singapore's Foreign Policy: The Search for Regional Order.* Singapore: World Scientific Publishing, 2008.

Barr, Michael D. *Lew Kuan Yew: The Beliefs Behind the Man.* Richmond, Surrey: Curzon, 2000.

Bercuson, Kenneth, ed. *Singapore: A Case Study in Rapid Development.* Washington, DC: International Monetary Fund, 1995.

Bhaskaran, Manu. *Re-Inventing the Asian Model: The Case of Singapore.* Singapore: Eastern Universities Press, 2003.

Bloodworth, Dennis. *The Tiger and the Trojan Horse.* Singapore: Times Books International, 1986.

Buckley, C. B. *An Anecdotal History of Old Times in Singapore 1819-1867.* Kuala Lumpur: University of Malaya Press, 1965.

Buchanan, Iain. *Singapore in Southeast Asia: An Economic and Political Appraisal.* .London: Bell & Sons, 1972.

Cherian, George. *Contentious Journalism: Towards Democratic Discourse in Malaysia and Singapore.* Seattle: University of Washington Press, 2006.

Chua, Beng Huat. *Communitarian Ideology and Democracy in Singapore.* New York: Routledge, 1995.

Chua, Beng Huat. *Life Is Not Complee Without Shopping in Singapore*. Singapore: Singapore University Press, 2003.

Chua, Beng Huat. *Political Legitimacy and Housing: Singapore's Stakeholder Society*. London: Routledg, 1997.

Collins, Alan. *Security and Southeast Asia: Domestic, Regional, and Global Issues*. Boulder, CO: Rienner.

George, T. S. C. *Lee Kuan Yew's Singapore*. London: Deutsch, 1973.

Hefner, Robert W. *Politics of Multiculturalism: Pluralism and Citizenship in Malaysia, Singapore, and Indonesia*. Honolulu: University of Hawaii Press, 2001.

Hill, Michael, and Lian Kwen Fee. *The Politics of Nation Building and Citizenship in Singapore*. Singapore: Times Books International, 1995.

Ho Khai Leong. *The Politics of Policy Making in Singapore*. Singapore: Singapore University Press, 2000.

Ho Khai Leong. *Shared Responsibilities, Unshared Power: The Politics of Policy-Making in Singapore* (Singapore: Eastern Universities Press, 2003.

Hong, Lisa, and Huang Jianli. *The Scripting of a National History: Singapore and Its Pasts*. Hongkong: Hongkong University Press, 2008.

Josey, Alex. *Lee Kuan Yew: The Crucial Years*. Singapore: Times Books International, 1986.

Kwan, Kevin. *Crazy Rich Asians*. London: Routledge, 2013.

Kwang, Han Fook, Warren Fernandez, and Sumiko Tan. *Lee Kuan Yew: The Man and His Ideas*. Singapore: Singapore Press Holdings, Times Edition, 1998.

Lee Kuan Yew. *The Singapore Story: Memoirs of Lee Kuan Yew*. Singapore: Prentice-Hall, 1998.

Lee Kuan Yew. *From Third World to First: The Singapore Story, 1965-2000; Memoirs of Lee Kuan Yew*. Singapore: Straits Times Press, 2000.

Lee Kuan Yew. *Hard Truths to Keep Singapore Going*. Singapore: Straits Times Publishing Company, 2011.

Leifer, Michael. *Singapore's Foreign Policy: Coping with Vulnerability*. New York: Routledge, 2000.

Lingle, Christopher. *Singapore's Authoritarian Capitalism: Asian Values, Free Market Illusions, and Political Dependency*. Fairfax, VA: Locke Institute, 1996.

Low, Linda. *The Political Economy of a City-State: Government-Made Singapore*. Singapore: Oxford University Press, 1998.

Low, Linda, and Toh Mun Heng, eds. *Public Policies in Singapore: Changes in the 1980s and Future Signposts*. Singapore: Times Minchin, James. *No Man Is an Island: A Study of Lee Kuan Yew's Singapore*. Boston: Allen & Unwin, 1986.

Minchin, James. *No Man Is an Island: A Study of Lee Kuan Yew's Singapore*. Sydney: Allen & Unwin, 1986.

Neo, Boon Siong. *Dynamic Governance: Embedding Culture, Capabilities and Change in Singapore*. Singapore: World Scientific Publishing, 2007.

Oei, Anthony. *What If There Had Been No Lee Kuan Yew?* Singapore: Mandarin, 1992.

Ortmann, Stephan. *Politics and Change in Singapore and Hong Kong: Containing Contention*. London: Routledge, 2010.

Peterson, William. *Theater and the Politics of Culture in Contemporary Singapore*. Middletown, CT: Wesleyan University Press, 2001.

Quah, Jon S. T., ed. *In Search of Singapore's National Values*. Singapore: Times Academic Press, 1990.

Rodan, Garry, ed. *Singapore Changes Guard: Social, Political and Economic Directions in the 1990s*. New York: St. Martin's Press, 1992.

Rodan, Garry. *Transparency and Authoritarian Rule in Southeast Asia: Singapore and Malaysia*. New York: Routledge, 2004.

Sandhu, Kernial S., and Paul Whatley, eds. *Management of Success: The Moulding of Modern Singapore*. Singapore: Institute of Southeast Asian Studies.

Selvan, S. *Singapore, The Ultimate Island: Lee Kuan Yew's Untold Story*. Melbourne: Freeway Books, 1990.

Seow, Francis T. *Beyond Suspicion: The Singapore Courts on Trial*. New Haven, CT: Yale University Southeast Asian Studies, 2006.

Seow, Francis T. *The Media Enthralled*. Boulder, CO: Rienner, 1998.

Seow, Francis T. *To Catch a Tartar: A Dissident in Lee Kuan Yew's Prison*. New Haven, CT: Yale University Southeast Asian Studies, 1994.

Seow, Francis T., and Ingrid Seow Stendhal, comp. *Confucius Confounded: The Analects of Lee Kuan Yew*. Kuala Lumpur, Malaysia: Berita Pub., 2010.

Shadrake, Alan. *Once a Jolly Hangman: Singapore Justice in the Dock*. Petaling Jaya, Malaysia: Strategic Information and Research Development Centre, 2010.

Singapore Institute of Policy Studies. *The Singaporean: Ethnicity, National Identity and Citizenship*. Singapore: Institute of Policy Studies, 1990.

Singapore Institute of Policy Analysis. *The IFER Report: Restructing Singapore's Economy*. Singapore: Times Academic Press, 2002.

Singh, Bilveer. *Whither Pap's Dominance? An Analysis of Singapore's 1991 General Election*. Selanger-Darol Ehsan, Malaysia; Pelanduk Publications, 1992.

Singh, Bilveer. *Politics and Governance in Singapore: An Introduction*. Singapore: McGraw Hill, 2007.

Slater, Dan. *Ordering Power: Contentious Politics and Authoritarian Levianthans in Southeast Asia*. New York: Cambridge University Press, 2010.

Sng Hui Ying and Chia Wai Mun, eds. *Singapore and Asia: Impact of the Global Financial Tsunami and Other Economic Issues*. Singapore: World Scientific Publishing, 2010.

Tammey, Joseph B. *The Struggle over Singapore's Soul: Western Modernization and Asian Culture*. New York: de Gruyter, 1996.

Tan, Andrew. *Intra-ASEAN Tensions*. London: Royal Institute of International Affairs, 2000.

Tan, Kenneth Paul, ed., *Renaissance Singapore? Economy, Culture, and Politics*. Singapore: Singapore University Press, 2007.

Tan Wah Piow. *Frame-Up: A Singapore Court on Trial*. Oxford: TWP Publishing, 1987.

Tan Wah Piow. *Let the People Judge: Confessions of the Most Wanted Person in Singapore*. Kuala Lumpur: Institute for Social Analysis, 1987.

Tay, Simon S. C., ed, *A Mandarin and the Making of Public Policy*. Singapore: Singapore National Univeristy Press, 2000.

Termewan, Chris. *The Political Economy of Social Control in Singapore*. New York: St. Martin's Press, 1994.

Trocki, Carl A. *Singapore: Wealth, Power, and the Culture of Control*. New York: Routledge, 2006.

Turnbull, C. M. *A History of Singapore, 1819-1988*, 2nd edn. Singapore: Oxford University Press, 1989.

Vasil, Raj K. *Asianising Singapore: The PAP's Management of Ethnicity*. Singapore:

Heinemann, 1995.

Vasil, Raj K. *Governing Singpore: Democracy and National Development*. Boston: Allen & Unwin, 2000.

Wilson, Peter, ed. *Challenges for the Singapore Economy After the Global Financial Crisis*. Singapore: World Scientific Publishing, 2011.

Yao, Souchou. *Singapore: The State and the Culture of Excess*. London: Routledge, 2007.

Index

About the Contributors

DEREK DAVIES served as the editor of the Far Eastern Economic Review from 1964 to 1990. His distinguished newsweekly so displease government authorities in Singapore that he was sued for libel in 1988. After serving as a Fellow at the East-West Center in Honolulu in 1990-1991, he embarked on a pleasant retirement in Europe, where he commuted between homes in London and the French Alps. All contributors were saddened to learn of his death in 2002.

RICHARD A. DECK was a Fellow in International Peace and Security on a grant to study at the National University of Singapore and to write his dissertation at the Institute of Southeast Asian Studies from 1986 to 1988. Subsequently, he served as Vice President of Catalyst Concepts, a consulting and research firm in Berkeley, California, and Founding Director of the Asia-Pacific Regional Policy Research Institute. Currently, he lives on the East Coast.

MICHAEL HAAS was on the political science faculty at the University of Hawai'i at Mānoa from 1964 to 1998. During 1997, he was a Fulbright Fellow at the Institute of Southeast Asian Studies in Singapore. After his retirement, he moved to Los Angeles, where he is President of the Political Film Society and a member of the California Senior Assembly. Among his fifty published books, his latest are *Asian and Pacific Cooperation: Turning Zones of Conflict into Arenas of Peace* (2013) and the second edition of *International Human Rights: A Comprehensive Introduction* (2014).

CHRISTOPHER LINGLE, a former visiting economics professor at the National University of Singapore, fled the country when he believed that his op-eds in the *International Herald*

Tribune provoked surveillance; he was subsequently sued for libel but lost because he chose not to defend himself while outside the country. A professor of economics in the Institute of Human Studies, George Mason University, he has been a visiting professor in several countries, including China, Guatemala, Hongkong, Luxembourg, and South Africa. He is the author of *Singapore's Authoritarian Capitalism, Asian Values, Free Market Illusion, and Political Dependency* (1996), and *The Rise and Decline of the Asian Century: False Starts on the Path to the Global Millennium* (1998).

CLARK D. NEHER, former Director of the Center for Southeast Asian Studies at Northern Illinois University, has done field work for Singapore's Institute of Southeast Asian Studies. In 19xx, he retired from the Department of Political Science. With Professor Robert Dayler, he co-authored the fifth edition of his *Southeast Asia in the New International Era* (2013), including a chapter on Singapore.

FRANCIS T. SEOW was Singapore's Solicitor-General from 1967 to 1969. In 1988, when he sought to run for office as an opposition candidate, he was detained and tortured for seventy-two days by the Singapore authorities. The following year he was appointed a Fellow at Yale Law School, and in 1990 he became a Fellow at the East Asian Legal Studies Program, Harvard School of Law. He is the author of four books about Singapore: *To Catch a Tartar* (1994), *The Media Enthralled* (1997), *Beyond Suspicion: The Singapore Courts on Trial* (2006), and with Ingrid Seow Stendhal a compilation, *Confucius Confounded: The Analects of Lee Kuan Yew* (2010). He now lives in the Boston area.

KURT WICKMAN, a former visitng economics professor at the National University of Singapore, teaches at Gavle University, Sweden, and a Chulalongkorn University, Bangkok. He is the author of *Singpore: Föredome eller skräckexempel?* (1995) and several journal articles on Singapore and other topics on political economy.

www.ingramcontent.com/pod-product-compliance
Lightning Source LLC
Chambersburg PA
CBHW081147270326
41930CB00014B/3059